Signs and
Symptoms

PETER L. COOPER

Signs and Symptoms

Thomas Pynchon
and the
Contemporary
World

University of California Press
Berkeley | Los Angeles | London

University of California Press
Berkeley and Los Angeles, California

University of California Press, Ltd.
London, England

©1983 by
The Regents of the University of California

Library of Congress Cataloging in Publication Data

Cooper, Peter L.
    Signs and symptoms.

    Bibliography: p.
    1. Pynchon, Thomas — Criticism and interpretation.
I. Title.
PS3566.Y55Z58   1982   813'.54   82-6929
ISBN 0-520-04537-8   AACR2

Printed in the United States of America
1 2 3 4 5 6 7 8 9

For Karen and Jessica

Table of Contents

Preface

In this book I have attempted to understand the achievement of Thomas Pynchon by viewing his work in the context of literary, philosophical, and scientific aspects of modern thought. My first chapter creates a background for subsequent discussion of Pynchon: I consider important points of similarity and dissimilarity between him and recent American novelists, emphasizing his contemporaries and the general terrain of recent American fiction, rather than Pynchon himself, and suggesting topics to be developed more fully in the later chapters, which deal with Pynchon almost exclusively.

One note on format: since Pynchon uses ellipses liberally and suggestively throughout *Gravity's Rainbow,* I have placed brackets around my own when quoting from that work. The ellipses in quotations from other Pynchon works and from secondary sources are all mine.

I wish to express my gratitude to Professor Richard Lehan for his thoughtful and incisive criticism in the early stages of this work, always given with tact, friendliness, and an engaging pleasure in sharing ideas; to the academic readers who reviewed the manuscript in draft and made many valuable suggestions; and to Lydia Lesh for typing much of the final version. I will always remember the kindness and support both of my parents, James and Ruth Cooper, and my parents-in-law, John and Else Toron. The greatest debt I owe to my wife, Karen, who gave me more understanding, encouragement, and, especially, love than I had a right to expect. To her and to our daughter, Jessica, this work is dedicated.

Hopewell, N. J.
1981

Abbreviations

The following abbreviations designate works by Thomas Pynchon discussed in the text.

E   "Entropy," *Kenyon Review* 22 (1960), 277 – 92.

49   *The Crying of Lot 49* (New York: Bantam Books, 1967).

GR   Gravity's Rainbow (New York: The Viking Press, 1973). Bracketed ellipses within quotes from *Gravity's Rainbow* are the present author's; ellipses appearing without brackets within quotes are Pynchon's.

L   "Low-lands," *New World Writing* 16 (1960), 85 – 108.

MMV   "Mortality and Mercy in Vienna," *Epoch* 9 (Spring 1959), 195 – 213.

SI   "The Secret Integration," *Saturday Evening Post* 237 (19 December 1964), 36, 39, 42 – 44, 46 – 49, 51.

V.   *V.* (New York: Bantam Books, 1964).

W   "Journey into the Mind of Watts," *Man Against Poverty: World War III: A Reader on the World's Most Crucial Issue,* ed. Arthur I. Blaustein and Roger R. Woock (New York: Random House, 1968), pp. 146 – 58.

Pynchon's Literary Context

The Counterrealists

Reading Pynchon, or, certainly, writing about him, should make us self-conscious, for as readers and critics, we ape the plights and practices of the characters about whom we read. Pynchon is deeply ambivalent about this human compulsion to find—or to make—patterns of experience and then interpret them. Such patterns always falsify reality to some unknowable degree, and they run the risk of reducing its rich varieties, contingencies, and singularities to mechanical regularities, dull predictabilities, and sterile uniformities. He parodies the urge to systematize, and he frequently vilifies analysis and classification, the mental functions encouraged by it. He points out that perception of continuity or discontinuity, sameness or difference, may simply depend on perspective; he notes that the lines of categorical division that structure a system and constitute its meaning may describe the limits of the formulator's vision rather than the nature of reality. But despite all his misgivings and qualifications, Pynchon finally sanctions the building of interpretive systems or models of the world. They are imperfect but necessary.

Acting on his sanction but recalling his admonitions, I think one can best appreciate Pynchon in context by placing contemporary American fiction writers at one of two poles: those who inherit, extend, or modify the traditions of realism and naturalism; and those who consciously react against the traditions in practicing "counterrealism," as John Barth calls it in "Muse, Spare Me." Pynchon belongs in this latter group. I do not mean to suggest that he and the other counterrealists are more alike than distinct: a spectrum of authors, each unique, spans the two poles, and few fit into either category with perfect ease. Some, such as Norman Mailer and Ralph Ellison, can alternate between poles within a single work, and authors who seem clearly aligned with one end of the spectrum may produce a work that leans toward the other: consider Updike's *The Centaur* or Bellow's *Henderson the Rain King*. I am not trying to make a rigorous, schematic division, nor am I trying to establish a "school" or write a comparative study. But I believe that it will be easier to understand and assess Pynchon's particular achievement by introducing it in the light of recent trends in American fiction.

Neorealists and Counterrealists

Compared to the works of counterrealists, the neorealists' writing presents a recognizable, detailed, and plausible social surrounding — plausible given the bizarre quality of twentieth-century American life. A would-be writer in Mailer's "The Man Who Studied Yoga" complains that "reality is no longer realistic," an observation echoed by the works of the whole range of contemporary authors. But apart from verisimilitude and historicity of setting, neorealists present rounded, individuated characters who are explained, or, as E. M. Forster says, made explicable, through attention to their psychology and motivation. A coherent and consistent narration focuses on their conflicts, introspections, formation of values, personal and social interactions, adjustments and accommodations. One has the sense that the characters and their worlds function pretty much by cause and effect, by regular and fixed rules that are familiar or at least knowable in theory. With such people in such a world, logical explanation is possible, and so is the human ability — not always realized — to face the conditions of life and society: to work out a resolution in the face of opposition and affirm one's own integrity, worth, or identity. Usually the neorealists show their characters as trying to reach a tenable mode of being with themselves, with others, and with their civilization. These authors ask us to suspend our disbelief, to concede that the events they portray have happened or could happen to a real person. Writers with an affinity for this kind of realism include Saul Bellow, John Updike, Philip Roth (Joseph Heller moves this way in *Good as Gold*), James Gould Cozzens, Herbert Gold, John Cheever, J. D. Salinger, Ernest Gaines, Frank Conroy, John A. Williams, James Baldwin, Joyce Carol Oates, William Styron, Truman Capote, Robert Coover, John Gardner—even Bernard Malamud, despite his reliance on the quest motif and fable form.

But a number of American authors, typically younger and more recently active, recognize their fundamental divergence from the principles and practices of realism. John Barth has said of himself and his contemporaries, "The differences between what we are doing are much more conspicuous and striking than the similarities. Which isn't to say that there isn't some kind of shared temperament."[1] Granting the real differences to which Barth alludes, I find that "shared temperament" most thoroughly and powerfully expressed in the work of Thomas Pynchon: a general uncertainty about the reality and hospitableness of the world, a fascination (sometimes horrified) with epistemological dilemmas, a recognition of the need for fictional versions of reality, and a simultaneous apprehension of their dangers and insufficiencies that leads to narrative disruptions and to self-parody. Besides Pynchon and Barth, the counterrealists include Joseph Heller (*Catch-22*), Ken Kesey (*One Flew Over the Cuckoo's Nest*), Kurt Vonnegut Jr., Donald Barthelme, William Burroughs, John Hawkes, William Gaddis, Tom Robbins, Ishmael Reed, Henry Van Dyke, Susan Sontag, Vladimir Nabokov, and Jorge Luis Borges. Perhaps these writers differ most obviously from the neorealists in their portrayal of the human being as a relatively flat, insubstantial figure adrift in an alien world. That world, sometimes rendered with great particularity, is typically fantastic, grotesque, absurd, mysteriously threatening, filled with unforseen events or shocking juxtapositions—a labyrinth, oddly animated by plots that seem deliberately and malevolently opposed to human priorities. When preexisting forces shape reality, the individual is shrunk to insignificance. Authors may enforce this point by populating their works with two-dimensional, cartoon-like props, a strategy not appreciated by some critics. Shimon Wincelberg complained of *Catch-22*

---

[1] Annie Le Rebeller, "A Spectatorial Skeptic: An Interview with John Barth," *Caliban* 12 (1975), 94.

that the characters "can be summed up in terms of a joke, which might make them easy for a reviewer to describe, but greatly limits their ability to grow, develop, or expose themselves to revelation."[2] This, I think, misses the point: unlike more realistic characters, they are not *supposed* to grow, develop, or expose themselves to revelation. Their limitations reveal how puny and ineffectual they are before the plots and power structures of the world or the indifference — perhaps hostility — of the cosmos. The characters seem unreal even to themselves because they are impotent in the face of conscious manipulation or chaotic circumstance. Vonnegut says of *Slaughterhouse-Five*, "There are almost no characters in this story, and almost no dramatic confrontations, because most of the people in it are so sick and so much the listless playthings of enormous forces."[3]

Just as identity is not substantial and dimensional in counterrealistic fiction, neither is it absolute. The human caricatures seem to be multiple, shifting, contingent surfaces that cover little, if anything. They can switch roles and identities (there is seldom a difference) as easily as they can alternate masks, and the new surface may become more genuine than the original. In Vonnegut's *Mother Night*, Kraft, the Soviet agent-disguised-as-artist, becomes one of the great contemporary masters. Vonnegut announces at the outset, "We are what we pretend to be, so we must be careful about what we pretend to be."[4] Such protean possibilities inhere in most of Barth's characters, in Heller's "miracle ingredient" Yossarian, and in Kesey's comic-book-hero pastiche. Similarly, James Purdy suggests in *Cabot Wright Begins* that one's identity may be "suppositious," a product of the media. Ellison's "Proteus" Rinehart can change identity at will, perhaps because he has a "rind heart," as the author has said — a zero at the middle. And the narrator, even in his own eyes, almost assumes Rinehart's identities simply by putting on Rinehart-type glasses. Pynchon's Fausto Maijstral takes on a sequence of provisional

[2]Shimon Wincelberg, "A Deadly Serious Lunacy," in *On Contemporary Literature*, ed. Richard Kostelanetz (New York: Avon Books, 1964), p. 390.

[3]Kurt Vonnegut, Jr., *Slaughterhouse-Five: Or, The Children's Crusade* (New York: Dell Publishing Co., 1971), p. 164. All subsequent references cited in the text as *(SF)*.

[4]Kurt Vonnegut, Jr., *Mother Night* (New York: Dell Publishing Co., 1974), p. v. All subsequent references cited in the text as *(MN)*.

"selves" to expose "the false assumption that identity is single, soul continuous" (V., p. 287), and plastic surgeon Shale Schoenmaker (V.) in effect creates new people by retooling their surfaces.

Some of the authors whom I see as counterrealists are not very concerned with social forces, but their human figures are diminished nonetheless. John Barth, for example, admits that he "can't in fiction get very interested" in such things as current world problems, which he calls "the conditions of [life,]" but he is very interested in metaphysical constraints, which he calls "the facts of life."[5] Because his absurd cosmos offers no absolute values or ultimate verities, his characters become dwarfed and immobilized not by impersonal powers but, paradoxically, by a superfluity of freedom and choice. Jake Horner in *The End of the Road* is so aware of endless alternatives that even if he were a single, coherent self he could not settle on a course of action. The "serpents of Knowledge and Imagination," by offering him too much, bind his limbs as they did Laocöon's and literally paralyze him. He is overwhelmed not by external controls but by their complete absence: too many possibilities have the same effect as too few, and he feels "as though there were no Jacob Horner." Most of Barth's main characters suffer from some form of the problem that Horner epitomizes.

Other counterrealistic characters are dwarfed not so much by their social or the cosmic context as by their aesthetic one. Barth's later, more self-conscious work can "metaphysically" disturb us, the author says, by suggesting the ultimate paranoia: that we are characters in someone else's fiction. Such subservience again belittles the human figure. Similarly, Andrew Field has observed that Nabokov's fictional patterns, like chess problems, "have a fascination which is quite independent of the people (or rather figures) who participate in them. Nabokov has always had a marked predilection for the view from above."[6] Though writers like Heller, Vonnegut, Burroughs, and Pynchon also make their figures less substantial, less dimensional, less real than the forces that

---

[5]John Enck, "John Barth: An Interview," *Wisconsin Studies in Contemporary Literature* 6 (Winter-Spring 1965), 13.
[6]Andrew Field, "The Defenseless Luzhin," in *On Contemporary Literature*, ed. Richard Kostelanetz (New York: Avon Books, 1964), p. 474.

dominate them, these authors do so largely to illustrate man's position in a public world of technology, institutions, and interlocking power structures beyond his ken. On the other hand, authors like Nabokov and the later Barth, who delight in elaborate and self-referential structures, show that *they*, not some master cabal, manipulate their characters for greater rigor of design.

Most counterrealists and some neorealists evince a degree of social and cosmic anxiety over the tendency of all closed systems, human or intergalactic, toward stasis, a tendency to which some apply the scientific term *entropy*. (Usages of the term are generally metaphorical and rather loose; Pynchon's is the most sophisticated and scientifically informed — see chapters 2 and 4.) Unlike Bellow or Updike, who are also preoccupied with the phenomenon, counterrealists present entropic change not so much as a recognizable fact of life but rather as a malevolent, magical potency that works through fantastic landscapes, mysterious agencies, or even perverse single agents. Burroughs' fiction, played against a backdrop of surrealistic filth, makes repeated reference to a dying universe and often depicts higher forms of life being broken down into lower forms and those broken again into undifferentiated waste. "Thermodynamics has won at a crawl," he writes in *Naked Lunch*. John Hawkes frequently sets his action against a vista of spreading decay, degeneration, and barren indistinction. His waste landscapes, real and potent, overwhelm the tenuous characters. In *The Beetle Leg*, the desert envelopes a little town and actually consumes men and machines. The spectre of universal decline haunts even the private aesthetic patternings of Nabokov. "Time's arrow" in *Lolita* points mockingly toward degradation, but not so much in the external worlds of social organization and cosmic heat death as in the world of one's own conceptions. Humbert recalls a misplaced photograph of Annabel Leigh "amid the sunny blur into which her lost loveliness graded." Just before losing Lolita, he finds himself overtaken by a "slow awfulness," a purely personal analogue for the "slow apocalypse" of Fausto Maijstral in *V*. In *Pale Fire*, the character Gradus embodies this process of "graded" loss. As an agent of the "communal eye," Gradus is the enemy of any "special reality" or unique structuring. As his name suggests, he signifies the *gradual* degeneration of order to chaos, concentration to diffusion, surprise to probability, singularity and distinction to repetition and sameness. He is portrayed as a foolish bungler, but he arrives nonetheless. The force he represents is everywhere and closely parallels entropy as presented by Pynchon. John Shade, Gradus's victim, observes that "time means succession, and succession, change." Charles Kinbote, who believes that he is Gradus's intended target, writes more paranoiacally and pointedly that "spacetime itself is decay; Gradus is flying west."

The Grotesque and the Absurd in the Work of the Counterrealists

In depicting the entropic slide of the contemporary world, the counterrealists are much more prone than the neorealists to update traditions of the grotesque in art and literature. Some authors comment on the fear that humankind is singly and collectively losing its humanity by writing novels in which characters appear to themselves, other characters, or the reader as machines and automata. Besides Pynchon, especially in *V.*, Heller, Kesey, Vonnegut, Burroughs, and Ellison provide examples of this strategy. In *Invisible Man*, various black characters — the shoeshine boy, Tod Clifton, the narrator himself — are set dancing like animate puppets or mechanical dolls. Lieutenant Scheisskopf of *Catch-22* is obsessed with perfect parades: he wants to "sink pegs of nickel alloy into each man's thighbones and link them to the wrists by strands of copper wire with exactly three inches of play." Chief Bromden of *Cuckoo's Nest* sees the "acutes" on the ward "fidgeting and twitching, responding to the dials in the [Big Nurse's] control panel." The "chronics" are "machines with flaws inside that can't be repaired." *Breakfast of Champions* presents people as machines, a view from which only the author and a few of the characters are delivered in the course of the book.

These authors create worlds that make the reader respond with simultaneous laughter, horror, and disgust. Their worlds are grotesque by John Ruskin's definition — both ludicrous and terrible. Modern technology may amplify grotesque effects, just as in *Cat's Cradle* a microphone amplifies Papa Monzano's "death rattles and all sorts of spastic yodels," bouncing them off the city's buildings while the gathered crowd awaits his speech. The grotesque world is poised fearfully atop underpinnings of a wacky causality. A monstrous disproportion exists between events and their consequences, and dreadful results mushroom from innocuous beginnings. Wolfgang Kayser identifies this convention of the grotesque as the "whirlpool," employed especially by Friedrich Theodor Visher: it is "the turbulent accumulation of incidents and the demonic nature of a mechanism which, once triggered, tumultuously unfolds itself and completely disintegrates a whole segment of reality."[7] Uncontrollable acceleration often marks the rush from trivial cause to terrible effect, a rush in which people are swept up, helpless.

Technology seems to plunge us toward destruction; our capabilities grow in geometric proportion to our moral sense of how to apply them. Hence the threat of apocalypse always lurks behind the ominous logic of recent history—or perhaps it leaps out at us openly. *Cat's Cradle* begins with a chapter entitled "The Day the World Ended" and closes with a catastrophe that plays itself out like a Rube Goldberg machine to destroy life on earth. In *Breakfast of Champions*, Vonnegut's "robo-Magic" starts out as an appliance company and moves into munitions via a mechanism for controlling the wash cycle. Pynchon's Yoyodyne makes a similar jump from toys to real sixty-foot missiles. Not just technological "progress" but the general course of events in a counterrealistic novel is described by bizarre developments growing out of and into other bizarre developments at an increasingly rapid rate. To take just a couple of examples, in *The Crying of Lot 49* the Tristero blossoms "exponentially," and in *Catch-22* Milo rises by progressively larger leaps from officious mess sergeant to raingod whose "graven images" overlook "stone altars red with human blood."

Although occasional figures such as Milo appear larger than life, the individual is more typically a puppet at the mercy of mysterious and hostile forces, as in Burroughs' worlds, where abysmal powers shape what passes for reality. Often the sources of estrangement do not fully reveal themselves or their purpose, even though their influence cannot be escaped or

---

[7]Wolfgang Kayser, *The Grotesque in Art and Literature*, trans. Ulrich Weisstein (New York: McGraw-Hill Book Co., 1966), p. 113.

controlled. Charles Harris quotes Jan Kott's description of the grotesque experience: the recognition that "the absolute is absurd . . . not endowed with any ultimate reasons; it is stronger, and that is all."[8] John W. Hunt's words about Pynchon apply generally to the authors I have called counterrealists: "the absurd nature of life [is] something with which he begins rather than ends"; it "assumes more and more the position of premise rather than conclusion."[9] Within the individual or within the larger world, the authors destroy the bond that one expects to find between cause and effect; they playfully violate the chain of logical links between events that the reader or the character needs to orient himself. Anything can happen at any time for any reason—or for no reason.

Consider the apparent reversal of stimulus and response that undermines the laws of causality in *Gravity's Rainbow*: Slothrop has a sexual encounter and *then*, seemingly as a consequence, a V-2 obliterates the area. In *Catch-22*, a warrant officer gets malaria instead of the clap for his "five minutes of passion on the beach." Yossarian inadvertently catches the clap when he steps out of his tent in Marrakech one night to get a candy bar and a Wac he has never seen before calls him into the bushes. "'That sounds like my dose of clap, all right,' the warrant officer agreed. 'But I've still got somebody else's malaria. Just for once I'd like to see all these things sort of straightened out, with each person getting exactly what he deserves. It might give me some confidence in this universe.'"[10] The world does not work by cause and effect, and neither, apparently, do people. Conversations between characters repeatedly thwart our expectations that some reasonable and discernible motivation underlies the behavior. When Clevinger *(Catch-22)* asks Halfoat why he plans to die of pneumonia, the Chief counters, "Why not?" Pynchon's Benny Profane and the Whole Sick Crew will perfect this method of accounting for

---

[8]Charles B. Harris, *Contemporary American Novelists of the Absurd* (New Haven: College and University Press, 1971), p. 30.

[9]John W. Hunt, "Comic Escape and Anti-Vision: The Novels of Joseph Heller and Thomas Pynchon," in *Adversity and Grace: Studies in Recent American Literature*, ed. Nathan A. Scott (Chicago: University of Chicago Press, 1968), p. 91.

[10]Joseph Heller, *Catch-22* (New York: Dell Publishing Co., 1961), p. 175. All subsequent references cited in the text as *(C-22)*.

their actions in *V*. As distinct from neorealists, the counterrealists present characters and worlds that are finally inexplicable.

The counterrealists tend to divide between those who emphasize sociological sources of absurdity and those who concentrate on metaphysics. Borges, Barthelme, Nabokov, and Barth exemplify the latter contingent. Todd Andrews, narrator of *The Floating Opera* concludes that *"Nothing has intrinsic value"* and that *"There is, therefore, no ultimate 'reason' for valuing anything,"* including life and death. Vonnegut occupies something of a middle position, seeing personal efficacy as undermined not only by technological disasters but also by a universe described in *The Sirens of Titan* as "composed of one-trillionth part matter to one decillion parts black velvet futility", a universe not "schemed in mercy." In *Jailbird*, twenty years after *Sirens*, Starbuck observes, "The human condition in an exploding universe would not have been altered one iota if, rather than live as I have, I had done nothing but carry a rubber ice-cream cone from closet to closet for sixty years." Pynchon's absurdism investigates both sociological and metaphysical sources in greater depth, but he stresses the sociological. Reality may be only a state of mind, but the state of mind fostered by the here and now is deranged. One sees in his novels a tension between absurdities arising from too little structure (a cosmos and a civilization drifting toward maximum entropy) and too much structure (a world congealing into bureaucracies and intermeshing power groups). Heller and Kesey portray the latter kind of institutional absurdity, although without the breadth of historical and philosophical concerns (e.g., the ideas of Max Weber) that one finds in Pynchon. Yossarian of *Catch-22* and Chief Bromden of *Cuckoo's Nest* must live in a system that becomes insane because it is *too* organized, *too* devoted to self-serving method and routine. In counterrealistic fiction, there are neither metaphysical nor social standards by which to judge sanity. The protagonists may seem crazy, but who in their worlds is saner? Heller applies a Catch-22 of his own to his characters: any "well-adjusted" person on Pianosa must be demented. "McWatt was the craziest combat man of them all probably, because he was perfectly sane and still did not mind the war"

(C-22, p. 61). The same catch applies to those in Kesey's ward, Pynchon's San Narciso, Hawkes' post-war Germany, and Burroughs' "Reality Studio."

Control, Conspiracy, and Paranoia

Some of the counterrealists who focus on societal grotesqueries and absurdities posit some molding force beyond the unconscious nightmare of history. Characters, narrators, and perhaps authors develop the "paranoid" conviction that some all-encompassing conspiracy just beyond the point of clear identification seeks to crush and control life. Such worlds contrast with Heller's; despite the emphasis on form, rank, and routine, nobody rules in Heller's world but accident. Even the Peckems, Dreedles, and Minderbinders who ride the random course of events do not control it or their own destinies. The officers at the top are clowns, and ex-P.F.C. Wintergreen—the lowest-ranking man in the European theater—is one of the most powerful. Scheisskopf haphazardly floats to the head command; he never could have done so if some master group manipulated all events. Vonnegut also mocks the belief in conspiracies, suggesting that crazy circumstance has produced things as they are. In *The Sirens of Titan* he pushes the notion of plotted history to comic and cosmic extremes: the entire course of human civilization and precivilization has been arranged—for a bathetic purpose—by Tralfamadore, a planet about 150,000 light-years away. And in *Jailbird* the majority stockholder of the sinister cartel proves to be a shopping-bag lady.

At the other extreme, William Burroughs presents nightmares of domination by alien powers, "Senders," and viral agents. Comparable fears arise in Pynchon when, for example, Oedipa senses "magic, anonymous and malignant" (49, p. 11) or when the narrator of *Gravity's Rainbow* reveals that our planetary "mission" is "to promote death" (GR, p. 720). Pynchon, however, distances himself a bit by putting questionable characters and narrators between such opinions and himself. Burroughs is more easily identified in his fictional vehicles: his *Naked Lunch* persona, William Lee, was his pseudonym for *Junkie*, and Burroughs has voiced his views in a BBC interview.[11] Kesey's Chief Bromden is subject to this type of paranoia: the Chief's Combine is a Pynchonesque power group never visible except in its effects; it mechanizes not only people but all aspects of life.

Norman Mailer's work offers the prospect of human as well as suprahuman conspiracies. In his treatment of character and plot, Mailer is not typically counterrealistic. In general, his narratives are less defiantly fragmented and implausible, and his characters are rounder, more explicable, more likely to achieve freedom or existential authenticity. But Stephen Rojack of *An American Dream* comes to sound rather like Oedipa Maas of *Lot 49:* he believes "in grace and the lack of it," in spirits, demons, evil potencies, and omens. In Mailer one receives none of those hints, recurrent in Pynchon, that such perceptions may just be projections. On the contrary, espousing what Norbert Wiener calls the "Manichean" view of entropy as an active evil, Mailer posits something "whose joy is to waste substance," sounding a bit like a latter-day version of Pynchon's "Scurvhamite": "Nothing for a Scurvhamite ever happened by accident." Creation was a vast, intricate machine. But one part of it, the Scurvhamite part, ran off the will of God, its prime mover. The rest ran off some opposite Principle, something blind, soulless; a brute automatism that led to eternal death" (49, p. 116). Again Pynchon raises the notion but puts it at a remove from himself, assigning it to a questionable sect in a questionable history. Besides demonism, political power plays and conspiracies pervade Mailer's fiction, as in *Barbary Shore* or *An American Dream*. In the latter, the character Kelly has ties to the CIA, FBI, White House, Mafia, and other channels; such interlocks suggest an organized complicity to foster death and control. In a less extreme expression of the same attitude, Ellison's invisible man sees everyone in New York as directed by "some unseen control."

Even in the most fantastic counterrealism, the paranoid vision can take hold. Borges's "The Babylon Lottery" raises the possibility that all events in a supposedly "infinite game of chance" are guided by "the Company" and its ubiquitous, invisible agents. And Barth's Eben Cooke (*The Sot-Weed Factor*) speculates that Baltimore and Coode, the arch-

---

[11]Extracts of the interview are printed in *Les Langues Modernes* (January–February 1965).

antagonists whom no one has ever seen, are really in collusion, feigning a rivalry "to hide some dreadful partnership." In the words of *Gravity's Rainbow*, the history of Maryland seems to be a Them-like conspiracy, "not always among gentlemen, to defraud" (*GR*, p. 164).

The Problem of Knowing

Some plots are devised by others. But to confound matters, we continually (and often unconsciously) invent our own plots, which we usually cannot distinguish from those imposed on us. In *Giles Goat-Boy*, George Giles hears two lovers, supposedly in a passionate moment, discussing whether one can know things directly or see only the "screen" onto which one projects incessant personal patternings. Epistemological problems and quests, presented comically or not, abound in counterrealistic fiction, especially Pynchon's (see chapter 5). Heller's chaplain tries to confront the "immoral logic" of Catch-22, but he is confused in his endeavor by such forms of paramnesia as *déjà vu, jamais vu*, and *presque vu*, as well as by experiences that fall into no category—for example, his sighting of a naked man in the tree at Snowden's funeral. As does Oedipa in her investigation of the Tristero, the chaplain starts to think that what he saw "was either an insight of divine origin or a hallucination: he was either blessed or losing his mind. Both prospects filled him [as they do her] with equal fear and depression." Perhaps he suffers from "an aberration of memory rather than of perception"; perhaps "he never really *had* thought he had seen what he now thought he once did think he had seen" (*C-22*, p. 276). "There was no way of really knowing anything, he knew, not even that there was no way of really knowing anything" (*C-22*, p. 274).

The chaplain is trapped in an epistemological circle: he can verify his own perceptions and memories only with more of his own perceptions and memories. Like Oedipa as she gazes down the corridors of Genghis Cohen's rooms, the chaplain senses with trepidation "how far it might be possible to get lost in this" (*49*, p. 69). With "so many monstrous events" taking place, the chaplain loses confidence in his ability to tell "which events *were* monstrous and which *were* really taking place" (*C-22*, p.287). In one instance, he "recognized himself as the source of the turbulent roar that was overwhelming him" (C-22, p. 282). Unlike Pynchon, Heller exploits the comic possibilities of the circle very glibly and with little real anxiety. Sometimes he resolves the puzzle himself, providing the reader with a knowledgeable perspective from which to laugh with condescending sympathy at the poor character: "The possibility that there really had been a naked man in the tree [as there really had been] . . . never crossed the chaplain's mind" (C-22, p. 280).

Vonnegut combines humor and pathos in the epistemological plights of his characters. Although, as he says, "nobody ever understands," understanding seems almost possible—just out of reach and just barely missed. Characters in The Sirens of Titan fret and brood over "what life is all about" so often that the phrase becomes a sort of refrain. And yet that novel travesties the attempt to find a purpose in the pattern of history, a design in the design. Figures from later books are driven by the same unquenchable need: Dwayne Hoover (Breakfast of Champions) is launched on a homicidal rampage by his search for "what life is all about." Early or late, the author stresses the futility and danger of the quest. Vonnegut's work abounds in images that evoke uncertainty, in particular the confusion between self and external reality. Howard Campbell and Resi Noth (Mother Night) stand in front of a window and see themselves superimposed on the scene beyond it, much as Nabokov's John Shade sees his living room "hung" on the snow scene outside. Campbell looks at this overlap of subject and object, wondering "what the allegory was." He finally falls prey to a complex of forces he cannot comprehend; he becomes a character in a plot too intricate and far-reaching for him to unravel, especially when his personal projections are superimposed on it.

Nabokov frequently evokes confusions like Campbell's by presenting images in which one view overlays or interferes with another. His main figures, for example Humbert Humbert, Charles Kinbote, and John Shade, often try to see through some "semi-translucent" medium, or they depend for vision on some tricky combination of window and mirror. In other words, one cannot tell—perhaps they cannot tell—to what extent the patterns they see merely reflect their own inventive powers, psychotic or artistic. Humbert, the deranged solipsist, often

stands alone, confined in narrow and nearly viewless quarters,
straining to see past uncanny obstacles. His thwarted attempt
to spy on nymphets resembles his frustrated endeavor to
detect the design of his fate. His world is filled with strange
coincidences, not all of which, he suspects, are purely
coincidental. He tries to read the pattern of his destiny and
finds it easy to see in hindsight but not while it is unfolding;
"McFate" does not italicize its clues. Humbert believes that
certain events along the way are revelatory but that their path
is "so slight as to be practically undistinguishable from a
madman's fancy."[12]

The suggestion of insanity in the narrator, of course,
complicates the epistemological issues. Perhaps feigning
madness for the jury, perhaps not, Humbert assumes causal
connection in simple coincidence: the McCoo's house burned
down, he declares, "possibly, owing to the synchronous
conflagration that had been raging all night in my veins"
(*L*, p. 35). He recalls Cincinnatus of *Invitation to a Beheading*,
who upon reviewing his sojourn in prison finds himself
"involuntarily yielding to the temptation of logical
development, involuntarily (be careful, Cincinnatus!) forging
into a chain all the things that were quite harmless as long
as they remained unlinked." Cincinnatus "inspired the
meaningless with meaning, and the lifeless with life."[13] After
abducting Lolita, Quilty mires Humbert in a "cryptogrammatic
paper chase" of veiled allusions, anagrams, and numerology.
As for Oedipa, everything becomes a potential clue; the
frenzied detective wonders how he can know if he is seeing
bits of evidence or finding patterns that don't exist, perhaps
superimposing them over patterns that do and so confounding
his search.

Charles Kinbote's commentary in *Pale Fire* raises the same
epistemological problems that Humbert's confession does.
Kinbote also sees causality where only temporal correlation
exists: "My fall acted as a chemical reagent on the Shades'
sedan, which forthwith budged and almost ran over me."[14]

[12]Vladimir Nabokov, *Lolita* (New York: Berkley Publishing Corp., 1966), p.
196. All subsequent references cited in the text as (*L*).
[13]Vladimir Nabokov, *Invitation to a Beheading*, trans. Dmitri Nabokov (New
York: Capricorn Books, 1965), p. 155.
[14]Vladimir Nabokov, *Pale Fire* (New York: Berkley Publishing Corp., 1974), p.
12. All subsequent references cited in the text as (*PF*).

And in his notes to the poem he fully indulges his propensity for seeing meaningful designs where there may be none; much as Herbert Stencil "Stencilized" Mondaugen's story (V.), Kinbote transforms Shade's poem. But Kinbote's detective work meets severe impediments. He attains his only knowledge of the poet's creative activity by "peeps and glimpses, and window-framed opportunities." The window frame recalls the sharp limitations of Kinbote's solipsistic vantage point — the preponderance of enclosing opaque wall, or even the machinations of nature in the obstructing greenery. So beset, Kinbote sometimes has to rely on the reflection of a "kindly mirror," but, as often in Nabokov, the mirror could suggest the mind and the mind's need to see itself reflected in all things, to remake external "reality" in its own image. In forging his story of Zembla, Kinbote has yielded in his own way to a human compulsion that drives the fictional poet and the author himself. On reading two Shadean lines, Kinbote comments that one might wish to sink "back into oblivion's bliss," but a "diabolical force" urges one "to seek a secret design in the abracadabra,"

> 812 Some kind of link-and-bobolink, some kind
> 813 Of correlated pattern in the game (PF, p. 135)

Although he professes to "abhor such games," his Zembla, like Shade's poem, exists only as a complex pattern of correlations drawn between the "drab prose" of his outer world and the "strange poetry" of the inner.

Because they are absorbed by the problems and processes of knowledge, Nabokov, Pynchon, Borges, Barth, and many other contemporary authors are fascinated by correlated patterns and labyrinthine structures within structures, infinitely regressing. Consider the proliferations of Sudarg's mirror, of V. in love, of doors in Genghis Cohen's hallway, of forking paths, or of Barth's tales within tales. Such configurations bear on the theme of knowing not only because they overwhelm the mind but also because, as Barth notes, preoccupation with intricate patterns can betoken madness:

> One manifestation of schizophrenia as everyone knows is the movement from reality toward fantasy, a progress which not infrequently takes the form of distorted and fragmented representation, abstract formalism, an increasing preoccupation, even obsession, with pattern and design

for their own sakes — especially patterns of a baroque, enormously detailed character — to the (virtual) exclusion of representative "context."[15]

Nabokov is just one of several counterrealists who build their books around schizophrenic, paranoid, or otherwise unreliable characters obsessed with patterns. Pattern precedes content for such characters; they believe, as does Oedipa Maas, that there is to "outward patterns a hieroglyphic sense of concealed meaning" (49, p. 13), and they feel, as does John Shade, that *"Life is a message scribbled in the dark. / Anonymous"* (PF, p. 29). They are compelled against the odds to decipher the message if they can, to discover its author (or authors), to trace out some thematic design.

Of course, even if the pattern tracer is not clearly unstable, many epistemological problems remain. Barth suggests some of these in his first novel, where narrator Todd Andrews explains why he builds his story around the metaphor of the floating opera:

> It always seemed a fine idea to me to build a showboat with just one big flat open deck on it, and to keep a play going continuously. The boat wouldn't be moored, but would drift up and down the river on the tide, and the audience would sit along both banks. They could catch whatever part of the plot happened to unfold as the boat floated past, and then they'd have to wait until the tide ran back again to catch another snatch of it, if they still happened to be sitting there. To fill in the gaps they'd have to use their imaginations, or ask more attentive neighbors, or hear the word passed along from upriver or downriver. Most times they wouldn't understand what was going on at all, or they'd think they knew, when actually they didn't. . . . I needn't explain that that's how much of life works.[16]

The situation described here recalls Vonnegut's *Sirens of Titan:* when subject to mind-control techniques, "Unk" perceives the world in "blanks and glimpses" but still struggles to discover "what life was all about." Barth presents "the facts of life" as he sees them and Vonnegut presents an intergalactic fantasy — satire, but the characters face the same

[15]John Barth, *Lost in the Funhouse* (New York: Bantam Books, 1969), p. 115. All subsequent references cited in the text as *(FH).*
[16]John Barth, *The Floating Opera* (New York: Doubleday & Co., 1972), p. 7. All subsequent references cited in the text as *(FO).*

impediments to their efforts to know. Likewise, Humbert and Kinbote have only intermittent, "window-framed opportunities." Characters in *Gravity's Rainbow*, most notably Franz Pökler, perceive "reality" in broken intervals, as a succession of separate frames that gives the illusion of continuity. These inescapable "delta t's" (time intervals) designate gaps in perception that one might reduce but never eliminate; to sense any kind of meaningful design, one must fill such gaps in perception by fabricating what is missed. One makes the structure one interprets, writes the message one reads.

This attempt to make and interpret design is especially taxing because, as the narrator of *Gravity's Rainbow* proclaims, "*everything is connected,* everything in the Creation" (GR, p. 703). Todd Andrews concurs, "I think that to understand any one thing entirely, no matter how minute, requires the understanding of every other thing in the world" (FO, p. 6). This, of course, makes it impossible for him to discover the "objective truth" about any event, much less a design of events broken by delta t's. When Betty June Gunter attacks him, apparently with intent to kill, he realizes that he can "interpret a number of possible significances, often conflicting, sometimes contradictory," but all equally plausible.

The world of the floating opera seems completely undetermined; at least, causes can never be known, especially in the realm of human behavior. Todd writes, "there is no will-o'-the-wisp so elusive as the cause of any human act" (FO, p. 214). One can gather masses of information, as Todd does in his *Inquiry into the Circumstances Surrounding the Self-Destruction of Thomas T. Andrews.*

> But it is another thing to examine this information and see in it, so clearly that to question is out of the question, the *cause* of a human act.
> In fact, it's impossible, for as Hume pointed out, causation is never more than an inference; and any inference involves at some point the leap from what we see to what we can't see. (FO, p. 214).

Though the attempts of Pynchon's characters to understand their world can be described more accurately as "paranoia" than as simple inference, Pynchon also posits the need to leap over the unknown, to fill in "what we can't see" if we would supply some sense to events. This, of course, raises the issue of projection; one may impose on circumstances a design or meaning not there at all. Pynchon demonstrates through his Heisenbergian references what Todd Andrews knows: the very fact of an observer precludes objectivity. Todd's subjective influences will always get mixed up with the data in ways he cannot control or even measure. Nevertheless, in keeping the *Inquiry* on his father he also collects notes on himself, the note-taker. Both aspects of the *Inquiry* are endless; just as Todd cannot ultimately grasp the *cause* of Betty June's or his father's actions, neither can he finally know himself. Like the world and anything in it, he comprises too many possibilities.

In *The Sot-Weed Factor,* Barth demonstrates a point that Pynchon makes through Fausto Maijstral and other characters: epistemological problems arise because the subject as well as the object is mutable. As Henry Burlingame instructs Eben Cooke, "The very universe is naught but change and motion"; forms seem stable because "our coarse vision fails to note their change."[17] Life is constituted in a jumble of endlessly moving and interweaving plots that would be impossible to sort out even if one had a stable, definitive vantage point, which of course one does not. The single and continuous self, Henry tells Eben, "lives only in your fancy, as doth the pointed order of the world. In fact you see a Heraclitean flux: whether 'tis we who shift and alter and dissolve; or you whose lens changes color, field, and focus; or both together. The upshot is the same, and you may take it or reject it." (SWF, p. 349). But if one cannot reliably interpret the pattern before one's eyes, it is hopeless to grasp "the truth" in history. Like Pynchon, but with less urgency in his playfulness, Barth shows that history is subjective, a welter of irreconcilable and generally unreliable versions and distortions that offer no possibility of final knowledge. Even the chapter titles debunk the attempt to find a design:

THE POET WONDERS WHETHER THE COURSE OF HUMAN HISTORY IS A PROGRESS, A DRAMA, A RETROGRESSION, A

[17] John Barth, *The Sot-Weed Factor* (New York: Grosset & Dunlap, 1960), p. 140. All subsequent references cited in the text as (SWF).

CYCLE, AN UNDULATION, A VORTEX, A RIGHT- OR
LEFT-HANDED SPIRAL, A MERE CONTINUUM, OR WHAT HAVE
YOU. CERTAIN EVIDENCE IS BROUGHT FORWARD, BUT OF AN
AMBIGUOUS AND INCONCLUSIVE NATURE.

Ebenezer Cooke, in a period of despair, posits another answer:
blind chance. In a moment of paranoia, he jumps to the
opposite conclusion: conspiracy. But these are unverifiable
suppositions, like any other theory. "Tis our fate to search,"
declares Burlingame, and yet we have no hope of final
discovery, or even of stable reference points to guide us on the
quest. Barth underscores this inherent uncertainty with an
image that Pynchon employs to the same end in *The Crying of
Lot 49* and *Gravity's Rainbow.* Burlingame demonstrates to
Eben that the very constellations by which they chart their
course are spurious, not real patterns at all. Epistemologically,
morally, or physically, there are no fixed coordinates to which
one can always look for direction. Right and wrong are "like
windward and leeward, that vary with standpoint, latitude,
circumstance, and time" (SWF, p. 515).

Giles Goat-Boy is a *Bildungsroman* that ironically
undermines all the characters' attempts to know, perhaps
more radically than does *The Sot-Weed Factor.* Neither George
Giles nor the reader can say what the goat-boy's assignment
was, or whether he proved himself Grand Tutor. Barth lends
imagistic support to his theme with pervasive references to
light and darkness, visibility and invisibility, eyes and mirrors,
spectacles and scopes of all kinds. (Ellison employs very
similar images in *Invisible Man,* his modified *Bildungsroman,*
in order to depict the narrator's problems of perception and
discovery, but he does so without the professed counterrealist's
degree of fantasy, self-conscious juggling of myth, self-
announcing artifice, and insistent fabulism.) Even in his work
that aspires to have "no content except its own form, no
subject but its own processes," Barth still shows interest in
epistemology, as in the story "Night-Sea Journey." "Ambrose
His Mark" treats the human propensity to read signs and find
in events a veiled significance, a meaning that takes form
primarily from the viewer's own subjective workings, fears,
and hobbyhorses. In "Lost in the Funhouse," Ambrose cannot
know external reality because it is multiple and because his
observing self gets in the way; but the same impediments
thwart Ambrose when he tries to study himself, as Todd

nds upon one's ability to manipulate or even create
rns of experience, not just perceive them; the pattern
r can build his "own special reality," a world that offers
ents of joy and "combinational delight." Hence Nabokov's
s abound in imaginative games—patterns of allusion,
stion, reflection, and wordplay. These form an artistic
se against the horror of shapeless, undefined "reality"
efuses to doff the quotation marks it brandishes, as
kov has said, like sharp claws. An epistemological gap
s remains. Like a vacuum, it draws out the subjective
ructions that give one a sense of knowledge, an illusion
omprehensible whole. Just as electricity binds the earth
er, Nabokov told an interviewer, "the act of individual
on . . . [must] animate a subjectively perceived texture,"
lity begins to "rot and stink" like a corpse.21

ookov's "act" is similar to Pynchon's "projecting a world"
th's "reinventing" it, although Pynchon's term is more
iological than self-consciously aesthetic. In each case a
n—sometimes deliberate, sometimes not—provides the
s that allow characters to act. And such fictions, even the
st conspiracy paranoias, might actually describe the
l with at least metaphoric validity: the intricately woven
of relationship could duplicate the texture of reality, as
bokov's "contrapuntal theme" and Barth's "tangled
," A character from *Chimera* says, "The truth of fiction
t Fact is fantasy; the made-up story is a model of the
."22 For Pynchon, paranoia is the model of a cosmos in
l "*everything is connected*" and of a world in which
ocking interest groups *do* manipulate events to some
tain degree.

anoia is also a viable model of the worlds of *Catch-22* and
oo's Nest. Yossarian at first appears to be a textbook case,
the novel progresses — or circles — one sees a few MP's,
some other characters, observes the world outside the
tal, and comes to feel that Yossarian is not so crazy after
ief Bromden is "paranoid schizophrenic" in clinical
. The first sentence of his narrative could come from
Pynchon's works: "They're out there." But here, as in

er, *City of Words*, p. 33, quotes Nabokov.
Barth, *Chimera* (Greenwich, Conn.: Fawcett Publications, 1972), p.
subsequent references cited in the text as (C).

Andrews did: "In the funhouse mirror-room you can't see
yourself go on forever, because no matter how you stand, your
head gets in the way" (*FH*, pp. 81–82).

Inventing Reality: Action Inside the Unknown

Perhaps epistemological issues pervade counterrealistic fiction
because the authors disbelieve in impersonal reality, or at least
in its accessibility. Borges has written, "Really, nobody knows
whether the world is realistic or fantastic, that is to say,
whether the world is a natural process or whether it is a kind of
dream, a dream that we may or may not share with others."18
The border between invented reality and impersonal reality
cannot be defined or even shown to exist. Consequently, and in
accord with the interest in structural complication I mentioned
above, Borges invents a reality in which a character invents a
reality in which others invent a reality in which the subject
forms his world in the act of perception. The narrator of "Tlön,
Uqbar, Orbis Tertius" pieces together a theory that a benevolent
secret society has tried to "project a world" (Oedipa will use
the same phrase). They concoct *The First Encyclopaedia of
Tlön*, which states that geometry in Tlön depends on the
viewer: "As man moves about, he alters the forms which
surround him." Similarly, in Oedipa's descent from the
mountaintop to San Narciso, Pynchon demonstrates that the
nature of reality and the "forms which surround" one vary
with perspective.

But Pynchon, at least through his characters, is more
concerned than Borges with trying to define the border or
interface between the projected and the perceived. In his
attempt, he reveals greater interest and expertise in scientific
epistemology than do other counterrealists; for example, he
draws upon Einstein and Heisenberg in referring all back to
the observer. In addition, he makes that observer confront an
external something which, though not directly knowable, has
a political and historical impact. Pynchon shows the greater
social urgency. Borges, like Barth or Nabokov, stands closer
to uninhibited philosophical or aesthetic play: his Tlön is far
more subjective than San Narciso, which implicates the legacy

18Tony Tanner, *City of Words: American Fiction, 1950–1970* (New York:
Harper and Row, 1971), p. 40.

of America; the forms that compose Borges's projected world exist only when and as they are perceived or remembered.

The counterrealists recognize that there is no Reality — only subjective realities, or mental constructions of the world made from unique and imperfect vantage points. Such private authorship leans toward solipsism and schizophrenia, but the counterrealists acknowledge the insights of madness now that the external world (assuming it is not a dream) seems an unsafe arbiter of sanity. Paranoia could be perception, schizophrenia a viable alternative to collective craziness. They recognize that modern man must fabricate versions of reality to satisfy his need for understanding as he faces the epistemological barriers or the superhumanly scaled atrocities that his era has sprung upon him. Barth said in an interview with John Enck: "If you are a novelist of a certain type of temperament, then what you really want to do is re-invent the world. God wasn't too bad a novelist, except he was a Realist. . . . But a certain kind of sensibility can be made very uncomfortable by the recognition of the *arbitrariness* of physical facts and the inability to accept their *finality*."[19] Barth is a counterrealist because he tries to reinvent the world in fictions that do not accept the primacy or finality of fact. He, Nabokov, and Borges invent characters who reinvent the world more self-consciously than Pynchon's do. Borges's writer Herbert Quain admits "that of the various pleasures offered by literature, the greatest is invention." Likewise, John Hawkes said, "I want to try to create a world, not represent it,"[20] and his narrators of *Second Skin* and *The Blood Oranges* are possessed of the same desire to play demiurge. Susan Sontag shows that the mind must remake the world to attain some resistance to it, or authority over it, and Donald Barthelme practices that advice.

One finds a similar feeling in Heller, Kesey, Vonnegut, and their main characters, although, as with Pynchon, the rationale is often a bit more practical and less aesthetic than with Barth, Borges, or Nabokov. Protagonists from either group may "reinvent the world" to give meaning and design to what might otherwise be unmanageable chaos. In "Funes, the Memorious," one of Borges' characters dies for lack of a system

[19]Enck, "John Barth," p. 8.
[20]John Enck, "John Hawkes: An Interview," *Wisconsin Studies in Contemporary Literature* 6 (Summer 1965), 154.

to organize and limit the mass of details su
perception and memory. Moreover, a fictio
events is necessary to motivate real actions
Kilgore Trout, Randle P. McMurphy, Henr
Fausto Maijstral come to realize. It is unlik
from Pianosa to Sweden (*Catch-22*), or tha
(*Cuckoo*) did all that he is supposed to hav
can inspire actual rebellions, and paranoia
together into what Pynchon terms a "We-sy
the "They-system."

These fabrications recall Bokonon's *fom*
or what Vonnegut calls the "comforting ho
to sustain us. Vonnegut's Eliot Rosewater r
wonderful *new* lies" if he is to continue wi
of living, just as Barth's Jacob Horner needs
Typically, Barth presents the comic *reduct*
without fictions that lend meaning to a giv
and Eben Cooke literally cannot move — bu
must act, to define themselves existentially
motion. As existence precedes essence, so i
reinvention precedes existence. Borges and
similar points: a reference to the imaginary
artifacts and an encyclopaedia; images from
become incarnate. Barth, thinking of Tlön,
"Literature of Exhaustion" that a fabricatio
prior reality," and Eben Cooke comes to fee
surrounding Baltimore and Coode are more

Any reinvention of the world is, as Eben
raised not e'en on sand but on the black and
the Pit.'" And yet he "'sees in the vain cons
nobleness allowed to fallen men'"; "blind l
codes nor causes," so "'what the cosmos la
ourselves supply.'" (SWF, pp. 670, 732). Ha
similar case. On the blue island, Skipper (S
reinvents his life, supplying what it lacked.
observes that far from giving us the "naked
narrator offers us a fabrication, a sort of ver
itself a protective "second skin." Skipper fi
power of his mind; the alchemy of his imag
him by transmuting his painful past into a g

For Nabokov, one's sense of reality — delt

Pynchon, one cannot dismiss the paranoid's vision. The Chief's distorted perceptions paradoxically reveal the truth. Bromden crushes one of the Big Nurse's pills: "For a tick of time, before it all turned into white dust, I saw it was a miniature electronic element . . . microscopic wires and grids and transistors."[23] These pills, of course, are barbiturates, which Ratched uses to control the "robots." McMurphy recognizes the method in the madness: "I didn't say it didn't make sense, Chief, I just said it was talkin' crazy" (CN, p. 210). The Chief carries this faith in metaphoric veracity one step further: "But it's the truth even if it didn't happen" (CN, p. 8). Kesey certainly meant for his readers to feel tolerance if not respect for madness. He writes in his introduction, "I studied inmates as they daily wove intricate and very accurate schizophrenic commentaries on the disaster of their environment" (CN, p. xi). He employs the metaphor of weaving also used by Pynchon in *The Crying of Lot 49* to suggest much the same point: self-made "tapestries" can faithfully represent the form if not the details of reality. Vonnegut in his preface to *Mother Night* asserts a belief common to the counterrealists: " . . . lies . . . can be, in a higher sense, the most beguiling forms of truth" (MN, p. ix). One might think of Pynchon's "Low-lands," where Dennis Flange ponders "the truth of a true lie," or of Barth's Mythotherapy that is "a true representation of the distortion that everyone makes of life," or of Nabokov's "special reality" that has "nothing to do with the average 'reality' perceived by the communal eye." Fabricated realities may be the only realities possible or inhabitable. One cannot find objective answers in *Pale Fire*, just as one cannot find the Crown Jewels. Perhaps that is the point. In a world of compulsive seekers, one never seems to find what is being sought, and yet one can find something else by remaining playfully open to sudden developments in the quest: a mountain instead of a fountain, texture instead of text, Zembla instead of the poem the communal eye would see. Viewed in this way, existence becomes a game of seeing and making designs, a game that offers sporting and aesthetic pleasure to those who play it well.

Such acts of creation can have a certain predictive validity:

[23]Ken Kesey, *One Flew Over the Cuckoo's Nest*, ed. John Clark Pratt (New York: The Viking Press, 1973), p. 33. All subsequent references cited in the text as (CN).

everyone actually is trying to kill Yossarian, Bokonon's *foma*
do foretell how the world ends, Billy Pilgrim can predict the
manner of his death, V.'s white comb does turn up on Malta,
and Humbert was being chased by someone intent on stealing
Lolita from him: they are right, Shade would say, about the
texture if not the text of events. In much of contemporary
American writing, the fictional versions of reality made to
"fill the blank," as Barth calls it, are vindicated. One cannot
dismiss a projected world just because fantasy helps in some
indeterminable measure to shape it. The hazy duality of
paranoia and perception, delusion and discernment, is the
closest one can come to reality.

Characters in Mailer, Burroughs, Ellison, Kesey, and Heller
keep asking whether and to what extent they perceive reality
or their own fabrications. Vonnegut seems less insistent, given
his and Bokonon's feeling that even if there is a purpose and
meaning to life, we can't know it. Pynchon, as always, offers
complementary perspectives: Mantissa suggests that Old
Godolphin's Vheissu may have been a hallucination, but
Godolphin responds, "Does it make any difference? . . . it was
not what I saw or believed I saw that in the end is important.
It is what I thought. What truth I came to" (*V.,* p. 190). And
yet perhaps more typically, characters like Oedipa (*49*) and
Slothrop (*GR*) sense that their mysteries have historical import,
and they want to know if their "projected worlds" illuminate
transpersonal reality. Hawkes, especially in *Second Skin* and
The Blood Oranges, appears to care more about the aesthetic
and therapeutic value of invented worlds than about their
epistemological value. Barth's Todd, Horner, Burlingame,
Giles, and the funhouse voices presume that one can playfully
concoct fictions at will and superimpose them on a blank page
without much danger, so long as one doesn't take the fictions
very seriously or expect others to do so. Nabokov believes that
if reality is unknowable and if we each must live enclosed in
our own invented world, we might as well accept it and, if
possible, make it aesthetically enjoyable. For the character
who is a self-conscious artificer, fictionalizing can provide
gratifying diversion and "combinational delight."

Such exhilaration in play could account for what Barth
finds especially pleasing in recent novels — "a kind of wild
inventiveness which you certainly didn't find a decade or so

previously."[24] The impossibility of discovering and disclosing
reality permits this kind of creative abandon, a sportive
contrivance that revels in its own compensating possibilities.
Todd knows that his *Inquiry* will never achieve "the truth."
But he adds, "It doesn't follow that because a goal is
unattainable, one shouldn't work towards its attainment.
Besides . . . processes continued for long enough tend to
become ends in themselves, and if for no other reason, I should
continue my researches simply in order to occupy pleasantly
two hours after dinner" (*FO*, p. 215). Todd sounds here
somewhat like Herbert Stencil working "for no one's
amusement but his own" (*V.*, p. 50). These characters divert
themselves with an epistemological quest just because they
cannot succeed. Todd, who perhaps sees the impossibility of
succeeding more clearly than does Stencil, worries less about
having to "approach and avoid" success. Sherry and the genie
in *Chimera* go still further: the "real" situation is just a pretext
for the play of language. Fictions can be "truer than fact . . . in
rare instances their beauty made them real" (*C*, 61, 25).

Nabokov is even more insistent about the necessity and the
pleasure of building one's own fictional world. Humbert says
he penned the story of Lolita "to save not my head, of course,
but my soul." Actually, *Lolita* is not about Lolita or even Lolita
and Humbert; in it, rather, Humbert considers his attempts to
transform his experience through language. In this he is like
Hawkes's Skipper, only more self-conscious. Nabokov has
said that the "initial shiver of inspiration" for the novel "was
somehow prompted by a newspaper story about an ape in the
Jardin des Plantes who, after months of coaxing by a scientist,
produced the first drawing ever charcoaled by an animal: this
sketch showed the bars of the poor creature's cage" (*L*, pp.
282 – 83). Humbert laments, "I see nothing for the treatment
of my misery but the melancholy and very local palliative
of articulate art" (*L*, p. 258). At least he has the chance of
diverting himself with the activity. This may not seem enough,
but there is no other hope: "Oh, my Lolita. I have only words to
play with!" (*L*, p. 32).

Pale Fire deals even more exclusively than *Lolita* with
"articulate art" as the only reality, for Kinbote has reinvented

[24]Enck, "John Barth," p. 3.

a world from John Shade's verbal reinvention, "Pale Fire,"
which itself we have only as an incomplete and partially
legible text. Somewhat as Humbert would paint the bars of his
cage, Shade would harmoniously arrange the coincidences he
perceives and the linguistic ornaments he makes to ensure that
he is "most artistically caged." The "viewless wings of poesy"
are not omnipotent. Shade, like the waxwing, is unable to fly
through window-mirrors that combine inner and outer worlds,
perception and self-reflection; but as an imaginative artist he
can exploit that semi-translucence where inner and outer meet,
using the coincidental doublings to build a "private universe"
he can understand, a world of "combinational delight" whose
pattern just might mirror that of "galaxies divine."

Shade achieves his "crystal land" by superimposing the
image of the inner room on the world outside the window.
Metaphorically, this is what Kinbote does with Shade's poem.
As he interprets the work, he recapitulates Oedipa Maas
projecting a world as she tries to lend "Meaning" (or, in
Kinbote's words, "human reality") to the legacy left by Pierce
Inverarity. Kinbote, of course, inherits "Pale Fire." He reads
the lines about "that crystal land" and exclaims: "Perhaps an
allusion to Zembla, my dear country" (PF, p. 54). In a way, he
is right: this is Zembla, "a land of reflections" where the inner
world of dreams and fantasy is "duplicated" and superimposed
on the world beyond the glass, beyond the semi-translucent
barrier that defines one's self and isolates it. Zembla is the
land of imaginative transformation where one magically alters
"the average 'reality' perceived by the communal eye" into a
"special reality," the necessary condition and sustaining
medium of art.

Self-conscious Authors, Narrative Techniques

Quite often, then, counterrealistic fiction will portray
characters who reinvent the world, either as paranoids,
self-conscious artisans, or some uncertain combination of the
two. Hence the authors themselves are usually self-conscious
about fiction making, seeing the characters' reinventions as
analogues for their own. Through a variety of technical
experiments, they demonstrate their appreciation of the
delights, difficulties, deficiencies, and even dangers of such

productions. For example, they generally appear to agree with Susan Sontag that the novel should be challenging, unfamiliar, and hard to process if it is to catch up with the other arts and be faithful to contemporary experience. Solipsism and epistemological problems typify that experience; Hippolyte, narrator of Sontag's *The Benefactor*, writes, "Despite the force with which I press myself against the line, I cannot jump outside the circle of my consciousness." Pynchon employs references ranging from Conrad to Goedel to Wittgenstein to Heisenberg in portraying characters who are similarly locked inside the towers or hothouses of their own minds. The characters—and perhaps the authors—often feel trapped and restless in any one reality, even a self-made one. Competing with the claustrophobic ambience of the novels, plot lines often feature characters who move to escape confinement or just simple stasis: Rojack, the invisible man, the Kerouac persona, Reed's Loop Garoo, Fariña's Gnossos, Orr, Yossarian and Chief Bromden at the end of their stories, Burroughs' William Lee, Humbert with Lolita, Burlingame, all of Pynchon's protagonists chasing or chased through an alien environment. Their movement represents the characters' inability to settle on a single view or understanding of the way things are, or to accept such a view.

Counterrealistic fiction also frequently presents narrators and narratives that are inconsistent and unreliable, a further acknowledgment of the impossibility of defining reality. The early Mailer tended to treat epistemology through plot, showing the character's struggle to apprehend the controlling forces that underlie and shape the patterns of existence: witness General Cummings trying to resolve those forces "to the form of a single curve." In *Why Are We in Vietnam?*, Mailer makes epistemological problems structural. The narrator undermines our confidence in our ability to know what is going on or even who our source is, reminding us, "You never know what vision has been humping you through the night." And Ellison veers toward counterrealism by abandoning the realistic treatment of the traditional picaresque novel for a surrealism that derives from the dreams, confusions, visual distortions, and hallucinations of the narrator. Barthelme's narration is frequently erratic, sometimes, as in *Snow White*, throwing unidentified voices at the audience. And Burroughs, especially in *Naked Lunch*, deploys a raiding party of masked voices to harry the reader, who becomes lost in the mechanical nightmares. The mechanical nightmare of Nurse Ratched's ward comes via a single voice, but a paranoid's. Even Borges's more metaphysical fantasies often arrive through an unreliable narrator, as in "Tlön, Uqbar, Orbis Tertius." John Hawkes has shown a special predilection for such possibilities of the first person, particularly in *Second Skin* and *The Blood Oranges*, in which real life, fantasy, wishful waking dream, and paranoid projection are hard to sort out. The reader faces an epistemological dilemma of his own. Nabokov, whom Hawkes greatly admires, may have given us the definitive modern version of this device. His Catch-22 is that we cannot trust Humbert whether he appears sane or insane. If Humbert is a madman, we must suspect the plots and patterns he sees; if Humbert is a conscious and deceptive artist or a calculating deceiver of psychiatrists, juries, and readers, then we must suspect the plots and patterns he makes. He is probably a bit of all three. Similarly, Charles Kinbote seems mad and compulsive at some times but conscious and artistically calculating at others. Again, madness and art may coexist; one can never be sure to what extent any given piece of his commentary is paranoid or aesthetic fabrication. Also like Humbert, Kinbote employs rhetoric, often sounding as if he writes to justify himself to doctors or detractors.

Heller adopts the first person in *Something Happened*, but without intending or achieving profound epistemological effects: the inconsistencies in Bob Slocum's personality may disclose the author's failure to focus clearly on just who Slocum is. *Catch-22* more tellingly conveys bewilderment in the inconsistencies and circlings of its third-person narration. Important scenes are retold several times, each time in greater detail and with a change of tone, usually toward grimness. Heller said, "I wanted people to laugh and then look back with horror at what they were laughing at."[25] As in other "black humor" novels, especially Pynchon's, such contrary perspectives deny the reader any stable vantage point from which he can order his responses to the world; the author undercuts the reader's sense of security and complacency as much as that of any character by juxtaposing comic-strip

[25]"So They Say," *Mademoiselle* 57 (August 1963), 234.

humor with grisly, realistically depicted horrors like Snowden's death or Esther's nose job. For the comedy, Heller and Pynchon present the outlandish as commonplace: Yossarian sees nothing exceptional in the escapades of the Halfoat family or in the sleeping arrangements of Hungry Joe and Huple's cat, nor does Oedipa startle at hearing the Fort Wayne Settecento Ensemble's variorum recording of the Vivaldi Kazoo Concerto, Boyd Beaver, soloist. But Heller much more than Pynchon achieves his absurdity by simple contradiction or inversion: in the Pianosa base hospital "the Texan turned out to be good-natured, generous and likable. In three days no one could stand him" (*C-22*, p. 10). Or he exploits the comic circularity of Lewis Carroll-like exchanges and of Catch-22 in its various permutations.

In Vonnegut, too, the third-person narratives often cause more uncertainty than do first-person accounts such as those in *Mother Night* or *Cat's Cradle*. *Slaughterhouse-Five*, for example, moves in a somewhat Pynchonesque direction; one cannot be sure whether or to what degree the events are "Pilgrimized." Bokonon recognized—and made us recognize—his *foma*. Billy's time and space travel could be mental travel, a fantastic tapestry woven from threads of association between past war experiences, present situations, and futuristic Kilgore Trout novels. If so, Billy does not feel the self-doubt of Oedipa Maas, nor does he playfully exercise his creative power as do the more self-conscious fabricators of Nabokov and Barth. Sometimes the narrator, Vonnegut himself, identifies Billy's experiences as "true" or fantasized, but usually he leaves the reader unaided. As in Heller and Pynchon, at times the humor is satiric, directed at a particular target and implying a philosophical norm; other times it is just grotesque. For either purpose, Vonnegut, like Heller, relies on bald incongruities and tonal disparities. He also treats the preposterous as matter-of-fact but opts more for interplanetary fantasies than bureaucratic absurdities. And he is more akin to Heller than Pynchon in his use of the short gag, sentence, paragraph, chapter, and—in his case—novel. He describes his books as "mosaics made up of a whole bunch of tiny little chips; and each chip is a joke."[26] Pynchon's mosaics are far

---

[26]Kurt Vonnegut, Jr., *Wampeters, Foma, and Granfalloons* (New York: Dell Publishing Co., 1976), p. 258.

more varied and inclusive, his chips larger and more weighty. Pynchon, for example, draws upon contemporary science with greater knowledge and profundity of purpose (see chapter 4). Vonnegut may employ the same concepts, but he does so with an easy and often superficial glibness: Winston Niles Rumfoord (*Sirens of Titan*) exist as a wave-phenomenon after being "chrono-synclastic infundibulated."

Oddly enough, and for all his expansiveness, Barth likes to work the short joke—typically a paradox, philosophical puzzle, möbius strip, or circular trap. Jake (*The End of the Road*) and Eben Cooke must have selves to act, but, existentially speaking, they must act to have selves. In *Letters*, the mad Harrison Mack, Jr., "fancied himself, not George III sane, but George III mad; a George III, moreover, who in *his* madness believed himself to be Harrison Mack sane." And for all Barth's complexity, tone and speaker are often more consistent than one might expect; the cool, witty, smug voice warms up only when excited by the ingenuity of its "wild inventiveness." Although Burlingame worries Eben with the epistemological problems occasioned by mutable subjects and objects, the "lens" of the novel remains very steady, as perhaps it must to follow the eighteenth-century format Barth exploits. Pynchon, though, demonstrates issues like the ones Burlingame raises by playing havoc with point of view (see chapter 7). Barth's first-person narrators, admittedly quirky, still seem able and willing to give an accurate, rational account (perhaps Giles goat-boy least so).

Barth's epistemological concerns appear less in inconsistencies of tone and voice than in self-conscious statements and structural curiosities. Todd says he eschews a logical narrative sequence because he feels, like Tristram Shandy, that to explain anything well he must explain everything. But then how can one be linear? (I discuss Pynchon's response *sans* explicit self-questioning in chapter 7.) Pynchon's mood is part paranoid, part mystic, and part post-Einsteinian; Barth's mood is more insouciant. Both, however, demonstrate the point by fracturing narrative continuity and proceeding by association. In *Letters*, everything bears on everything else, precluding the possibility of straight plot line from beginning to middle to end; the novel is composed of uncentered fragments, epistles in this case, that point in many directions at once. *Giles Goat-Boy* mocks the hope of complete knowledge and disclosure, for its construction undermines its own textual authenticity: the various frames, postscripts, footnotes, and the like all cast doubt on one another as well as on the tapes that constitute the story proper. Hence the reader experiences the confusion and frustration of being unable to verify any version of reality.

Barth perhaps marks the extreme of an important counterrealistic impulse: to violate realistic illusion, to prevent a suspension of disbelief by insisting on the complexity of plotting and structure, the freedom of invention and distortion, the sport of stylistic and allegorical contrivance, the artifice of fabulism. He says, "*Affirm* the artificial element in art (you can't get rid of it anyhow), and make the artifice part of your point."[27] Generally, Borges, Nabokov, Hawkes, and Pynchon are closer to Barth in this than are the other writers I have discussed. Borges is a special case: he condenses the maze and yet preserves its maddening convolutions. For him it is enough, as Barth noted, to suggest to the reader's mind labyrinths and infinite regressions. With their intricate contrapuntal structures, Hawkes and Nabokov, and especially Pynchon and Barth, carry the reader down mazed paths, exhausting possibilities where Borges only posits them. For example, Barth fits tales within tales in *The Sot-Weed Factor* and goes even further in "Menelaid"; Pynchon fits versions within versions in "Mondaugen's Story" or fantasies within fantasies in *Gravity's Rainbow*. Each has to see how far and in how many possible ways he can push a game or a complication, sometimes to the reader's regret. Here Barth may seem more perverse because the contortions are so premeditated, self-conscious, and self-satisfied. In *Chimera* and *Letters*, he multiplies layers of self-reflection. These works are like halls of mirrors in which the laws of optics and light behavior depend on the whims of the author. He champions the baroque as Borges defines it: "that style which deliberately exhausts (or tries to exhaust) its possibilities and borders on its own caricature."[28]

At the opposite counterrealistic extreme is a writer like

[27]Enck, "John Barth," p. 6.
[28]I quote from Barth's "The Literature of Exhaustion," in *On Contemporary Literature*, ed. Richard Kostelanetz (New York: Avon Books, 1964), p. 672.

William Burroughs, who fears the power of fabricated systems — even his own — to enthrall the mind. Burroughs sees fiction as potentially akin to the thought-control conspiracies of his Senders or Dr. Benway, and so he advocates and practices a kind of guerrilla warfare on the entrapping form. He introduces spontaneity and accident with his "cut-up" method, hacking apart and rearranging the declarative sentence. That sentence he villifies as an outgrowth and perpetuation of Aristotelian "either/or" thinking, a shackle to the Western mind. Expanding his suspicion of logical structure beyond the sentence, he destroys plot line, narrative continuity, and consistent point of view in his novels; the fragmentary episodes of *Naked Lunch* may not even be bound by parallel relation, as are the episodes of *Gravity's Rainbow* (see chapter 7). Pynchon too inveighs against either/or thinking, analysis, and classification, and he suspects that organized plots threaten the free, spontaneous workings of life and the imagination. He too has compared reality to theater and to a film that the audience cannot or will not recognize as such, and he is wary of being trapped inside a confining delusion. He too sees "salvation," or possibility, in the unstructured. His Osbie Feel shouts in battle cry, "We piss on Their rational arrangements" (GR, p. 639). But Pynchon also speaks of "assertion through structure," which he practices. He makes the reader seek meaningful patterns and thus imitate his characters. The later Burroughs in particular tries to destroy this habit, frustrating the reader out of the search. His tack is diametrically opposed to those of Nabokov and Barth, who revel in design-making, reinvented worlds, correlated patterns, and contrapuntal themes.

Donald Barthelme, like Pynchon, occupies something of a middle ground between the extremes. His fiction shows the need for fantasy and reinvented worlds, yet it also prizes the indeterminate, the changeful, and the unfixed. Barthelme values the freedom to construct different versions of reality and yet to stand apart from all of them. In "The Balloon," people enjoy a mysterious globe that suddenly appears over their city, simply because its meaning, purpose, and origin cannot be explained by any one theory; rather, it calls forth a multitude. Because it can "shift its shape," the balloon "offered possibility, in its randomness, of mislocation of the self, in contradistinction to the grid of precise, rectangular pathways under our feet." Barthelme similarly mislocates his narratives, breaking them up and undermining the reader's usual habits of reading, organizing, and synthesizing. Like Pynchon he connects epistemology with literacy, equating reading and understanding the world with reading and understanding fiction. He too sees possibility as well as entropy in randomness and shows a corresponding fascination with recycled junk, reprocessed literary modes, and haphazardly accreting catalogue sentences. His vision of exponentially growing trash piles and his suggestion that we learn to "appreciate" their "qualities" bring to mind "Low-lands," *The Crying of Lot 49*, and *Gravity's Rainbow*, although his backdrop of fairy tale and fantasy as opposed to historical crisis makes for obvious tonal differences.

The counterrealists on the middle ground and even those at the extremes feel the simultaneous need to make and unmake fictional structures: thus they can escape enclosing form, acknowledge that certainty or final versions are impossible, or simply enjoy the play of mind. Most of the writers I have discussed combine all these motives, but in different proportions and degrees. Those who want most to escape confinement will unmake their structures through use of dissolving points of view and narrative disruptions. Those who enjoy authorial gymnastics will unmake their structures through self-parody, typically by caricature of the traditional methods they often use. Pynchon is one of the very best practitioners of either method. But even the more aesthetically motivated counterrealists share some of his anxieties, though perhaps to a lesser extent. Borges, for example, is enchanted with the mind's power to create systems, and he acknowledges the need of such with the story of Funes. But as he shows with the library of Babel, the labyrinth can become a horrible, inescapable prison. In "Tlön," he notes that "any symmetrical system whatsoever" can cast dangerous, enchanting spells that lead people into atrocities. Moreover, he finds any system finally unjustifiable in a relative universe because, he has written, "a system is nothing more than the subordination of all aspects of the universe to some one of them"; inevitably the schema of the system falsifies reality.

Hawkes also portrays both the freeing and the confining

sides of the imagination. His characters become absorbed, possessed by their constructs, somewhat as Pynchon's are by their "hothouses"; these constructs tend to be evil in the early works. The later Hawkes sees in them a good, even a kind of salvation, but he still recognizes that Skipper's imagination reinvented the world as a paradisiacal blue island *and* a hellish black one. Also reminiscent of Pynchon, John Hawkes reveals his ambivalence about reconstructing events by writing a parody of a detective story: *The Lime Twig*, though, is built around a sporting event, not the collapse of the Western ethos, as is *V.* Similar issues arise in *The Recognitions.* There William Gaddis considers at great length whether one can recognize reality as anything more than a reproduction, or what Barth might call a reinvention. As in *Pale Fire*, the characters try to discover, interpret, or verify not objective reality but an artistic reinvention of the world. Copies are needed to replace the gradually fading, decomposing original, but like Oedipa's "act of metaphor," copies can lead or mislead, clarify the form and meaning of the original or impose a false surface that offers its own delights and insights while obscuring those of the original. In raising these questions about pictorial art, the long and convoluted novel makes some discoveries about its own art form.

Vonnegut is much briefer and more direct, but he also recognizes the dual potential of creations and invented realities. Jonah says in *Cat's Cradle*, "Anyone unable to understand how a useful religion can be founded on lies will not understand this book either."[29] Bokononism always makes fun of itself and exposes itself as a fiction, always expresses a "cruel paradox": "the heartbreaking necessity of lying about reality, and the heartbreaking impossibility of lying about it" (CC, p. 189). But there are hazards, too: it was from reading a Kilgore Trout novel that Dwayne Hoover in *Breakfast of Champions* got the delusion that sent him on a violent rampage, and so as in *Mother Night*, Vonnegut again warns that one never knows how one's fictions will be taken.

Nabokov, for all his delight in self-contained "special reality," also sees the threat of solipsism when the special

---

[29]Kurt Vonnegut, Jr., *Cat's Cradle* (New York: Dell Publishing Co., 1970), p. 14. All subsequent references cited in the text as (CC).

becomes the only reality. Consequently, he builds his novels around characters who are in a literal or figurative prison — a reigning obsession that dominates the mind and its processing of experience. As in Pynchon, the obsession is largely epistemological; the character tries to decode a pattern of events, but, ironically, instead of reaching a shared truth he only barricades himself further in his solitary confinement. Through some sort of "criss-cross cause and effect," Humbert strengthens the bars of his cage by painting them. While recognizing that each person must forge his or her own version of reality, Nabokov parodies all such attempts in order to show his knowledge of the insufficiency of any one version and also to save himself from getting immured in his own constructions. For example, Kinbote objects to Shade's "here time forked" passage because "the whole things strikes . . . [him] as too labored and long, especially since the synchronization device has been already worked to death by Flaubert and Joyce" (*PF*, p. 140). But Kinbote's entire commentary relies upon such devices; in his very next note he synchronizes — with some labor and length — the movements of Shade and Gradus. And Humbert, like his "McFate," becomes a "synchronizing phantom." Nabokov tells of his same predilection in *Speak, Memory*: "I like to fold my magic carpet, after use, in such a way as to superimpose one part of the pattern upon another"; this allows "the highest enjoyment of timelessness."[30]

Barth's views on the possibility of knowledge almost enforce his fictional aesthetic. He is so radically skeptical that he doubts any version of reality, even his own. He realizes at once the need for fiction — to fill in the blank and provide a basis for action — and the inevitable shortcomings of any fiction, thus effecting a tension that hallmarks his work from *The Floating Opera* to *Letters*. Such a tension belongs to "the literature of self-parody," as defined by Richard Poirier: it "makes fun of itself *as it goes along.* It proposes not the rewards so much as the limits of its own procedures; it shapes itself around its own dissolvents; it calls into question not any particular literary structure so much as the enterprise, the activity itself of creating any literary form, of empowering an idea with

---

[30]Vladimir Nabokov, *Speak, Memory: An Autobiography Revisited* (New York: G. P. Putnam's Sons, 1966), p. 139. All subsequent references cited in the text as *(SM)*.

style."[31] Somewhat as Pynchon's Fausto fabricates selves to undermine the notion of the self, so Barth invents fictions to expose the nature of fiction. In "The Literature of Exhaustion" he calls The Sot-Weed Factor and Giles Goat-Boy "novels which imitate the form of the Novel, by an author who imitates the role of Author."[32] For example, he caricatures what he terms "aboriginal forms and narratives"—the "roots of the English novel" in The Sot-Weed Factor, "classical myth and the oriental tale" in Giles Goat-Boy and Chimera, and the epistolary novel in Letters.[33]

Counterrealists who enjoy the sport and liberation of self-parody often build their fictions around not one but a number of literary modes and subgenres, or even non-literary materials, all of which they exploit but also mock and undercut; thus they suggest the multiplicity and inadequacy of possible perspectives. Barthelme and Pynchon bring in everything from myth to comic book to fairy tale to pornography. Vonnegut, as in Mother Night or Cat's Cradle, may present a narrative comprising parts of imaginary books, magazines, letters, tapings, and so on. Barth's The Sot-Weed Factor has been called a mock-epic, a farce, a satire, a Bildungsroman, a picaresque tale, an historical romance, a parody of one or all of the above, and more. Of Giles Goat-Boy Poirier has written that Barth creates "a blurring excess of meanings . . . . nightmarish fusions among literary, political, sexual, anthropological, and historical myths."[34] Pynchon, especially in Gravity's Rainbow, draws encyclopaedically upon the full range of our cultural heritage and exploits science and technology more fully than Barth does, despite Goat-Boy's WESCAC; his novels offer a miscegenation of perspectives, disciplines, and systems, often showing how these overlap or inform one another.

But while Barth, like Pynchon, attacks the systems that he defines—attacks even the urge to systematize—he does so comically, irreverently, as if without fear or even recognition of

[31]Richard Poirier, The Performing Self: Compositions and Decompositions in the Languages of Contemporary Life (New York: Oxford University Press, 1971), pp. 27–28.
[32]Barth, "The Literature of Exhaustion," p. 670.
[33]LeRebeller, "A Spectatorial Skeptic," p. 103.
[34]Poirier, The Performing Self, p. 26.

their power to control the mind. The author's playful exercise of sovereignty over the material frees him from it. Parody for him is a diversion, not a means to examine the shortcomings of some established way of organizing reality. In *Giles Goat-Boy*, for example, Barth does not seem worried so much as amused and even inspired by the labyrinthine ramifications of consciousness; these permit a kind of lexical gamesmanship where fun for fun's sake, and not "truth," becomes the norm. Barth seems not to believe or feel the need to believe in any of the patterns, myths, or syntheses as reality. In fact he appears to need *not* to believe, to preclude belief by incessant undercutting. He values the materials as pieces in a game; they allow him the sport of intellectual play, parallel construction, and fanciful allegorizing. Rather than unify his sensibilities by submitting them to the monomyth, he fractures the monomyth by making it submit to his ironic sensibilities. His narrative conforms to a design in order to explode it, to show the author's ability to master and manipulate it. The main point of *Giles Goat-Boy* is the cleverness of the maker, not some statement about our inability to know, not some assessment of our myths or cultural heritage in terms of their "content." One senses that another set of myths with wholly different implications about human reality might have served just as well if Barth and his readers had been equally familiar with that lore, and if the myths offered the same opportunities for elaborate, parodic constructions. Barth told John Enck that such scholars of myth as Lord Raglan and Joseph Campbell, who furnished him with much material for *Goat-Boy*, may be "cranks" for all he knows or cares.

Pynchon's Place in Contemporary American Fiction

As I have suggested, the counterrealists employ a variety of methods to involve their readers in the same confusions and epistemological problems that their characters face within fictional worlds. Nabokov writes that "in a first-rate work of fiction the real clash is not between the characters but between the author and the world." The novelist, like the chess player, poses "problems," and "a great part of a problem's value is due to the number of 'tries' — delusive opening moves, false scents, specious lines of play, astutely and lovingly prepared to lead the would-be solver astray" (SM, p. 290). Pynchon and Barth also make the reader go on a difficult quest for meaning, make him search through a partially realized, gradually emerging pattern of tenuously related events. At least it *seems* to be a pattern; the reader may feel uncertain because he is often seduced into seeing correlation as causation, arcane fact as fantasy. He shares the characters' pique or even their sense of release and renewed possibility at being unable to verify any version of reality, for these elaborate counterrealistic works make him sense that his own version is but another unverifiable, imperfect fiction.

Pynchon is a central figure in contemporary American fiction not only because his works are important in their own right but because he shares deeper affinities with a broader range of counterrealists than does any other writer I have included in this general temperament. Like Heller, Kesey, Burroughs, Vonnegut, and Reed, he wants his fiction to refer back to some kind of shared external world. He too responds to sociological and metaphysical anxieties with genuine dread and with humor that is sometimes satiric, sometimes purely grotesque. But he typically shows more philosophical profundity, historical knowledge, scientific learning, literary allusiveness, and fabulistic ingenuity than they do. Fundamentally, his writing has more in common with the work of Barth and Nabokov.

The fictions of Nabokov and Pynchon are similar in this respect: both exploit the compulsive tendency we have as human beings and especially as readers to look at phenomena and see meaningful patterns that perhaps do not objectively exist. Both build narratives upon a web of echoes, reflections, and repeated details that *seem* to be interlocking clues — one never knows for certain if they are. With this tantalizing web of partial revelation, both inveigle the reader into mimicking solipsistic and paranoid protagonists who isolate themselves even more profoundly in the course of their epistemological quests. And both withhold from the reader any final certainty, any firm ground of knowledge, any sure means for determining reality. In the Heisenbergian terms Pynchon employs, both arrange things so that one cannot even tell to what degree subjective influences have "perturbed" the events one observes. Also, while remaining skeptical, both accord a metaphoric validity to the fabrications of the protagonists, a validity that Nabokov calls "special reality" and Pynchon "the truth of a true lie." This validity is perhaps the only reality and truth available. Consequently, both writers evince some ambivalence about fabricated designs and envisioned meanings, such as fictional plots, and so both employ parody and self-parody to keep themselves uncommitted.

But here Nabokov and Pynchon begin to separate. While both, in Page Stegner's words, show "structural and thematic concern with the infinite levels of perception," Nabokov is much more insistent in "his attempt to escape the spherical prison of time by creating in his art a subjective world" that supplants the "communal" one.[35] Each person cannot help inventing his world to some uncertain degree, so he may as well build his own special reality self-consciously, aesthetically — that is, decorate his cage without too many qualms about objective truth. Ultimately, then, Nabokov tends to dismiss the epistemological problem of whether the phenomenal world is perceived or projected; his main concern is whether the projection is controlled and artistically sound. Pynchon's characters, who worry about what is "really" going on, tend to be detectives — Nabokov's are often artists or artists manqués, deliberate, manipulative, and self-directing rather than subject to large, mysterious, and impersonal forces. Hence they typically experience more "combinational delight" than paranoia when they encounter the "web of sense." Humbert recalls "those dazzling coincidences that logicians loathe and poets love" (L, p. 31). He cherishes and employs that which obsesses Stencil, goads Oedipa, and frightens Slothrop.

John Dewey has written that an experience "is esthetic in as far as it is final or arouses no search for some other experience."[36] This applies well to Nabokov novels, which point not so much to the outer world as to their own felicities of language manipulation and contrapuntal structure. Contemptuous of "messages," Nabokov declares: "For me a work of fiction exists only insofar as it affords me what I shall

---

[35]Page Stegner, *Escape into Aesthetics: The Art of Vladimir Nabokov* (New York: Dial Press, 1966), p. 50.
[36]John Dewey, *The Quest for Certainty, A Study of the Relation of Knowledge and Action* (London: George Allen and Unwin, 1930), p. 235.

bluntly call aesthetic bliss, that is a sense of being somehow, somewhere, connected with other states of being where art . . . is the norm" (L, p. 286).

Whereas Nabokov's intricate patterns compose a realm of "non-utilitarian delight," Pynchon's point back to the communal world and make rather didactic statements about historical conspiracies, economic oppression, social entropy, and so forth. In V., for example, Pynchon juxtaposes episodes from past and present not to afford "aesthetic bliss" through a "contrapuntal theme" so much as to enforce a vision of modern Western decadence. In light of these different objectives, it does not matter whether Kinbote is really Botkin or Charles Xavier, whether Shade really wrote the commentary or Kinbote the poem, as some have wasted time arguing. It matters more whether V. is a paranoid fantasy or the key to the master cabal of the century, whether the Tristero is a reality, a hoax, a hallucination, a salvation, or a destruction. V. or the Tristero could reveal an historical trend even if they are only fantasies, and one senses a need in Pynchon to relate "true lies" back to some shared reality, to find something in them "that mattered to the world," as Oedipa says (49, p. 136). Consequently, Pynchon often makes it hard to distinguish the border between his invented plots and actual historical events or scientific experimentation.

Pynchon, then, is more concerned with sociology and public solutions than is Nabokov. Both authors demonstrate that human patterning faculties are aroused by unrealized design, but in Nabokov the design will be the nymphet or the 999-line poem; in Pynchon it will be "the ultimate Plot Which Has No Name." The first allows for individual contribution; the second may leave little room for viable action. Pynchon's world often seems beyond human control, a closed system running down. Nabokov's world is highly controlled and stylized, even self-contained and static. The figures that populate it rarely move from one condition to another, as Pynchon's characters Stencil, Oedipa, and Slothrop do. Nabokov's figures, like artists, have *already* created a complicated and contrapuntal world, a complete system of correspondences. They play with anagrams; they imaginatively repattern elements already present in order to produce a new meaning. Pynchon characters play with acronyms; they hunt for meaning by projecting beyond the individual clues or letters and trying

to guess at their larger import. For Nabokov, that larger
significance lies within the available set of conditions and
can be achieved through art.

Like Pynchon, John Barth recycles "exhausted" materials.
He also shares the younger writer's fascination with intricate,
complex structures and displays of technical virtuosity. For
Pynchon, "names by themselves may have no magic, but the
act of naming" does (GR, p. 322). For Barth, the story-telling is
the story; "the key to the treasure *is* the treasure" (C, p. 16). Yet
both writers believe that in making such constructs one may
falsify "the case," impose a nonexistent order on what might be
chaos. Instead of retreating into simplicity or primitivism, each
takes the opposite tack of building labyrinths so complex as to
subvert themselves. Here Barth, speaking of himself, could also
be describing Pynchon: "Some people have a gift for making
very complicated things simple. With me it's the reverse: I
make simple things complicated."[37] But when they begin with
complicated things . . . . Pynchon and Barth see the world as an
extremely complex, endlessly ramifying mental construct,
"reality" as subjective and multiple. Any version of it will
inevitably be incomplete; any epistemological inquiry or
artistic rendition will fall short. Hence in their fictions,
self-parody accompanies heterogeneity and encyclopaedic
all-inclusiveness. Both affirm that there is much to know and
no chance, really, to know it. Barth says, "Christ knows what
the 'objective truth' is. The word 'truth' [like Nabokov's
"reality"] simply does not exist without quotation marks."
Even our public life could well be a fiction plotted by power
groups: "No wonder a writer like Pynchon finds his main
theme in paranoia. How can he not?"[38]

Here Barth identifies the key to distinguishing between
himself and his contemporary. Bernard Bergonzi comments:
"There is a . . . division in absurdist fiction, between writers of
whom one can posit some kind of relationship to American
reality, or reality in general, and those who are much more
concerned with establishing their own individual reality, in a
self-contained verbal universe. . . . John Barth is a distinguished
practitioner of the latter approach."[39] Pynchon practices the

[37]LeRebeller, "A Spectatorial Skeptic," p. 100.
[38]Ibid., p. 106.
[39]Bernard Bergonzi, *The Situation of the Novel* (Pittsburg: University of
Pittsburg Press, 1970), p. 90.

former. Barth says, "Muse, spare me (at the desk, I mean) from Social-Historical Responsibility, and in the last analysis from every other kind as well, except Artistic."[40] And he aspires, as he says in *Chimera*, to write fiction that "will represent nothing beyond itself, have no content except its own form, no subject but its own processes" (p. 266). The anatomical and parodic structures of Pynchon's works point beyond the literature they inhabit to address systems or organizing forces both objective and subjective, to address both the world and the human mind that registers and responds to the world.

In fact, the problematic relation between mind and world is central to Pynchon. Barth's characters, more like Nabokov's, tend to dismiss the problem by assuming that impersonal reality is unknowable and personal reality but a fiction. This "knowledge" frees them to play with fictionalizing, to be self-consciously and openly arbitrary in their fabrications. They write their own scripts and act out their own roles with the conviction that they merely "fill in the blank," supply "what the cosmos lacks," as Barth says. Pynchon knows that man "embroiders" plots to fill the epistemological gap between himself and the unknowable, but he does not suggest that we design purely self-reflective fictions where the only norm is aesthetic bliss or intellectual sport; nor does he suggest that his own fictions are such endeavors. Moreover, he seems unsure that the plots one creates are entirely one's own, that one is in control or is even aware of the shaping mechanism. While registering a profound uncertainty and seeing the need for alternate realities, Pynchon keeps trying, as do some of his characters, to decode the ominous logic of reality and to make his fictions reflect it.

Barth's "Glossolalia" points out "that language may be a compound code, and the discovery of an enormous complexity beneath a simple surface may well be more dismaying than delightful." So it is with "*anything* examined curiously enough" (*FH*, p. xi). Barth usually confines himself to ethics and epistemology—lately, just to language and literature. Pynchon will examine "*anything*." He confronts the entire world.

---

[40]"Muse, Spare Me," in *The Sense of the Sixties*, ed. Edward Quinn and Paul J. Dolan (New York: Free Press, 1968), p. 440.

*A Control That Is Out
Of Control*

In his first nationally published story, "Mortality and Mercy
in Vienna" (*Epoch*, 1959), Thomas Pynchon takes up his
consistent theme: the depiction of contemporary society and its
effects on human nature. And from this outset, Pynchon shows
human beings as dwarfed and dominated by quasi-animate
forces that seem to lurk inside social change, grinding
individuals into anonymity and conformity. These
people-assimilating forces begin to appear conscious and
malignant; Cleanth Siegel wonders rather paranoiacally if it
"was a question of compulsion," if there was "something
which linked people . . . some reason which gave them no other
choice" (MMV, p. 202). Siegel first noticed this insidious
process at Harvard when he witnessed how rapidly his
"majestically sneering" roommate degenerated into an effete
puritan after suffering "the first tiny rent in that Midwestern
hauteur which he had carried up to now as a *torero* carries his
cape" (MMV, p. 202). That Siegel fears a similar loss of self
becomes apparent when he employs the bullfight metaphor to
describe his own social situation—the Washington crowd,
precursor to The Whole Sick Crew in V., threatens to absorb
him: "Moment of truth. *Espada* broken, *muleta* lost, horse
disembowelled, picadors sick with fear. Five in the afternoon,
crowd screaming. Miura bull, sharp horns, charging in"
(MMV, p. 213).

This minatory levelling process that so concerns Cleanth
Siegel also concerns his author. In various guises and
situations (though seldom named), it appears in all of
Pynchon's fiction to inform themes, dominant symbols and

imagery patterns, narrative structures, and prose style. In delineating the nature and consequences of this process, Pynchon draws metaphorically and rather broadly on the concept of entropy as understood by the scientist considering thermodynamic systems, the information theorist regarding communication systems, or the historian contemplating social systems. Definitions vary with discipline, but in each case entropy is a measure of disorder, randomness, and probability. Energy concentrations, special arrangements, ordered hierarchies, and organized structures in which forms and distinctions exist are improbable.[1] That is, they typically require energy to be shaped and sustained; they could hardly occur by chance. But all systems tend toward an arrangement— or disarrangement—that would be produced by chance; all tend to dissipate into a chaos without order or differentiation. This chaotic equilibrium reflects the random and even distribution of parts or energy. It precludes physical work in a thermodynamic system, information transfer in a communication system, and the coordinated interchange that allows productive activity in a social system.

The distinguishing barriers between Cleanth Siegel and the Washington Crew members are breaking down, but this only intensifies his sense of isolation. Siegel notes that everyone around him has become alike in becoming solipsistic; each person has built a temple "to the glory of some imago or obsession . . . decorated inside with the art work of dream and nightmare, and locked finally against a hostile forest, each 'agent' in his own ivory tower, having no windows to look out of, turning further and further inward" (MMV, p. 212). Such solipsistic characters recur throughout Pynchon, for example in the persons of Herbert Stencil (V.), agent in his hothouse, or Oedipa Maas (49), the maiden held captive in the tower. In decorating their enclosed temples, they recall Nabokov's characters making their cages "artistic." But whereas Nabokov builds novels around the sport and value of such activity, assuming that one must live in a cage of one's own making anyway, Pynchon and his characters show an urgent need to break through the enclosing walls and reach some transpersonal reality.

[1]Norbert Wiener, *The Human Use of Human Beings: Cybernetics and Society* (New York: Avon Books, 1967), p. 20.

Their need typically yields to their fear of meeting reality in the form of that entropic force which leaves people no choice, that "anonymous and malignant" magic, as Oedipa thinks of it (49, p. 11). And their need yields to resignation. Like Conrad's Kurtz, Siegel at first hopes to bring light to the partygoers' inner darkness, but he eventually gives up the struggle, saying in effect: "Exterminate all the brutes." He leaves his party to a homicidal attack, speculating that such a violent rending of the tower walls will be a "very tangible salvation" to the solipsists. Herbert Stencil chooses to "approach and avoid" the resolution of his mystery, Oedipa Maas begins her "many demurs" during her first visit to Zapf's Used Books, and Tyrone Slothrop (GR) gives up his quest for whatever enlightenment the Rocket might bring him.

Isolation and Conformity: The Inanimate Self

Ultimately, Pynchon's characters cannot escape their solitary confinement or help others to do so. Yet paradoxically, they are no more individual for being isolated. In all of Pynchon's work, defining contours dissolve in the general malaise. This is Pynchon's "entropic vision," which Charles Harris correctly identifies as his concern not so much with a moribund cosmos as with "the dehumanizing processes of mechanistic society that transform animate man into inanimate automaton."[2] Fausto Maijstral best summarizes the situation: "Decadence, decadence. What is it? Only a clear movement toward death or, preferably, non-humanity." In becoming "more inanimate," people move "closer to the time when like any dead leaf or fragment of metal they [will] be finally subject to the laws of physics" (V., p. 301). In an imaginary conversation with SHOCK and SHROUD, two synthetic humans made to measure the effects on us of peculiarly modern hazards, Benny Profane learns that the mannequins represent what we already are becoming in the mass:

> "Me and SHOCK are what you and everybody will be someday.
> . . . If somebody else doesn't do it to you, you'll do it to
> yourselves. . . . None of you have very far to go. . . . Remember

[2]Charles B. Harris, Contemporary American Novelists of the Absurd (New Haven, Conn.: College and University Press, 1971), p. 78.

the photographs of Auschwitz? Thousands of Jewish corpses, stacked up like those poor car-bodies. Schlemihl: It's already started" (V., pp. 266, 267, 275).

In Pynchon, this mass trend is often portrayed — or perceived by the characters — as being conscious and malignant, perhaps because it stimulates a kindred urge in the human psyche. Wylie Sypher notes that "under the guise of the death wish Freud gave psychoanalysis its own version of the theory of entropy. If, he says, the tendency of instinct is toward repeating or restating an earlier condition, then the desire to return to the inorganic is irresistible, and our instinct is to obliterate the disturbance we call consciousness."[3] In other words, man — at least in part — seeks to become "subject to the laws of physics"; the death wish is "what Freud himself called a kind of 'psychical entropy.'"[4] Similarly, Walter Benjamin has observed that in this age of mechanism and decadence, mankind "can experience its own destruction as an aesthetic pleasure of the first order."[5]

Pynchon often presents this "aesthetic" pleasure as sexual perversion. The emphasis on stylization, the primacy given technique, and the ensuing treatment of oneself or others as inanimate objects all conduce to that machine-age fetishism and sado-masochism figuring so prominently in his fiction. In "Mortality and Mercy in Vienna," the jaded Debby Considine, a prototype of V., is magnetically attracted to the "Windigo psychotic," Irving Loon, not knowing that she, like many Pynchon characters after her, has become sexually fascinated with the cause of her own death. Sex and death, especially fetishistic love for the instrument of one's demise or subjugation, are recurrent and related themes, most notably in V. and Gravity's Rainbow. The masochistic Esther is sexually aroused by her graphically described nose job. Shale (as in rock) Schoenmaker, a plastic surgeon with an apt name, works on her "gently, like a lover," and then makes love to her urgently, like a working professional: "Come. We'll make believe it's your operation. You enjoyed your opertion, didn't you. . . . Lie on the bed. That will be your operating table. You

[3]Wylie Sypher, Loss of the Self in Modern Literature and Art (New York: Random House, 1962), p. 75.
[4]Harris, Contemporary American Novelists, p. 84.
[5]Walter Benjamin, "The Work of Art in the Age of Mechanical Reproduction," in his Illuminations (New York: Harcourt, Brace & World, 1968), p. 244.

are to get an intermuscular injection.'" (*V.*, pp. 96–97). V. with her lovers, especially Mélanie l'Heuremaudit (cursed hour), epitomizes this urge to stylize the act, to be self-conscious, to reduce one's partner and oneself to an inanimate object, *"une fétiche."* Even Benny Profane, who usually fears inanimate objects, wonders before sex with Rachel Owlglass if someday "there would be an all-electronic woman. Maybe her name would be Violet [sustaining the pattern of "V" references]. Any problems with her, you could look it up in the maintenance manual" (*V.*, p. 361).

As Richard Lehan notes, "Pynchon believes that the machine age pushed the Puritan fear of women—that is, of sex—to its final destructive conclusion, led modern man 'deeper into fetish country' until the woman 'became entirely and in reality . . . an inanimate object of desire.'"[6] For such a world, the Rocket holds an irresistible fascination. On the one hand, it is the ultimate sexual-technological fantasy for the machine-age fetishist or for anyone who might be "in love, in sexual love, with his, and his race's, death" (*GR*, p. 738). Scientist Franz Pökler "found delight not unlike a razor sweeping his skin and nerves, scalp and soles, in ritual submissions to the Master of this night space and of himself, the male embodiment of a technologique that embraced power not for its social uses but for just those chances of surrender, personal and dark surrender, to the Void, to delicious and screaming collapse" (*GR*, p. 578). Its "great airless arc" appears to Katje Borgesius "as a clear allusion to certain secret lusts that drive the planet [. . .] over its peak and down, plunging, burning, toward a terminal orgasm" (*GR*, p. 223). As is typical of his work from "Mortality and Mercy in Vienna" on, Pynchon will state his theme in a variety of tones, ranging from vituperative to sorrowing to coarsely burlesque. Counterpointing Katje's serious vision, rocket limericks relate the woes that befall a host of young fellows having affairs with different parts of the V-2.

Besides those sexually aroused by destruction, the Rocket also speaks to those like Brigadier Ernest Pudding who feel the need for "something real, something pure" to blast away the

---

[6]Richard Lehan, *A Dangerous Crossing: French Existentialism and the Modern American Novel* (Carbondale: Southern Illinois University Press, 1973), p. 160.

"stuffed paper illusions and military euphemisms" that stand between man and the "truth," that clog the cycle of life and death. Similarly, Pudding's masochism satisfies a "need for pain," which arises from his guilt over losing seventy percent of his troops in World War I. And Katje, who inflicts that pain as Domina Nocturna, needs suffering as "reassurance for her. That she can still be hurt, that she is human. . . . Because, often, she will forget" (GR, pp. 234, 662). Sado-masochism might even lend a kind of community in which the injured and the injurer "are joined in the behavior of the whole injury," but generally it proves a pathetic solution. The chain of interlocking perversities aboard the *Anubis* travesties the Great Serpent as much as does Their use of the benzene ring.

Even Pynchon characters other than fetishists or sado-masochists behave so as to dissolve the borders not only between recognizable individuals but also between animate beings and inanimate objects. Benny Profane and The Whole Sick Crew, a rootless bunch of effete pseudointellectuals, wed *dépaysement* with mechanization in their characteristic pastime, yo-yoing. To yo-yo, one simply goes underground (like so many Pynchon characters) and shuttles back and forth indefinitely between two subway terminals. The point of the practice is pointlessness: motion without any motive but to be moving. Yo-yoing thus travesties the quest of Herbert Stencil, adopted arbitrarily and sustained merely to stave off *ennui* with enforced activity. Meaningless motion appears throughout Pynchon's fiction. Ensign Morituri says of the *Anubis* Sick Crew, "We'll all just keep moving, that's all. In the end it doesn't matter." But for him drifting may be the best alternative. When Slothrop pushes, "Is that all you want, just to 'keep moving'?" the Ensign replies, "I want to see the war over in the Pacific so that I can go home [. . . .] and once I'm there, never to leave Hiroshima again" (GR, pp. 479–80).

Pynchon raises the unsettling possibility that motion is meaningless but that stasis is death. When faced with these distressing options, most of those in a position to choose would join the Crew. But meaningless motion degrades one to the condition represented by SHOCK and SHROUD—not dead but not really alive either. Benny resigns the purposeful self-direction of an organism and becomes more like an automaton, or at least an appendage of the machine. Consequent is a typical Pynchon irony: the means used to escape a condition merely reinforce the condition. Benny yo-yos, as Stencil pursues V., to keep some sense of animateness, but in doing so each plays unwittingly into the hands of entropic forces. Stencil's quarry proves to represent, if any one thing, the urge to become inanimate. And the self-directing will that Benny loses apparently transfers to the subway train, which "disgorged passengers, took more on, shut up its doors and shrieked away down the tunnel" (V., p. 29). Meanwhile, the passengers resemble "vertical corpses, eyes with no life, crowded loins, buttocks and hip-points together. . . . All wordless. Was it the Dance of Death brought up to date?" (V., p. 282). Death, emptiness, barrenness, the void — these are always forcing themselves upon the city-dwelling characters, even on the relatively insouciant and oblivious Profane; he fears vistas "where nothing else lived but himself. It seemed he was always walking into one: turn a corner in the street . . . and there he'd be, in alien country" (V., p. 12). The urban-based themes of death and the machine fuse in Benny's nightmare of mechanical disassembly, a nightmare of the twentieth century given archetypal form in the dismemberment of V. disguised as the Bad Priest — she is composed almost entirely of artificial parts.

Pynchon's metaphoric use of entropy reveals the inroads that the animate and the inanimate are making into one another's realms. Working with modern materials, the author urges a hypothesis traditional in grotesque art and literature: the alive are not so alive, but the dead seem to be taking on a life of their own. Pynchon's use of yo-yoing, for example, makes contemporary the convention of the human puppet driven by some inhuman motive power.[7] Benny discovers that a "mad Brazilian" named Da Conho has developed an emotional relationship with his machine gun. "When he found out not long after this that the same thing was with Rachel and her MG, he had his first intelligence that something had been going on under the rose, maybe for longer and with more people than he would care to think about" (V., p. 14). This malevolent, partially hidden, seemingly conspiratorial plot to equate the animate and the inanimate could be the central concern of the novel,

[7]My discussion of this tradition in the literature of the grotesque is based on Wolfgang Kayser's The Grotesque in Art and Literature, trans. Ulrich Weisstein (New York: McGraw-Hill Book Co., 1966).

uniting the meanderings of Benny Profane and the questings of Herbert Stencil.

V., as Stencil perceives her career, devolves from a woman into a grotesque automaton, tracing the analogous course of Western civilization. And as many critics have noted, her degeneration parallels that of Henry Adams's Virgin into dynamo. In the first chapter, a Christmas carol celebrating the virgin birth gives way to "suck hour," during which rowdy sailors guzzle beer from mechanical imitation breasts. With insistent repetition that itself becomes mechanical, the novel graphically portrays humanity or sexuality degraded into mechanism, a motif climaxed when Mélanie dies accidentally impaled on a spear during a dance entitled "Sacrifice of the Virgin." Through this modern-day grotesquerie, Pynchon updates an older social pessimism recounted by Harrington: "'As death comes after life,' Spengler prophesied, 'civilization is the inevitable destiny of culture.' For him, and for many others, this formula meant the triumph of a mechanized, rootless existence ('civilization') over the rich organic life ('culture')."[8]

The Crying of Lot 49 is also built around this seemingly calculated confusion of the inanimate with the animate. Los Angeles becomes a monstrous junkie with freeways for veins and human beings for "melted crystal" (49, p. 14). Similarly, San Francisco's "capillaries" are "mashed together in shameless municipal hickeys" (49, p. 87). San Narciso becomes an agent, an intention, a state of mind, an avatar of a dead man's "will"; quasi-animate, it defies Oedipa to come to terms with it. Objects retain (or are thought to retain) traces of the lives that have invested in them. Pierce Inverarity seems somehow encoded into San Narciso, just as the old sailor is encoded into his mattress or as Mucho's car owners are encoded into their traded-in automobiles. An aching sense of pathos informs the catalogue of items that Mucho finds in the cars—random tidbits that had been "truly refused" or, "perhaps tragically," lost. A person as "thin-skinned" as Mucho cannot separate the disordered effluvia from the owner's life: "a salad of despair, in a gray dressing of ash, condensed exhaust, dust, body wastes" (49, pp. 4, 5). The car

[8]Michael Harrington, The Accidental Century (New York: Macmillan, 1965), p. 14.

lot dissolves the barriers not only between animate and
inanimate but also between distinct individuals. The owners
have rather fetishistically identified themselves with mass
producible machines, making their cars "motorized, metal
extensions" of themselves, which they exchange for "a dented,
malfunctioning . . . futureless automotive projection of
somebody else's life. As if it were the most natural thing. To
Mucho it was horrible. Endless, convoluted incest"
(49, pp. 4, 5).

Gravity's Rainbow continues to explore the grotesque
encroachments of the inanimate into the animate, and vice
versa, positing more strongly than before that conscious,
deliberate, organized powers may direct or create the type
of world where their fusion is all but inevitable. Objects,
especially the Rocket, behave or are thought to behave like
organic beings. Katje puts on a "lifeless nonface" for Slothrop
and tells him that the Rocket "lives an entire life" in its
trajectory (GR, pp. 222, 209). Miklos Thanatz (from thanatos)
refers to the Rocket "as a baby Jesus, with endless committees
of Herods out to destroy it in infancy [. . . .] it really did
possess a Max Weber charisma" (GR, p. 464). Whole
"Technologies" such as "Plastics, Electronics, Aircraft" are
spoken of as having desperate, vampirish needs that "dictated"
the war: "dawn is nearly here, I need my night's blood, my
funding, funding, ahh more, more" (GR, p. 521). Conversely,
people on this side of the grave have become "only the shell —
with the soft meaty slug of soul that smiles and loves, that feels
its mortality, either rotted away or [. . .] picked at by the needle
mouths of death-by-government — a process by which living
souls unwillingly become the demons known to the main
sequence of Western magic as the Qlippoth, Shells of the Dead"
(GR, p. 176). Such death belongs to contemporary urban
existence, "a set of ways in which the natural forces are turned
aside, stepped down, rectified or bled to ground" (GR, p. 661).

Manifest Entropy: Urban and Suburban
Waste Landscapes

From his first short story, Pynchon has suggested that there
may be a plot to reduce individuality and humanity to inert
equilibrium and inanimateness, to material subject to "the laws

of physics." Of course the laws Pynchon has in mind are the
laws of thermodynamics. The loss of distinction between
individuals or between the animate and the inanimate is a loss
often deliberately hastened by the "death wish" that Freud
labeled "psychical entropy." Following the lead of Henry
Adams, whom he mentions in "Entropy" and parodies in V.,
Pynchon applies the concept of entropy metaphorically to
describe a social devolution that necessarily comprises all of
the individual psychical entropies. In Pynchon's world,
ordered, complex, unique selves are disappearing. Pynchon's
few multifaceted characters have trouble organizing their
disparate needs, drives, and emotions into integrated selves
that can sustain a coherent and consistent pattern of action.
Stencil, Oedipa, and Slothrop all become increasingly
"scattered." But most denizens of Pynchon's fiction are not
dimensional enough to become scattered. Characters often
assume identities not in themselves but as members of groups
that subsume individual personalities. Such is the case with
"The Playboys" and most of the Whole Sick Crew in V.,
Marvy's Mothers or the homosexual inmates in Gravity's
Rainbow, and the uncounted bands, cults, secret societies, and
so forth that patronize W.A.S.T.E. in The Crying of Lot 49. All
the barmaids at the "Sailor's Grave" (V.) share the same role,
the same identity, and the same name, Beatrice.

These bizarre groups appear randomly scattered across the
social landscape. Each seems to have an internal logic,
consistent in its own terms but unrelated to those of other
groups. There is no common context or set of terms, no
informing whole that unifies the groups into a coherent society;
they would be eccentric, but there is no center from which to
deviate. Rudolf Arnheim's notion of entropy describes this
condition. In its intermediate stages, entropic dissolution
reveals not complete randomness but "disorder," "the clash
of uncoordinated orders," limited and randomly dispersed.[9]
Pynchon's "Nueva York," San Narciso, or the Zone appear
as disorder moving toward the advanced stage of entropy
characterized by Vheissu in V.: total barrenness, stillness,
and indistinction.

Pynchon depicts similar "entropic" changes in the

[9]Rudolf Arnheim, Entropy and Art: An Essay on Order and Disorder
(Berkeley: University of California Press, 1971), p. 13.

appearance of cities — progressive levelling into characterless, uniformly jumbled waste landscapes. Dennis Flange in "Low-lands" escapes into a dump surrounded by a chaotic sprawl of "housing developments and shopping centers and various small, light-industrial factories" (L, p. 93). Similarly, the children of "The Secret Integration" prefer the junkyard to the world outside it; at least the dump shows the failure of the machine to take over, demonstrating the fallibility of the inanimate. The kids feel an instinctive aversion to the dreary, repetitive prospect of the housing tract, which offers no accidents, no surprises, no singularities, "no small immunities, no possibilities for hidden life or otherworldly presence" (SI, p. 43).

Such incoherent waste landscapes form the background for Pynchon's fiction. In V. one encounters the Slough of Nueva York, phasing at the edges into "towns" composed of "Chinese restaurants, seafood palaces and split-level synagogues" (V., p. 16). The Crying of Lot 49 focuses most consistently and sharply on the character and effects of the contemporary urban landscape. San Narciso is a nebulous abstraction, something beyond Eliot's "unreal city": "Like many named places in California it was less an identifiable city than a grouping of concepts — census tracts, special purpose bond-issue districts, shopping nuclei, all overlaid with access roads to its own freeway" (49, p. 12). Moreover, it has no center. Oedipa hears an ad for Hogan's [Hogan Slothrop's?] Seraglio in "downtown San Narciso" and wonders where that could conceivably be.

Apart from having no physical center, the "city" also lacks an intelligent shaping principle to control its development. The narrator dubs San Narciso "grotesque," and so it is in the traditional sense defined by Wolfgang Kayser as discussed above. Exemplifying Montaigne's use of "grotesque," it is "monstrous . . . pieced together of the most diverse members, without distinct form, in which order and proportion are left to chance."[10] San Narciso appears as a weird assemblage of "auto lots, escrow services, drive-ins, small office buildings and factories. . . . beige, prefab, cinderblock office machine distributors, sealant makers, bottled gas works, fastener factories, warehouses, and whatever" (49, p. 14).

[10]Kayser, The Grotesque, p. 24.

It is also grotesque in being at times gruesome as well as ridiculously self-satirical. With no forces to guide its growth but profit incentive and the craving for new amusement, it can spawn a recreational facility like the Fangoso Lagoons, which sounds like a submarine version of Nathanael West's Hollywood:

> It was to be laced by canals with private landings for power boats, a floating social hall in the middle of an artificial lake, at the bottom of which lay restored galleons, imported from the Bahamas; Atlantean fragments of columns and friezes from the Canaries; real human skeletons from Italy; giant clamshells from Indonesia—all for the entertainment of Scuba enthusiasts. (49, p. 18)

Gravity's Rainbow enfolds a myriad of such chaotic congeries. Recalling the detritus and "dressing of ash" in Mucho's cars, the layers of junk piled on Slothrop's desk cover a "base of bureaucratic smegma that sifts steadily to the bottom" (GR, p. 18). Such heaps are more than disordered; they seem to defy the possibility of order, to reveal the workings of inexorable, irresistible entropy. Randomly arranged, shapeless assemblages recur throughout Pynchon's fiction as a structural—or anti-structural—principle, often described in catalogues that seem likewise unorderable and potentially indefinite. The randomizing principle manifests itself everywhere: in small areas, such as Slothrop's desk and auto interiors, or in whole landscapes, such as Nueva York, San Narciso, bombed-out London, and the Zone.

The entropic sprawl has engulfed Pynchon's world. Spreading with the no longer "identifiable city," entropy actually constitutes the city's present form—or formlessness. For Oedipa, San Narciso finally gives up "its residue of uniqueness" and merges "back into the American continuity. . . . San Narciso had no boundaries" (49, pp. 133, 134). Michael Harrington could be speaking of San Narciso or any of Pynchon's urban settings when he writes: "The city . . . no longer had limits. It ceased to be a nucleus of civilization set in the countryside and reached out, obliterating the immemorial distinction between town and nature. As a result, man could not escape himself."[11] The city has become as inescapable as Oedipa's tower, and contemporary urban life, no doubt, has

---

[11]Harrington, *The Accidental Century*, p. 19.

much to do with the size, shape, and strength of the towers inhabited by all of Pynchon's isolates.

Pynchon characters rarely escape from their solipsisms to touch one another; similarly, they seldom escape from the amorphous but ubiquitous urban world. Paola and McClintic Sphere drive away from Nueva York and into the Berkshires as the latter resolves to "keep cool but care" (V., p. 343), yet the chapter ends here; we never see the couple in the country, and the next scene yo-yos us back to Benny Profane and the Whole Sick Crew. Neither Oedipa nor anyone else in The Crying of Lot 49 really gets outside of the city. All action takes place in San Narciso, Los Angeles, San Francisco, or Kinneret—with the exception of Oedipa's "religious instant" on the hill overlooking the municipality. Her picnic excursion with Metzger "would stop short of any sea," reaching instead the Fangoso Lagoons. Gravity's Rainbow, somewhat more hopefully, posits a "green uprising" at least as strong as our death-dealing civilization, and Enzian speculates, "Somewhere, among the wastes of the World, is the key that will bring us back" (GR, pp. 720, 525). But rarely does anyone benefit from an extra-urban experience. After sharing love with Roger Mexico in the rural Kent cottage, Jessica Swanlake returns (at the War's end) to her safe, predictable husband. Tchitcherine spends years in Central Asia but fails to be transformed by the beauty of the land, by the love offered him, or by his approach to the Kirghiz light. When last seen, though, he is under Geli Tripping's love spell; forgetting his vendetta against Enzian, he "goes back to his young girl beside the stream" (GR, p. 735). Yet the scene ends here, and the next chapter begins in a monstrous city of the future. The novel itself, like its characters, returns to the blasted urban chaos with which it opens.

Inability to remove oneself from the city is associated with inability to stand at a remove from the events of contemporary life and achieve some comprehensive view of them. Looking down the mountain, Oedipa senses some higher, nearly perceptible order, some shaping principle hidden beneath the surface disorder of the landscape. But she cannot quite hold onto the entire picture and comprehend it: the "revelation . . . trembled just past the threshold of her understanding" (49, p. 13). Moreover, the alluring intimation of order lasts but an "instant." When she descends from the mountain to the city, she finds a senseless scatter of buildings "whose address numbers were in the 70 and then 80,000's. She had never known numbers to run so high. It seemed unnatural" (49, p. 14). Yoyodyne, San Narciso's big source of employment, also grew with "unnatural" acceleration, jumping in a couple of decades from making toys to building sixty-foot missiles. Don Hausdorff observes that "the beaming president of the company [who figures in all three novels] has a name that nicely fuses the trivial and the horrible: Bloody Chiclitz. The name of the company itself blends the technological symbols of Henry Adams and Thomas Pynchon,"[12] and "yo-yo" recalls from V. the more or less willing subjugation of man to machine.

Contemporary Confusion: The Barriers of Complexity and Rationality

With both the landscape and the company, accelerated growth and diversity preclude human comprehension. The human mind cannot keep pace with such multiplicity, rates of change, or jumps in scale, and understanding gives way to confusion. For example, Yoyodyne short-circuits the seemingly natural relation of "one man per invention" (49, p. 64) urged by Ruskin and Pound, requiring would-be inventors to sign away patent rights and to join "task forces" that must follow predetermined procedures. Huge modern corporations like Yoyodyne begrudge the individual worker "the privilege of thinking for himself so that he can move beyond his immediate problem and perceive its general relevance."[13] The worker becomes alienated and discontent. Similarly, Franz Pökler in Gravity's Rainbow does not know the importance of his work on the 00000 project.

To describe workers' alienation, Pynchon draws on sociologist Max Weber, whom he mentions in Gravity's Rainbow. Weber would describe the workers' perplexity and disgruntled apathy as effects of "rationalization." Protestant cultures in particular sublimate the "irrational" and "charismatic" impulses they fear by building "rational" systems to control, regulate, and distance those impulses—that is, by imposing self-made orders on vital but unpredictable

[12]Don Hausdorff, "Thomas Pynchon's Multiple Absurdities," Wisconsin Studies in Contemporary Literature 7 (1966), 265.
[13]Wiener, The Human Use of Human Beings, p. 71.

nature, by putting colored lines and marks "where before there were only blank spaces on the map" (*V.,* p. 156). Such systems are rational because they rely on ever more complex organization and procedure; in doing so, they "routinize" charisma, spontaneity, and creative intuition. Consequently, Weber associated rationalization with deadening monotony, depersonalization, and a general loss of freedom or vitality for the individual caught in the rational organization.

Stating the case more harshly, Pynchon sees "pornography" and "reminders of impotence" in what one character calls "Europe's Original Sin": intellectual analysis, evident especially in the "mania" for "dividing the Creation finer and finer" (*GR,* pp. 567, 722, 391). At one point the narrator refers to such abstraction as "dusty Dracularity, the West's ancient curse" (*GR,* p. 263). Again and again, especially in *Gravity's Rainbow,* one sees originality, vitality, and emotional or spiritual potence being systematized and made manageable. Magic and death rites fall to "the Committee on Idiopathic Archetypes," and the Harz country witchcraft succumbs to the "coven politics" of the Hexes-Stadt "where the only enterprise is administering" (*GR,* pp. 625, 718). Entropically, the "Brocken-complex" has lost its uniqueness and become like the rest of the world—"rationally" organized.

But as society or any system becomes more "rational," more complexly divided and arranged, the individual becomes less able to grasp the totality of the system—to see it whole, to observe how it functions, to explain it. Society—or a single component of it, like Yoyodyne—may comprise many subsystems which, even if internally consistent and comprehensible, are mutually alien and unintelligible because there is no one perspective from which the whole can be viewed and understood. Detail and number overwhelm the imagination, and one loses any sense of an informing whole, a unifying principle, a plan or purpose that links apparently uncoordinated developments to each other and to their effects. "The Situation," Sidney Stencil muses, is beyond human understanding or control. No single intelligence determines its course, but rather the "mongrel" figments of a heterogeneous collective mind. Even Roony Winsome, the Whole Sick Crew's self-proclaimed "king of the decky dance," has no idea of how his scene functions or what will happen next: one typical night, for no reason and "without anyone realizing it, there was a party." It just happened, by accident.

The "decky dance" mirrors the Dance Macabre of modern urban life. Sociologist Michael Harrington refers to our present epoch as the "accidental century": "Technology has literally been creating a new civilization. But since this process has taken place . . . without conscious direction, thought has not kept pace with technology."[14] Our "rationalized" society may be incomprehensible and inexplicable from any one perspective, but one perspective might be needed in order to coordinate the transformations wrought by electronic communications, new media such as television and film, long-range atomic weapons systems, cybernetics, synthetics, and so on. The forces that reshape, or misshape, our world may be unguided, and so the causes of change stand "in little or no relation to the effect — a new order of human life."[15] The disparity between events and consciousness leads to terrifying and ludicrous incongruities, a truly grotesque society marked by loss of scale and accelerating unreality: a toy company becomes a munitions manufacturer, an incoherent landscape spreads like cancer.

In the world as represented by Nueva York, San Narciso, and *Gravity's Rainbow*'s wartime Europe, an impotent despair sets in: people resign themselves to being controlled and directed by the incomprehensible, impersonal forces of corporate and bureaucratic necessity, much as Benny Profane resigns himself to being shuttled about by the subway. "Lacking human values to give direction to our 'progress,' we will tend increasingly to derive our values from the needs of our machines, thus becoming merely an echo of our own technology," writes Peter Abernathy, suggesting one interpretation of the narcissus motif in *The Crying of Lot 49*.[16] Similarly, Harrington notes that failure to assume control can lead to a dangerous social mentality: "If it is the machines alone which have created all these changes, then the best that one can do is to pray to the computers and production lines that they will become more benign. Such an approach leads to a modern animism that

[14]Harrington, *The Accidental Century*, p. 239.
[15]Ibid., p. 28.
[16]Peter L. Abernathy, "Entropy in Pynchon's *The Crying of Lot 49*," *Critique* 14, no. 2 (1972), 21.

invests technology with the spirits that once inhabited trees and storms."[17] Pynchon gives us his version of modern animism by showing the confusion of animate and inanimate.

Power Without Principle

The superstitious veneration for technology gives the man with means the stature and power of a god, even though he be in social consciousness and insight something far less. Modern methods and materials permit plastic surgeon Shale Shoenmaker to become a false deity, to remake what nature made, to replace "God's will" with—whose? Perhaps not anyone's will, but instead a generalized, faddish taste, conditioned by popular movies, ads, magazine illustrations— "unreality." Trendiness wields a transforming power, but one without principle: change is without guiding purpose, motion without meaning. By remodelling unique faces and bodies according to a popular norm, Schoenmaker accelerates cultural entropy, what he calls "cultural harmony" (*V.,* p. 91). He eradicates natural differences and imposes a characterless uniformity, or conformity.

Pynchon argues that humankind and not technology is responsible for the social grotesqueries that he documents so voluminously. Like Harrington, he warns against the modern animism that ends in apathy. Enzian considers here the dangers of such resignation:

> Yes but Technology only responds [. . .] "All very well to talk about having a monster by the tail, but do you think we'd've had the Rocket if someone, some specific somebody with a name and a penis hadn't *wanted* to chuck a ton of Amatol 300 miles and blow up a block full of civilians? Go ahead, capitalize the T on technology, deify it if it'll make you feel less responsible—but it puts you in with the neutered, brother, in with the eunuchs keeping the harem of our stolen Earth for the numb and joyless hardons of human sultans, human elite with no right at all to be where they are—" (*GR,* p. 521).

Pynchon and Harrington both suggest that our fatalism concerning the effects of technology may have produced a hazardous concentration of power. Harrington maintains that computers and cybernation in particular "could conceivably

[17]Harrington, *The Accidental Century,* p. 25.

eliminate the middle levels of executive decision," thus
creating "an even tinier elite and a larger, [more] alienated
mass" than existed before.[18] Pynchon supplies the perfect
fictional example: the founder of Inamorati Anonymous was a
Yoyodyne executive replaced on his job by the IBM 7094 and in
his wife's bed by the efficiency expert who had him replaced on
the job. But aside from the satirical humor, Pynchon posits—
more seriously, it appears, in each novel—a "tiny elite" of
"human sultans" who may have attained a panopticon from
which they direct the social and economic trends that seem
accidental. The technological revolution that now reshapes our
world may be "a control that is out of control," to borrow a
phrase from Gravity's Rainbow (p. 277). Or perhaps a few do
stand above the rationalized organizations and cartels that
interweave into a plot too labyrinthine for the unorganized and
uninitiated masses to comprehend; so buffered, "They" exert
control for Their own advantage.

And yet even Their control may be out of control: "The
System may or may not understand that it's only buying time."
It "sooner or later must crash to its death, [. . .] dragging with it
innocent souls all along the chain of life" (GR, p. 412). Beneath
Them, camouflaging and semiconsciously promoting Their
schemes, are the bureaucracies that Weber deemed the
inevitable outcome of rationalized social process. Pynchon
writes that throughout the final months of World War II, "a
million bureaucrats are diligently plotting death and some
of them even know it" (GR, p. 17). But this "mass nature of
wartime death [. . .] serves as spectacle, as diversion from the
real movements of the War [. . . .] The true war is a celebration
of markets" (GR, p. 105).

Walter Rathenau (who speaks at a seance in Gravity's
Rainbow) predicted as early as 1917 in Von kommenden
Dingen that autonomous and interlocking megacorporations
would come to dominate the economy, producing their own
resources and manipulating rather than answering to the
market. Currently, they have achieved a dangerous degree of
both independence and interconnectedness. As Pynchon
demonstrates in his tale of Byron the immortal light bulb,
Their world of bureaucratic, political, military, and corporate
interlocks has developed to the point where an event in one

[18]Ibid., p. 172.

sector will ramify to all the others. As a consequence the entire system moves toward inflexibility, oppressive stability, or—in Weber's terms—"routinization." No exceptional, disruptive event can long survive, if it manages to occur at all. Those on the outside, like Oedipa Maas or the people of Watts, feel burdened by the "exitlessness," the "absence of surprise to life" (49, p. 128). The "Devil's Advocate," a figure in Pirate Prentice's dream, divines that social organization has reached a "critical mass": "Once the technical means of control have reached a certain size, a certain degree of *being connected* one to another, the chances for freedom are over for good" (GR, p. 539). Pynchon adds apocalyptic overtones by reminding his reader that a nuclear weapon can explode only if it has a "critical mass" of radioactive material.

Perhaps most nefariously, They have disrupted "Nature"—interfered in its cycles. Pynchon makes this point emphatically when commenting on Kekulé von Stradonitz's dream, which suggested a way to synthesize the aromatic benzene ring. After such knowledge, what forgiveness? It led quickly to the formation of cartels such as I.G. Farben. Kekulé dreamt of a

> Great Serpent holding its own tail in its mouth, the dreaming Serpent which surrounds the World. But the meanness, the cynicism with which this dream is to be used. The Serpent that announces, "The World is a closed thing, cyclical, resonant, eternally-returning," is to be delivered into a system whose only aim is to *violate* the Cycle. Taking and not giving back, demanding that "productivity" and "earnings" keep on increasing with time, the System removing from the rest of the World these vast quantities of energy to keep its own tiny desperate fraction showing a profit: and not only most of humanity—most of the World, animal, vegetable, and mineral, is laid waste in the process [. . . .] Living inside the System is like riding across the country in a bus driven by a maniac bent on suicide. (GR, p. 412).

Perversely, They use the Serpent as a clue on how to break the cycle: "No return, no salvation" (GR, p. 413).

But in doing so, They have made possible the announcement of Plasticity's central canon: that chemists were no longer to be at the mercy of Nature" (GR, p. 249). They are independent of it, much as They are of the individual investor, the market, and the masses. Pynchon underscores the dangers here by noting that Their favorite "target" properties in new synthetic molecules are "Strength, Stability and Whiteness (*Kraft*,

Standfestigkeit, Weisse: how often these were taken for Nazi graffiti)" (*GR,* p. 250). And They misuse information as well as energy: keeping "brain-dossiers on latencies, weaknesses, tea-taking habits, erogenous zones [and special skills] of all, all who might someday be useful," They move people like Pirate Prentice into appropriate positions (*GR,* p. 77) Unlike Maxwell's demon, They sort human beings and potential energies not to sustain the system through recycling but to drain power out of it for Themselves.

One cannot say for certain to what extent Pynchon holds these views, for at times he presents them through paranoid or otherwise unbalanced characters. Nonetheless, he must share the concern of such a sane and perceptive historian of science as A. E. E. McKenzie: "Science is now so much an integral part of modern civilization that it is no longer merely the private activity of individuals. . . . It is a social function." However, "most research in applied science in western countries is planned, not by the State but by large combines or cartels, such as Imperial Chemical Industries, the General Electric Company, the Standard Oil Company, Bell Telephone Laboratories, Du Pont, Schneider Creusot and I. G. Farben."[19] Pynchon asks what insures Their socially responsible use of science and technology. His "paranoid" characters may perceive a terrible reality to which the "sane" have become inured.

Probable Outcomes: Fast or Slow Apocalypse

In his fiction, Pynchon attempts nothing less than to delineate the forces and patterns of economics, technology, politics, group and individual psychology, history, and culture that have brought the world to its present state; concurrently, he examines what worlds or what modes of human life could most probably arise from this juncture. Given his diagnosis of the contemporary social malaise, the prognosis he offers is grim. Pynchon forecasts two main possibilities: what Fausto Maijstral calls "slow apocalypse," in which Western civilization drifts entropically down through decadence to inanimateness, becoming "finally subject to the laws of physics" (*V.,* pp. 296, 301); and what one might call "fast

[19]A. E. E. McKenzie, *The Major Achievements of Science* (Cambridge: Cambridge University Press, 1960), I, 347, 348.

apocalypse," in which internal conflicts blow the system apart with a purging violence. In fact, Pynchon alternates his predictions, sometimes hinting at both eschatologies within the same work. "Mortality and Mercy in Vienna" ends with Cleanth Siegel allowing the "fast apocalypse," in the person of Irving Loon, to overwhelm the "slow," as represented by the Washington milieu. Pynchon typically uses religious terminology and imagery to portray fast apocalypse. Siegel permits a "miracle" to happen; he brings the decadent partyers a "very tangible salvation" by allowing Irving Loon to attack them with a Browning Automatic Rifle. As in *Gravity's Rainbow*, salvation or "truth" might be achieved only in a moment of ultimate violence proceeding from some "charismatic," "deeply irrational" force.

Pynchon's "Low-lands" broods and sometimes snickers over various facets of the "slow apocalypse." Written by a twenty-two year old, it shows a surprising preoccupation with aging, physical disintegration, cultural and marital heat loss, and devolution of the self into "something not so rare or strange" (L, p. 102). In escaping from the "relentless rationality" of his wife's world, Dennis Flange flees to a dump surrounded by a typical Pynchonian waste landscape. As he descends to the landfill floor, Dennis has an apocalyptic vision of the slow, inexorable process of entropy. Society is chewing up resources and spitting out wastes (like himself, he feels) at such a rate that it will one day be overtaken by them:

> one day, perhaps fifty years from now, perhaps more, there would no longer be any hole: the bottom would be level with the streets of the development, and houses would be built on it too. As if some maddeningly slow elevator were carrying you toward a known level to confer with some inevitable face on matters which had already been decided. (L, pp. 94 – 95).

As the title makes obvious, "Entropy" advances the same concerns, and here Pynchon makes his first extended application of thermodynamics to psychology and sociology. Again he presents an ongoing wild party composed of pseudointellectuals who live empty lives and mouth anti-establishment cant while working for the government, usually in some facet of communications. Having no coherent or unified culture of their own, they stitch together a rather grotesque substitute, a patchwork of clashing, unrelated parts — Armenian delicatessens covered with bullfight posters, and so on.

On the floor above, Callisto and Aubade have tried to seal themselves off from the party and the whole outer world. They create a "hothouse jungle," "a tiny enclave of regularity in the city's chaos, alien to the vagaries of the weather, of national politics, of any civil disorder" (E, p. 279). Despite the changing weather, Callisto notes that the temperature outside stays at 37°F, and in this uniformity of heat energy he sees "omens of apocalypse" — not the sudden, violent advent of "Mortality and Mercy in Vienna" or *Gravity's Rainbow* but rather the slow apocalypse of Henry Adams or Fausto Maijstral. When Callisto reaches middle age, the "spindly maze of [thermodynamic] equations" he learned in his youth becomes "a vision of ultimate, cosmic heat-death" (E, p. 282).This vision in turn becomes "an adequate metaphor" by which to analyze American society; he discovers in the public world

> a similar tendency from the least to the most probable, from differentiation to sameness, from ordered individuality to a kind of chaos. He found himself, in short, restating Gibbs' prediction in social terms, and envisioned a heat-death for his culture in which ideas, like heat-energy, would no longer be transferred . . . intellectual motion would, accordingly, cease. (E, pp. 283–84).

But "intellectual motion" has effectively ceased within the hothouse, which neither person can leave for fear of disturbing its delicate balance. Pynchon equates the actions of Callisto and Aubade with a convoluted, lifeless dance in which the partners are strangely separate. Certainly, each is in a closed sphere within the closed system — Callisto "helpless in the past," Aubade living "on her own curious and lonely planet," both locked in the hothouse (E, pp. 292, 280). Aubade tries in her own world (just as desperately as Callisto does in his) to stave off disorder and maintain an artificial unity. One sees in her mind "arabesques of order competing fugally with the improvised discords of the party downstairs. . . . That precious signal-to-noise ratio, whose delicate balance required every calorie of her strength, seesawed inside the small tenuous skull" (E, p. 287). Like Callisto, she illustrates the recurrent Pynchon device, perhaps inherited from Poe, of mixing up design with chaos in the perceptions of a disturbed intellect.

Also, the mention of calories reveals that she and Callisto expend energy in their futile attempts to maintain order, and so they hasten the very processes they work to forestall.

Callisto tries to prevent the death of one of the birds in his hothouse by transferring heat to it from his own body, but again Pynchon employs a musical motif to describe the inevitable winding down to endgame: "the heartbeat ticked a graceful diminuendo down at last into stillness" (E, p. 292). Naturally, Callisto sees in the bird's death the ominous logic of entropy: "'Has the transfer of heat ceased to work? Is there no more . . .' He did not finish" (E, p. 292). At this point, the strain of maintaining the balanced system finally becomes too much for Aubade, who acknowledges the inevitable by smashing the window that had buffered them from the world and turning

> to face the man on the bed and wait with him until the moment of equilibrium was reached, when 37 degrees Fahrenheit should prevail both outside and inside, and forever, and the hovering, curious dominant of their separate lives should resolve into a tonic of darkness and the final absence of all motion. (E, p. 292)

This passage recalls the ending of Poe's "Masque of the Red Death," another tale of attempted and unsuccessful retreat for protection against the destructive forces of the world. Abortive attempts at retreat appear throughout Pynchon's fiction.

Pynchon works both types of apocalypse into V., but he does not present the possibilities with equal seriousness. Fausto sounds as reasonable as anyone else in the novel when he speaks of slow apocalypse, and Mehemet, the time-traveling skipper, also seems to talk with insight. Although born in the age of the Virgin, he shows a feeling for the age of the dynamo and the lessons of thermodynamics: "'Both the world and we, M. Stencil, began to die from the moment of birth. . . . The only change is toward death. . . . Early and late we are in decay. . . . The body slows down, machines wear out, planets falter and loop, sun and stars gutter and smoke'" (V., pp. 432–33).

On the other hand, most suggestions of fast apocalypse are undercut in one way or another. For example, the Navy—monolithic, impersonal, bureaucratic—"had decided to remove all of Ploy's teeth" and give him a "regulation set of upper and lower plates" (V., p. 3). In microcosm, this episode reflects a main concern of the novel—that large, inhuman, and possibly conspiratorial forces direct themselves against the individual, levelling his idiosyncracies, imposing inert uniformity, and reducing him to inanimate parts. On waking from surgery, "Ploy saw apocalypse." But it is a ludicrous one: "He stood five feet nothing in sea boots and was always picking fights with the biggest people on ship, knowing they would never take him seriously." He also vents his righteous wrath by "leaping without warning to swing from the overhead like an orangutan, trying to kick officers in the teeth," or by filing his new teeth into points and biting people on the buttocks (V., p. 3).

Father Fairing, another Pynchon character with an apocalyptic vision, became convinced during the Depression that man would soon perish and that rats would inherit the earth. Consequently, he went into the New York sewers to convert the rats to Roman Catholicism. He "put an eternal blessing and a few exorcisms on all the water flowing through the sewers between Lexington and the East River and between 86th and 79th Streets. . . . He considered it small enough sacrifice" on the part of the rodents "to provide three of their own per day for physical sustenance, in return for the spiritual nourishment he was giving them" (V., pp. 105–06). There is also the suggestion that the rat Veronica satisfied his sexual needs in his moments of weakness. Roony Winsome wants to tape the atomic destruction of Moscow for "the version to end all versions of Tchaikovsky's 1812 Overture" (V., p. 111). And R. W. B. Lewis proposes that Roony's comically jaded Whole Sick Crew might have been "adapted and ironically modernized from Michael Wigglesworth's 'You sinful crew,' those Christ was dispatching to hell."[20] The Day of Doom is travestied again in Benny Profane's final scene. He is last observed running on momentum alone through the suddenly and mysteriously darkened streets of Valletta with one Brenda Wigglesworth, who will show herself to be an "inviolable Puritan . . . come marriage and the Good Life." At the moment, though, Brenda is "an American WASP who attended Beaver College and owned, she said, 72 pairs of Bermuda shorts." She also drinks sloe gin fizzes and writes admittedly "phony college-girl" poetry (V., pp. 426, 428). Two world wars are the closest our century has come to apocalypse, but V. treats

[20]R. W. B. Lewis, Trials of the Word: Essays in American Literature and the Humanities (New Haven, Conn.: Yale University Press, 1965), p. 228.

neither directly. The various "Armageddons" we glimpse exist mostly in the minds of F. O. operatives who seem to engage in music hall buffoonery (usually unintentional) as much as espionage. Their habitual phrase, "The balloon's gone up," prevents one from taking their "Situations" too seriously.

But if comedy undercuts the seriousness, seriousness underlies the comedy. The laughter is dark, albeit laughter. Even though the "Armageddons" may prove fantasies, projections, ridiculous mismatches, or unreal Situations, the recurring preoccupation with apocalypse signifies danger in itself. John May argues that "apocalypse is a response to cultural crisis. It grows out of that sense of loss that results from the passing of an old world view."[21] V. seems to record the passing of a world which justifies a faith in human agency, which registers the effect of an individual's virtú, which recognizes the primacy of the human and the organic. May also notes that "the cataclysm is usually attributed to the sins of mankind or to the decrepitude of the world," both of which are treated voluminously in V. Moreover, many aspects of the novel conform to age-old traditions in apocalyptic literature. Mircea Eliade writes in The Sacred and the Profane that "the extinction of fires, the return of the souls of the dead, social confusion of the type exemplified by the Saturnalia, erotic license, orgies, and so on, symbolized the regression of the cosmos into chaos."[22] Just a cursory glance at Pynchon's plot lines will uncover most of the elements that have characterized myths of cosmic cataclysm since primitive times, even down to the "extinction of the fires" as the lights go out on Malta for Brenda and Benny.

Eliade also notes that rituals bound up with apocalyptic myths testify to man's "thirst for the real and his terror of 'losing' himself by letting himself be overwhelmed by the meaninglessness of profane existence."[23] Man transcends profane existence in apocalypse: "the symbolic return to chaos is indispensible to any new creation . . . it is a sign that the profane man is on the way to dissolution, and that a new

[21]John R. May, Toward a New Earth: Apocalypse in the American Novel (Notre Dame: University of Notre Dame Press, 1972), p. 19.
[22]Mircea Eliade, The Sacred and the Profane: The Nature of Religion (New York: Harper and Row, 1961), p. 78.
[23]Mircea Eliade, Cosmos and History: The Myth of the Eternal Return (New York: Harper and Row, 1959), p. 91.

personality is about to be born."[24] The dismalness of V.'s eschatology, dark laughter aside, is that destruction of the old order does not point toward creation of the new. Benny was born Profane; he will not change, will not from all of his experiences learn a "goddam thing," much less attain sacred knowledge. Herbert Stencil, the focal point(s) for the other main subplot, is too obsessed and self-absorbed to learn much more. He says in his seventh "impersonation" that a "triangular stain swam somewhere over the crowd, like a tongue on Pentecost" (V., p. 79). W. T. Lhamon, Jr. argues convincingly that V. herself is associated with the Paraclete on several occasions.[25] Pentecost is similar to fast apocalypse in that it descends suddenly, violently, irrationally to sweep out the old order in a "rushing mighty wind," and to signify a new one with "cloven tongues like as of fire."[26] But nobody in V. really approaches such an awesome, transforming revelation. Stencil's artificially sustained and self-indulgent search, Fausto's "confessions," the escapades of the Whole Sick Crew, the gradual decadence of the lady V., and in fact the whole novel speak more resolutely about slow apocalypse.

More recently, though, Pynchon has reconsidered the fast apocalypse that he portrayed in miniature with his first story; each piece of writing since V. presents it as more and more possible — even viable — for a growing sense of political and sociological urgency informs the works. The Crying of Lot 49, like all of his fiction, renders the prospect in religious terms. The hint of imminent miracle runs throughout the novel, and a miracle, says Jesús Arrabal, is "another world's intrusion into this one" (49, p. 88). The character's name connects religious salvation and social plight: arrabal is Spanish for a suburb such as San Narciso. Pentecost is the Christian miracle of sacred communication, and allusions or direct references to it permeate the novel, perhaps even supplying its title: Pentecost is seven Sundays, or forty-nine days, after Easter. Oedipa enters San Narciso and experiences her "odd, religious instant" on a

[24]Mircea Eliade, Myths, Dreams, and Mysteries (New York: Harper and Row, 1967), pp. 80–81.
[25]W. T. Lhamon, Jr., "Pentecost, Promiscuity, and Pynchon's V.: From the Scaffold to the Impulsive," in Mindful Pleasures: Essays on Thomas Pynchon, ed. George Levine and David Leverenz (Boston: Little, Brown and Co., 1976), pp. 69–86.
[26]See Acts II. 1–6.

Sunday (49, p. 13). The novel ends at the auction, held on a Sunday afternoon perhaps forty-nine days later, with Oedipa feeling the onset of an awful, perhaps unmanageable revelation about the Tristero. And though it was not terribly effective, according to Bortz's history, the Tristero suggests the possibility —even the necessity—of violent retribution and the destruction of the old order; the name itself may play upon *dies irae* (49, p. 75).

The San Narciso landscape and the prospect of fast apocalypse recur in Pynchon's most important piece of nonfiction, "A Journey into the Mind of Watts". Los Angeles (parent of San Narciso) is the quintessential unreal city, its economy depending upon "various forms of systematized folly" (W, p. 148); in its midst is Watts, a "pocket of reality." Pynchon suggests that another explosion may follow the suppression of reality by unreality, showing again his predilection for applying the laws of physics to sociology and psychology. Violence in Watts "is never far from you: because you are a man, because you have been put down, because for every action there is an equal and opposite reaction" (W, p. 156). To the "innocent, optimistic child-bureaucrats, violence is an evil and an illness." But "far from a sickness, violence may be an attempt to communicate, or to be who you really are" (W, p. 156). This solution recalls "Mortality and Mercy in Vienna" and adumbrates *Gravity's Rainbow*, which was in progress at the time.[27] To underscore his message, Pynchon closes by describing a work he saw at the Watts Renaissance of the Arts festival:

> In one corner was this old, busted, hollow TV set with a rabbit-ears antenna on top; inside, where its picture tube should have been, gazing out with scorched wiring threaded like electronic ivy among its crevices and sockets, was a human skull. The name of the piece was *The Late, Late, Late Show*. (W, p. 158)

The possibility of imminent destruction pervades *Gravity's Rainbow* in the form of rocket strikes. And again, the sudden violence comes as a final revelation: the Rocket is referred to as "the one Word that rips apart the day," "a Word, spoken with no warning into your ear, and then silence forever" (GR, p. 25). This apocalypse is so fast that one hears it approaching only

[27]Jules Siegel, "Who Is Thomas Pynchon and Why Did He Run Away with My Wife?" *Playboy* 24 (March 1977), 170, 172.

after the fact. In a suitable inversion of chronology, Pynchon opens his latest novel with the aftermath of one such explosion: "A screaming comes across the sky. It has happened before, but there is nothing to compare it to now. It is too late. The Evacuation still proceeds, but it's all theatre" (GR, p. 3). He closes the book by threatening the audience, a theater crowd as jaded and unaware as Siegel's partyers, with a salvation just as awful: a salvation once again that razes tower walls. The violent advent poises barely outside the frame of *Gravity's Rainbow* — right before its beginning and after its ending:

> And it is just here, just at this dark and silent frame, that the pointed tip of the Rocket, falling nearly a mile per second, absolutely and forever without sound, reaches its last unmeasurable gap above the roof of this old theatre, the last delta-t.
>
> There is time, if you need the comfort, to touch the person next to you, or to reach between your own cold legs . . . or, if song must find you, here's one They never taught anyone to sing, a hymn by William Slothrop, centuries forgotten and out of print, sung to a simple and pleasant air of the period. Follow the bouncing ball:
>
> > There is a Hand to turn the time,
> > Though thy Glass today be run,
> > Till the Light that hath brought the Towers low
> > Find the last poor Pret'rite one . . .
> > Till the Riders sleep by ev'ry road,
> > All through our crippl'd Zone,
> > With a face on ev'ry mountainside,
> > And a Soul in ev'ry stone. . . .
>
> Now everybody — (GR, p. 760)

Pynchon's Solutions

The Moment and Its
Possibilities

Pynchon ends *Gravity's Rainbow*, his most recent work, with
a desperate affirmation—even at "the last delta-t," the last
infinitesimal moment, there is still time for redeeming action:
"There is a Hand to turn the time, / Though thy Glass today be
run" (GR, p. 760). As Leni Pökler says, "There is the moment,
and its possibilities" (GR, p. 159). Pynchon devotes a good deal
of space in his fiction to examining how people use or neglect
the real "possibilities" or solutions to those contemporary
problems discussed in chapter 2, depicting apocalypse, fast or
slow, as a possibility—perhaps even a probability—but not a
necessity. He charts the decay of the West, sometimes
despairingly, sometimes mockingly. But he also explores our
civilization's latent possibilities for reversing the trend.
Especially in works written after *V.*, he urges repeatedly that
things do not *have* to be the way they are. On quietly leaving
Winthrop Tremaine, a swastika merchant with a nice colonial
name, Oedipa castigates herself: "You're chicken.... This is
America, you live in it, you let it happen" (49, p. 112). Even the
passive at heart can wait for "another set of possibilities to
replace those that had conditioned the land to accept any San
Narciso" (49, p. 136).

The very atmosphere of uncertainty so peculiar to Pynchon's
work suggests that possibilities remain open even if unrealized,
that cultural heat death is not, as Callisto thought, inexorable
and irreversible. After all, America is not the closed system of
physics: it comprises human beings who, as Norbert Wiener
points out, are not themselves closed systems. They can amass
information and then use it to increase organization in "local

enclaves" of a generally entropic universe.[1] Cleanth Siegel
gazes terrified as the entropic, levelling force works first upon
others, then upon himself, and he wonders if it "was a question
of compulsion," if there is "something which linked people . . .
some reason which gave them no other choice" ("MMV," p.
202). Pynchon resolves that there is no compulsion, and so,
apparently, does his character. Siegel draws on his information
about the Ojibwa and exercises his freedom: he leaves the party
that threatens to devour him and allows Irving Loon to
massacre the guests.

Possibilities in Paranoia

Pynchon's first story offers, in addition to violence, another
means of coping: paranoia. Irving is, as the narrator tells us,
"paranoid," but his paranoia stimulates him to defend himself
against real, though misconstrued, danger. In the terms of
Gravity's Rainbow, paranoia has become "operational" (GR,
p. 25), for Debby Considine and the group do menace Irving
with a kind of annihilation. Debby, a prototype of V., is the
femme fatale, or rather sex machine, of the group; she collects
men from "undeveloped areas" which she visits as a
representative of the State Department, doing to them
something like what the bureaucracy does to their cultures. She
breaks, emasculates, "routinizes" the men: "Her exes either
assimilated in with The Group or found a niche in some other
group or dropped out of sight completely and forever"
(MMV, p. 207). Irving's "melancholia" signals not his
response to being assimilated but rather the onset of the
Windigo psychosis, a bizarre but actual malady peculiar to the
Ojibwa. Pynchon uses it as a paradigm of how the "preterite" —
the neglected, rejected, or "passed over" — achieve a notion of
self. In the dead of the Canadian winter, the starving Indian
hunter becomes a kind of deranged quester: "feeling a
concentration of obscure cosmic forces against him and him
alone, cynical terrorists, savage and amoral deities [somewhat
like Debby] . . . which are bent on his destruction," he identifies
himself with the Windigo, a cannibalistic spirit, and goes on a
murderous rampage (MMV, p. 208). Pynchon makes the same
point in his essay on Watts: paranoia allows the blacks to

[1]Norbert Wiener, The Human Use of Human Beings: Cybernetics and Society
(New York: Avon Books, 1967), pp. 20–21.

know themselves, to recognize the enemy, and to find a basis for action.

Herbert Stencil seems to adopt his V.-paranoia deliberately in order to give his life a purpose that enforces activity. "It may be that Stencil has been lonely and needs something for company," he says of himself (*V.*, p. 44). Paranoia offers him some last hope of escaping a seemingly terminal ennui that threatens to degrade him into a somnambulist or an automaton; it is for him what the subway is for Benny Profane—a means to keep moving. Convincing himself that "his quarry fitted in with The Big One, the century's master cabal," Stencil begins his dogged quest (*V.*, p. 210). He becomes so dependent upon his "acquired sense of animateness" that "having found this he could hardly release it, it was too dear. To sustain it he had to hunt V.; but if he should find her, where else would there be to go but back into half-consciousness? He tried not to think, therefore, about any end to the search. Approach and avoid" (*V.*, p. 44). On Malta, when faced with having to end his psychologically imperative quest, the panicked Stencil loses all pretense of mental balance and lapses into overt demonism, regarding V. as a malignant, indestructible, and all-powerful agency.

Although it causes him to distort the facts, paranoia helps Grover Snodd of "The Secret Integration" to realize a truth: that the adults are trying to control his life and his mentality. All Oedipa discovers for certain is that she needs to believe in a "transcendent meaning" behind the entropic waste landscape and that paranoia could supply it (49, pp. 136, 137). Before she experiences her "revelations," there "had hung the sense of buffering, insulation, she had noticed the absence of an intensity, as if watching a movie, just perceptibly out of focus, that the projectionist refused to fix" (49, p. 10). Somewhat like Herbert Stencil, she may be driven on a quest just to maintain a necessary sense of purpose and vitality. Pynchon here improves upon V. by making the object of Oedipa's quest less arbitrarily chosen, her motivation less self-conscious—or even conscious—and yet more human and complex.

Through viewing a Remedios Varo painting and talking to director Randolph Driblette, Oedipa comes to realize that she may, like a paranoid, be weaving together the pattern of events that she believes she is uncovering. Her desire to "project a world," in Driblette's phrase, reflects her felt but not entirely conscious need to imbue life with purpose, to restore lost intensity, to step outside of the tower that "buffers" her from something undetermined, to overcome what Alfred North Whitehead calls the "life tedium" that grips people who experience life as disconnected moments. Indeed, her visions of sacred and purposeful design—or evil conspiracy—often follow fast upon intimations of the void. For example, her "odd, religious instant" comes immediately after she sees that "nothing was happening" in San Narciso (49, p. 13). Oedipa recapitulates Varo's frail tower maidens "seeking hopelessly to fill the void" (49, p. 10). Similarly, her "intuition" that Mucho's letter would be "newsless inside" made her "look more closely at its outside," where she sees the warning: "REPORT ALL OBSCENE MAIL TO YOUR POTSMASTER" (49, p. 30). A misprint no doubt exists—perhaps even a pattern and a conspiracy—but Oedipa's degree of emotional involvement with surface shapes may stem from her psychological response to emptiness or impotence. Note that she finds Stanley Koteks, perhaps by using "subliminal cues in the environment," right after discovering that "there was nothing she could do" at the Yoyodyne stockholders meeting (49, pp. 60, 59).

The paranoid invents connections and so structures his or her experience. As the narrator of *Gravity's Rainbow* asserts, people need such a structure: "If there is something comforting—religious, if you want—about paranoia, there is still also anti-paranoia, where nothing is connected to anything, a condition not many of us can bear for long. Well right now Slothrop feels himself sliding onto the anti-paranoid part of his cycle [. . . .] Either They have put him here for a reason, or he's just here. He isn't sure that he wouldn't, actually, rather have that *reason*" (GR, p. 434). Paranoia counters the vision of chaos and the feeling of "life tedium" with "the onset, the leading edge, of the discovery that *everything is connected*, everything in the Creation, a secondary illumination—not yet blindingly One, but at least connected, and perhaps a route In for those [. . .] who are held at the edge" (GR, p. 703). The paranoid's function is similar to that of a sorting intelligence such as Maxwell's demon: the paranoid gleans information to build an improbable organization or energy concentration that motivates work, purposeful action, or even communication between formerly isolated parties. In the last instance paranoia is more than a personal response to the alien world: if it becomes truly "creative" it progresses beyond a "They-system" to posit a "We-system"; then group political action becomes possible (GR. p. 638; see below p. 94).[2]

Possibilities in Caring

The ability to care or even to love also fills the void, shapes apparent chaos, and lends meaning to motion. In Pynchon's world, though, love is far more rare and fragile than paranoia. Nonetheless, Pynchon does hold out love, either fraternal or sexual, as a possible form of salvation. When kicked out by his "austere and logical" wife (L, p. 91), Dennis Flange finds some much-needed companionship with Pig Bodine, Rocco Squarcione, and Bolingbroke. The friends retreat from the world into Bolingbroke's dump castle, jerry-rigged out of found materials, and there they enjoy the communal drinking and swapping of ribald stories so often seen in Pynchon. That night Flange also meets a beautiful elfin gypsy (perhaps in a dream) who seems ready to heal his frustrations and sense of personal decay by loving him.

Meatball Mulligan of "Entropy" demonstrates another application of caring. His party, while not an ideal mode of living, does not become a self-defeating closed system, nor does it despairingly give over to the chaos of the street. When three coeds from George Washington University crash the party, Sandor Rojas jubilantly cries, "Young blood." Infusion of the new staves off exhaustion. When the party really gets out of hand, Meatball realizes that he can retreat to the closet, his equivalent of Callisto's hothouse, but instead he goes to work. Very sensibly, he starts with himself; first he finds the tequila and begins "restoring order to his nervous system" (E, p. 281). Then he moves on to others, trying "to calm everybody down, one by one" ("E," p. 291). He will direct his energy toward creating order through interchange, communication,

[2]Mark Siegel considers some positive uses of paranoia in Pynchon: Creative Paranoia in Gravity's Rainbow (Port Washington, N.Y.: Kennikat Press, 1978). For another discussion of Pynchon's "creative" paranoia, see William M. Plater, The Grim Phoenix: Reconstructing Thomas Pynchon (Bloomington: Indiana University Press, 1978), pp. 187–98.

and treatment of individual cases, somewhat as Maxwell's sorting demon would. Meatball's solution, based on common sense and the need for community, is "more a pain in the neck, but probably better in the long run" (E, p. 291). A human intelligence and concern can retard entropy.

Pynchon makes essentially the same point in V., his least hopeful novel. McClintic Sphere's love for Ruby (Paola) makes him realize "that the only way clear of the cool/crazy flipflop was obviously slow, frustrating and hard work. Love with your mouth shut, help without breaking your ass or publicizing it: keep cool, but care. He might have known, if he'd used any common sense" (V., pp. 342–43). The jazzman-savant's common sense reminds one of Meatball Mulligan's choosing the practical course, Oedipa Maas's learning about excluded middles, and Roger Mexico's finding reality somewhere between 1 and 0. Paola suggests the redemptive possibilities of love not only by engendering such thoughts but also by returning to her husband, Pappy Hod, at the end of the book. When Pappy can simply say "I love you," she gives him as a token of her renewed faith the comb that symbolizes V.'s decadence and, by implication, the decadence of Western civilization.

Love confronts Benny Profane with the possibility of deliverance from his rootlessness and schlemihlhood. For example, Fina Mendoza finds him unconscious, yo-yoing on the subway, and feels that "she must help him" by taking him home to her parents. Benny and Fina run "through the station, beneath a chain of green lights," with "tropical birds peeking from her green dress whenever the black coat flew open" (V., p. 31). When the mechanical jaws of a subway door close on Benny, she saves him from a schlemihl's death: "With a frightened little cry she took Profane's hand and tugged, and a miracle happened. The doors opened again. She gathered him inside, into her quiet field of force" (V., p. 31). Rachel Owlglass, for whom Benny has his deepest feelings, even gets him to settle down with her and hold steady work at Anthroresearch Associates. Sexually or fraternally, Rachel cares for the downtrodden and does what she can to help: witness her concern for the masochistic Esther, who is sexually used by Schoenmaker and the Whole Sick Crew.

In her need for love and in her ability to care, Rachel

anticipates Oedipa Maas. Oedipa had hoped that Pierce Inverarity would prove the "knight of deliverance" who could rescue her from her tower and restore life's "intensity" (49, pp. 11, 10). That relationship failing, she married a disk jockey "from what has passed, [she] was hoping forever, for love" (49, p. 114). And she can respond to people, often upon seeing some weakness, defect, or sign of "preterition." She resists the lady-killer Metzger until she notices "a fat stomach the suit had hidden. . . . With a cry Oedipa rushed to him, fell on him, began kissing him to wake him up" (49, p. 26). Genghis Cohen's open zipper makes her feel "motherly," Mucho's problems with other women evoke "tenderness," and a premonition of how the broken old sailor will die makes her "overcome all at once by a need to touch him" (49, p. 93). Without her need and capacity for love, she would never have become "sensitized" to those clues that suggest "another mode of meaning behind the obvious" (49, p. 137).

Several characters in *Gravity's Rainbow* inherit the legacy of Meatball, McClintic, Rachel, and Oedipa. Leni Pökler believes in the power of love because, as she says, "I know there's coming together" (GR, p. 155). Despite the frustrations and reversals she suffers, she continues to believe and to care—for her daughter Ilse in particular. She can love because she has the strength to face uncertainty and death, to lose herself in her commitment to a person or an ideal, to "penetrate the moment" and see its "possibilities." Pirate Prentice shows something of the same grace under adversity. When he sees the vapor trail of an incoming V-2, he wonders: "Oughtn't he to be doing something . . . get on to the operations room at Stanmore [. . .] no: no time, really [. . . .] Run out in the street? Warn the others? Pick bananas" (GR, p. 7). In other words, do what you would be doing anyway. Picking bananas while the rocket falls may seem insane, but what would be saner? Pirate harvests the fruit to make a strange but sumptuous "banana breakfast" for his comrades—something unusual to break the routine of their day. He exemplifies the advice with which the narrator closes the novel: even as the Rocket reaches the last delta-t above your head, "There is time, if you need the comfort, to touch the person next to you" (GR, p. 760). The denizens of Pynchon's world confront forces that threaten to isolate, alienate, dehumanize, or even kill them. But they find chances for escape in caring and attempting human contact — either Pirate's fraternal sort or sexual love.

Threatening forces, even the proximity of death, stimulate and intensify love — not only the perverse but also the ennobling kind. The relation of love and death in Pynchon's work leads some critics to overstate their connection. William Plater, for example, writes that as "a force of equilibrium, love is another name for entropy and dying may thus be viewed as an act of self-love," adding later that for Pynchon "love, death, and life are the same."[3] Plater apparently takes at face value a pronouncement from V.: "the act of love and the act of death are one." (V., p. 385). But that view is not Pynchon's; rather it reflects V.'s fetishistic embellishments on the tradition of western Romanticism that the narrator debunks as "banal and exasperating" (V., p. 385). Love is not another name for entropy; it opposes entropy. Wallace Stevens wrote that "Death is the mother of beauty" — not that death is beauty or beauty death. Pynchon likewise asserts that the threat of death can quicken a love to counter it:

> In the trenches of the First World War, English men came to love one another decently, without shame or make-believe, under the easy likelihoods of their sudden deaths, and to find in the faces of other young men evidence of otherworldly visits, some poor hope that may have helped redeem even mud, shit, the decaying pieces of human meat [. . . .] while Europe died meanly in its own wastes, men loved. (GR, p. 616)

Imminent death also spurs heterosexual love. The correspondence between rocket strikes and Slothrop's sexual encounters baffles everyone and obsesses Pointsman. Unlike Pointsman, Roger Mexico does not seek to control all or reduce all to a mechanical explanation. Unlike Franz Pökler, he does not resist losing himself in "the moment." Because he is able to live with uncertainty, because he accepts risk and contingency as parts of life, Mexico, like Leni, can love. He and Jessica Swanlake manage one of the few affairs in Pynchon untainted by sado-masochism, fetishistic substitutions, experiments, symbolic role playing, and psycho-theatrics designed to titillate or gratify the participants' guilts and dark needs. It is an end in itself. Their love works as "real magic" (GR, p. 38),

[3]Plater, The Grim Phoenix, pp. 139, 155.

transforming both them and those around them: "They confuse everyone. They look so innocent. People immediately want to protect them: censoring themselves away from talk of death, business, duplicity when Roger and Jessica are there" (GR, p. 121).

Theirs is an "act of faith" (GR, p. 177). As such, it takes them "beyond the Zero" to the "trans-observable" where at times they lose the power "to tell which of them is which [. . . .] Roger and Jessica were merged into a joint creature unaware of itself" (GR, p. 38). Roger especially feels freed from subjection to the laws of physics, as Fausto would term it: "His life had been tied to the past. He'd seen himself a point on a moving wavefront, propagating through sterile history — a known past, a projectable future. But Jessica was the breaking of the wave. Suddenly there was a beach, the unpredictable . . . new life" (GR, p. 126). Through love, as one character points out, "isolation is overcome, and [. . .] that is the one great centripetal movement of the World. Through the machineries of greed, pettiness, and the abuse of power, *love occurs*" (GR, p. 440). Geli Tripping's love for Tchitcherine remains constant throughout the novel, and her love spell apparently transforms him. He does not recognize Enzian, whom he had vowed to kill, being "blind now to all but" her (GR, p. 734). The narrator concludes, "This is magic. Sure — but not necessarily fantasy. Certainly not the first time a man has passed his brother by, at the edge of the evening, often forever, without knowing it" (GR, p. 735).

Nor need loving and caring be confined to human givers and receivers. The constancy and depth of little Ludwig's devotion to Ursula, his pet lemming, rather comically recalls more serious loves. Ursula escapes, perhaps to a lemming's suicide, and Ludwig pursues her unswervingly through the Zone, despite all the dangers and depravities he must suffer: "Even knowing when she was a baby what they'd be in for someday, still Ludwig has always loved her. He may be thinking that love can stop it from happening" (GR, p. 556). Similarly, Roger hopes that Jessica could "always deny the dark sea at his back, love it away" (GR, p. 126). Somewhat as Leni did for her daughter Ilse, Ludwig sells himself to preserve Ursula, but both characters maintain the power to love despite the world's uses. Their power preserves them.

William Slothrop, Tyrone's eccentric and heretical first American ancestor, loved the pigs he had to drive from Berkshire to Boston for slaughter. He also "enjoyed the road, the mobility, the chance encounters of the day" (GR, p. 555). Like Roger and Leni, William can risk uncertainty, give himself to "the moment, and its possibilities." He can love. Tyrone gradually develops some of the same capacity, for human beings such as Tantivy Mucker-Maffick, and for nature: "Slothrop's intensely alert to trees, finally. When he comes in among trees he will spend time touching them, studying them, sitting very quietly near them and understanding that each tree is a creature, carrying on its individual life, aware of what's happening around it, not just some hunk of wood to be cut down" (GR, pp. 552–553). Going beyond even trees, some characters of Gravity's Rainbow begin to respect rocks as fellow members of creation: Felipe "believes (as do M. F. Beal and others) in a form of mineral consciousness not too much different from that of plants and animals, except for the time scale" (GR, p. 612). As noted previously, the novel closes with these lines from a William Slothrop hymn: "With a face on ev'ry mountainside,/ And a Soul in ev'ry stone. . . ." (GR, p. 760).

Possibilities in the Natural World

Such animism is common—and respected—in Gravity's Rainbow, perhaps because it applies to natural objects, as it does not in V. and The Crying of Lot 49. Pynchon wrote to Thomas F. Hirsch (8 January 1968) of his interest in the Herero religion and its pantheistic view of the cosmos.[4] The influence is often apparent in the novel's thematic statements and imagery patterns, as when Slothrop sees "a stout rainbow cock driven down out of pubic clouds into Earth, green wet valleyed Earth" (GR, p. 626). Frequently the rainbow designates a limit of the senses, a border of perception, or an interface between systems or cycles (GR, p. 203, 488, 524). But just as frequently it betokens love and earth-lust: Pan appears as a "beautiful Serpent, its coils in rainbow lashings in the sky" (GR, pp. 720–21). The two meanings come together in gravity, the integrating

[4]Joseph W. Slade, "Escaping Rationalization: Options for the Self in Gravity's Rainbow," Critique 18, no. 3 (1977), 29.

force—or geometry of relations—that functions like Kekulé's Great Serpent, binding "the World" together. Pynchon, finding the mystical in the physical, searches for the unnameable "Function" in patterns of energy (GR, p. 590). The narrator speaks of the "few" who had "looked into the heart of the solenoid, seen the magnetic serpent and energy in its nakedness, long enough to be changed, to bring back from the writhing lines of force down in that pit an intimacy with power, with glazed badlands of soul, that set them apart forever" (GR, p. 584). Through the Serpent that binds the world, Pynchon equates magnetic power with "soul." As George Levine notes, we were warned in the Wernher von Braun epigraph at the beginning of Gravity's Rainbow that "physics will become metaphysics."[5]

Pynchon does not portray humankind as stranded without hope in an alien and dying cosmos. Actually, as far back as "Entropy" he spoke of love and power as being "identical," entertaining the thought that "love therefore not only makes the world go 'round but also makes the boccie ball spin, the nebula precess" (E, p. 280). In Gravity's Rainbow, somewhat as in "Prometheus Unbound," physical forces appear to be spiritual, even loving if considered from a mystic's perspective: not only can people care for the Earth—it can care back. Lyle Bland, formerly of Them, discovers "that Earth is a living critter [. . .] that Gravity, taken so for granted, is really something eerie, Messianic, extrasensory in Earth's mindbody . . ." (GR, p. 590). An integrating force competes with the disintegrating one so conspicuous in this novel and dominant in V. The integrating force is a real alternative that calls for choice, not submission. Certainly it is not the false face of entropy.

Mehemet said, "the only change is toward death. . . . Early and late we are in decay" (V., p. 433). This simple formulation should not be taken as Pynchon's final statement. Again, I disagree with William Plater, who writes that "while it is the role of art and human invention to embellish and disguise simple facts, complex formulations can always be reduced to Mehemet's cheerful observation. Kekulé's serpent may offer a more elegant image, but it too brings the same message: Rebirth

[5]George Levine, "V—2," Partisan Review 40 (Fall 1973), 523.

is an illusion; the only transformation is, as Walter Rathenau expressed so well, 'from death to death transfigured.'"[6] The spirit of Rathenau speaks to a seance about "the persistence [. . .] of structures favoring death. Death converted into more death. Perfecting its reign" (GR, p. 167). But it is wrong to equate Pynchon's view with the spirit's or with Mehemet's. Rathenau's ghost lends just one more voice to a novel full of voices. Moreover, the voice hardly reaches us directly: its words are delivered in bizarre circumstances by a medium, Peter Sachsa, who himself comes to us only through the medium of an inconsistent, imperfect, and playful narrator. Pynchon's mediating structures should encourage the reader to question any statement that presents itself as conclusive and to give it no more than provisional assent. This mercurial narrator elsewhere undercuts Rathenau's pronouncements in the name of love, love that asserts itself in the face of death (GR, p. 616). And the narrator introduces Rathenau as "the architect of the cartelized state," a "corporate Bismarck" who helped consolidate "a rational structure in which business would be the true, the rightful authority" (GR, pp. 164, 165). Pynchon, relying on Max Weber, has spoken of the limits and dangers of rationalization throughout the novel. One should be wary of taking any character, spirit or no, as a mouthpiece for this author.

The "cartelized state" that Walter Rathenau actually prophesied and engineered becomes the system into which the Great Serpent is delivered, "a system whose only aim is to *violate* the Cycle. Taking and not giving back" (GR, p. 412). Plater argues that "the Great Serpent offers the illusion of return at the same time it cloaks the real action. After the transformation of depletion, there is 'no return, no salvation, no Cycle'" (GR, p. 413). But this is not the message of the Serpent, which announces that the world is "cyclical" and "eternally-returning"; rather it is Their "cynical" perversion of that message, and Their ways are not the Serpent's ways. They do not appreciate the difference, seeing in the Serpent only the means to synthesize the benzene ring along with other molecules whose "target properties" recall Nazi graffiti. At the seance, Rathenau tries to make Them see the implications of what They do; when he speaks of "the real movement" as being

[6]Plater, *The Grim Phoenix*, pp. 135–36.

"not from death to any rebirth" but "from death to death-transfigured," he means that "polymerizing is not resurrection," nor is "fanning the wastes of original waste over greater and greater masses of city" (GR, pp. 166, 167). He means that They are laying waste to the earth, not necessarily that the earth is on an unswerving path to its doom or even that waste need always oppose rebirth. Certainly Pynchon sees other potentialities. His world is not "moving in only one direction — toward death"[7]; Their world is. Pynchon looks beyond Their unilateral "taking and not giving back" to a larger cycle that promises return and renewal.

Pynchon's Herero woman buries herself up to her neck in the ground to "feel the incredible pressure [. . .] against her belly [. . . .] to be in touch with the Earth's gift for genesis" (GR, p. 316). Earth's pressure and gift appear again as gravity: "Earth's mindbody" has "hugged to its holy center the wastes of dead species" and then "rewoven molecules" — not synthesized them (GR, p. 590). The recycling magic operates on a smaller scale in Pirate Prentice's rooftop garden, where assorted wastes form an "unbelievable black topsoil in which anything could grow, not the least being bananas [. . . .] the politics of bacteria, the soil's stringing of rings and chains in nets only God can tell the meshes of, have seen the fruit thrive often to lengths of a foot and a half" (GR,p. 5 – 6). Pirate harvests the bananas to make breakfast for his comrades. This is not just "death-transfigured" but life-asserted. The waste-fertile soil as well as Pirate's caring gesture answers the threat of destruction, and so does the very aroma of the meal: it takes over "not so much through any brute pungency or volume as by the high intricacy to the weaving of its molecules, sharing the conjuror's secret" with the "rewoven molecules" in "Earth's mindbody" (GR, pp. 10, 590). Though "it is not often Death is told so clearly to fuck off" (GR, p. 10), it can happen, and people or nature can do the telling.

Possibilities in Waste

Circularity, as exemplified by both the Great Serpent and the politics of bacteria, opposes the linear movements of entropy and Their one-way exploitation of the earth. It affirms

[7]Ibid., p. 3.

possibility in the act of recycling. In "Low-lands" Pynchon begins to develop the notion of waste or garbage as potentially positive; certainly he suggests in the recurrent figure of junk piles that here, in the cast-offs of a blind and increasingly inhuman society, we may still encounter surprise and opportunity. At the dump with garbage men Rocco and Bolingbroke, Dennis Flange can establish a human bond not possible with his wife, Cindy. Pynchon often presents the recycling of waste as a solution to the unilateral exhaustion of both human and natural resources.

Pynchon, like his character Dennis Flange, romanticizes or idealizes the "disinherited," a tendency that surfaces in much of his writing. Society has, in effect, discarded the preterite as if they were waste, but they may offer an untapped source of wisdom and energy. Irving Loon seems in touch with some revitalizing natural force both hidden from and threatened by the Washington crowd. McClintic Sphere's jazz reveals the inventiveness needed to stave off the spiritual heat death into which the Whole Sick Crew is drifting. The Crew has only a finite number of ideas and terms to play with. " 'Mathematically,' " thinks Eigenvalue, " 'if nobody else original comes along, they're bound to run out of arrangements someday. What then?' What indeed. This sort of arranging and rearranging was Decadence, but the exhaustion of all possible permutations and combinations was death" (V., p. 277). A black man, Sphere (as in "closed thing, cyclical . . .") fits into the recent American literary tradition of using "national outsiders as cosmic insiders. Within V. itself the race the West has sought to exterminate provides the texts of its salvation."[8] It is McClintic who urges us to "keep cool but care."

The American majority has neglected the preterite as a source of redemption, relegating them to what it considers dumping grounds — Watts, for example. But they keep "hanging in there with what must seem a terrible vitality" (W, p. 147). To exemplify this vitality, Pynchon describes what he no doubt sees as an analogy to his own fictional statement and aesthetic (see chapter 7):

[8]Catherine R. Stimpson, "Pre-Apocalyptic Atavism: Thomas Pynchon's Early Fiction," in *Mindful Pleasures: Essays on Thomas Pynchon*, ed. George Levine and David Leverenz (Boston: Little, Brown and Co., 1976), p. 42.

An Italian immigrant named Simon Rodia spent thirty years gathering some of it [waste] up and converting a little piece of the neighborhood along 107th Street into the famous Watts Towers, perhaps his own dream of how things should have been: a fantasy of fountains, boats, tall openwork spires, encrusted with a dazzling mosaic of Watts debris. (W, p. 149)

The imagination recycles what is cast off by seeing in it new relationships, building blocks of wonder and surprise. The towers, of course, cannot eliminate the anger, frustration, and even despair in Watts. But they are far from being "a symbol" to Watts' people "of what is not, of the waste and debris of their own land from which nothing really new can ever be made."[9] On the contrary, the towers demonstrate that another response to the waste land is possible and, in fact, still practiced. At the "Renaissance of the Arts Festival" in memory of Simon Rodia, Pynchon finds many "fine, honest rebirths": for example "a roomful of sculptures fashioned entirely from found objects — found, symbolically enough, and in the Simon Rodia tradition, among the wreckage the rioting had left" (W, p. 157).

The children of "The Secret Integration" intuitively share Pynchon's faith in preterite possibilities and in recycling. Their black friend Carl is an invention, an unruly manifestation of their saving ability to imagine. As such, Carl relieves the monotony of their lives: Tim "did think of Carl as not only 'colored' himself, but somehow more deeply involved with *all* color. . . . Carl brought a kind of illumination, a brightening, a compensation for whatever it was about the light that was missing" (SI, p. 44). Carl opposes the homogeneous indistinction of white — the suburban way. The creative imagination reverses the tendency to exhaust materials and recycles Carl into being, putting him together

out of phrases, images, possibilities that grownups had somehow turned away from, repudiated, left out at the edges of towns, as if they were auto parts in Étienne's father's junkyard — things they could or did not want to live with but which the kids, on the other hand, could spend endless hours with, piecing together, rearranging, feeding, programming, refining. (SI, p. 51)

Thus Pynchon suggests that hope lies in the ability to see waste and imagine possibility, to take what has been spurned and integrate it back into our lives.

[9]Plater, *The Grim Phoenix*, p. 108.

This hope dominates *The Crying of Lot 49*. Oedipa's life has degenerated into "a fat deckful of days which seemed (wouldn't she be the first to admit it?) more or less identical, or all pointing the same way" (*49*, p. 2). The waste landscape of San Narciso forms no "identifiable city"; there is no "vital difference between it and the rest of Southern California" (*49*, pp. 12, 13). At the used car lot, Mucho can barely distinguish the car owners from their barely distinguishable cars or from one another. Oedipa comes to recognize the "continuity" of "alienations" and "disinheritance" that "she might have found . . . anywhere in her Republic . . . if only she'd looked," a whole other America "invisible yet congruent" (*49*, p. 135).

But *The Crying of Lot 49* presents a stronger challenge to entropy than does *V.* or most of Pynchon's preceding work. It conveys a greater sense of immediacy and unresolved tension because it looks to the present becoming the future rather than to the present trying—sometimes absurdly—to reconstruct its past. In *V.*, the track of the energy, as Henry Adams called it, is hardly decipherable; in *The Crying of Lot 49*, the track is still being laid. One feels throughout the book a sense of possibilities and alternatives, as crucial as they are barely beyond grasp. The strong suggestion of a hidden order, an integrating energy, "adds to the world's complexity, and demands not acquiescence, but conscious choice."[10] For example, Pynchon qualifies his theme of entropy with concepts such as information. John Nefastis claims to have invented a machine that violates the second law of thermodynamics because it " 'connects the world of thermodynamics to the world of information flow.' " Actually, he admits, "The two fields were entirely unconnected, except at one point: Maxwell's Demon. As the Demon sat and sorted his molecules into hot and cold, the system was said to lose entropy. But somehow the loss was offset by the information the Demon gained about what molecules were where" (*49*, p.77).

In the context of the novel, one might laugh off this notion, but contemporary scientists such as Norbert Wiener and Leon Brillouin have taken Maxwell's "thought experiment" quite

[10]Edward Mendelson, "The Sacred, the Profane, and *The Crying of Lot 49*," in *Individual and Community: Variations on a Theme in American Fiction*, ed. Kenneth H. Baldwin and David K. Kirby (Durham: Duke University Press, 1975), p. 188.

seriously. Brillouin may finally have answered the challenge in 1951 with "Maxwell's Demon Cannot Operate," an article in the *Journal of Applied Physics*. Maxwell, he argues, wrongly supposed that it costs no energy to gather information. Actually, to gain information one must use more than an equivalent amount of energy, as Oedipa realizes through common sense during her dialogue with Stanley Koteks: "'Sorting isn't work? . . . Tell them down at the post office, you'll find yourself in a mailbag headed for Fairbanks, Alaska, without even a FRAGILE sticker going for you" (49, p. 62). Brillouin explains more technically that if the light in the demon's chambers were in equilibrium with the gas, the demon would be unable to see the molecules; it has to draw upon some external source of light energy, and this precludes its operating a self-sufficient perpetual motion machine.

Nefastis believes he has solved the problem by building a machine that draws upon a nonphysical source of energy: human "sensitivity," something akin to what Pynchon calls "real magic" (GR, p. 38). The Tristero system may work just as the Nefastis machine is *supposed* to, but it counters social instead of thermodynamic entropy. As scientist W. Ehrenberg notes: "A practical system with immunity from the second law of thermodynamics would be . . . capable of returning the fuel after the work is done."[11] Pynchon's skillful coordination of motifs is evident here: in trying to take the human waste spit out by the social dynamo and recycle it through information and communication, the Tristero recalls the perpetual motion machine and the demon. The preterite who use the Tristero are, in a sense, human misprints, but the novel suggests that the answers to our contemporary plight may reside in misprinted envelopes, corrupted texts, and social rejects.

In standing for the potential value of waste and of the energy lost to a closed system, the Tristero also answers a need for an open system — a "yearning for diversity, a world of unprogrammed possibilities."[12] It serves, if not to free Oedipa from the tower, at least to jolt her out of her long series of identical days, out of her suburban routine and into another

[11]W. Ehrenberg, "Maxwell's Demon," *Scientific American* 217 (November 1967), 104.
[12]Tony Tanner, *City of Words: American Fiction, 1950–1970* (New York: Harper and Row, 1971), p. 178.

world—into what Michael Harrington calls "the other America." She acknowledges this "other," in fact, when she first uses the Tristero to mail the old sailor's letter. In doing so, she has recognized the "sufferings of another human being and simultaneously committed herself to the possibilities of other realities and to the viability of other modes of consciousness."[13] When she embraces the old man she steps outside of the role she takes in society and experiences a moment that could never happen within its prescribed routines; she has formed an unlikely, "unprogrammed" relation of just the sort that the Tristero symbolizes.[14]

Oedipa's encounter also gives her a sense of why some group like the Tristero is needed. She imagines the sailor's death after he or someone close by him falls asleep while smoking a cigarette and sets the mattress on fire. The lumpy mattress, like one of Mucho's cars, somehow retains not only the physical imprint of the sailor's body but "vestiges" of the owner's life: both the life and the record of it are destroyed together. Oedipa's vision reminds her of "John Nefastis, talking about his Machine, and massive destructions of information." All that the sailor had been or felt "would truly cease to be, forever, when the mattress burned. She stared at it in wonder. It was as if she had just discovered the irreversible process. It astonished her to think that so much could be lost, even the quantity of hallucination belonging just to the sailor that the world would bear no further trace of" (49, p. 95). Oedipa senses here just how much is squandered irretrievably if any person is let waste, prevented from recycling his or her "information" back into the public world. She begins to feel the political need of "a network by which X number of Americans are truly communicating whilst reserving their lies, recitations of routine, arid betrayals of spiritual poverty, for the official government delivery system" (49, p. 128). Her whole quest, in fact, stems from the same impulse: to recycle bits of information randomly scattered and lost, to sort clues instead of molecules into some system that "mattered," "to bring the estate into pulsing stelliferous Meaning"—ultimately, to "project a world" (49, pp. 136, 58, 59).

[13] Annette Kolodny and Daniel James Peters, "Pynchon's The Crying of Lot 49: The Novel as Subversive Experience," Modern Fiction Studies 19 (Spring 1973), 84.
[14] Mendelson, "The Sacred, the Profane," p. 216, has made a similar point.

As discussed above, the gravity of *Gravity's Rainbow*, linked
by imagery to Kekulé's Ouroboros, also suggests the possibility
of recycling "wastes" and "dead species" (GR, p. 590). More
intently here than in previous works, Pynchon affirms that
salvation lies in what we have cast off or learned to regard as
filth and garbage. A sick society, like the party aboard the
Anubis, will "throw everything of value over the side" (GR, p.
668). William Slothrop advocated such opinions in his
theological book *On Preterition*, arguing for "the holiness" of
the "'second Sheep,' without whom there'd be no elect [. . . .]
Could he have been the fork in the road America never took, the
singular point she jumped the wrong way from?" (GR, pp.
555 – 56). The "politics of bacteria" that operate in Pirate's
banana garden apply to human beings as well as to topsoil
created from rotted debris. Perhaps the West may escape its
"ancient curse" of "dusty Dracularity" by rooting itself in the
ground of "preterition." Lenin, Trotsky, Joyce, and Einstein all
frequented the Cafe Odeon: "dialectics, matrices, archetypes
all need to connect, once in a while, back to some of that
proletarian blood, to body odors and senseless screaming
across a table, to cheating and lost hopes" (GR, pp. 262 – 63).
This politics of recycling opposes Theirs of linear exhaustion,
just as the soil rings of Pirate's garden contrast with the
synthetic benzene ring developed by I. G. Farben.

According to the politics of recycling, one does not try, like
Blicero, "to break out — to leave this cycle of infection and
death" by fighting nature; one does not attempt to escape
gravity (GR, p. 724). Rather than ascend beyond the world, one
descends into it, like the Herero woman. Herero leader Enzian
believes that "somewhere, among the wastes of the World, is
the key that will bring us back, restore us to our Earth and to
our freedom." The narrator echoes this sentiment verbatim a bit
later in the book (GR, pp. 525, 667). Both Enzian and Blicero
perform symbolic actions in building and firing a rocket.
Blicero chooses the *via negativa*, renouncing and transcending;
his rocket is the 00000. But Enzian, just as he would look for
the key in the wastes of the world, assembles a missile out of
cast-off parts; his rocket is the 00001. Also, his gesture has
cultural — not just personal — significance. The Hereros are a
preterite people living transplanted in "this locus of death."
Enzian, therefore, takes preterite pieces and constructs a rocket
whose fin section and launching switch duplicate the form of

the sacred Herero village mandala (GR, p. 563). Symbolically, he reconstitutes the identity of his tribe. Then fulfilling the "logic of mandalas" (GR, p. 707) by shooting the 00001 due north, "death's region" in the Herero myth, Enzian reveals that his people can rise above the "Final Zero" of tribal suicide and be reborn. Mark Siegel draws upon Eliade to explain "Enzian's mythological rejuvenation" of his culture: "the mandala is primarily an 'imago-mundi,' a miniature representation of the cosmos of the pantheon, whose construction is equivalent to a magical recreation of the world,"[15] a recreation Enzian achieves through recycling waste and debris.

The narrator laments that

> *It is our mission to promote death.* The way we kill, the way we die, being unique among the Creatures. It was something we had to work on, historically and personally. To build from scratch up to its present status as reaction, nearly as strong as life, holding down the green uprising. But only nearly as strong.
>
> Only nearly, because of the defection rate. A few keep going over to the Titans every day, in their striving subcreation (how can flesh tumble and flow so, and never be any less beautiful?), into the rests of the folksong Death (empty stone rooms), out, and through, and down under the net, down down to the uprising. (GR, p. 720)

The circular motion, the conversion of death into life, and the suggestion of choice all assert that recycling can oppose entropy and decay, that it offers real grounds for hope and possibilities for action. Pynchon emphasizes this point with his many underground settings, to most of which he self-consciously (and sometimes mockingly) lends mythic associations of rebirth.

Political Possibilities: The Counterforce

To show that recycling of waste can describe a mass political solution, Pynchon often presents an "underground" of defectors or outcasts from the main "planetary mission." No such groups appear in the early fiction. There the possibilities inherent in sorting or recycling waste products are suggested or examined by individuals. But the children of "The Secret Integration" react against their parents by joining forces. The

---

[15]Siegel, *Pynchon*, p. 117.

kids are anarchists. Hating institutions such as the school, the railroad, and the PTA, they band together into a counterforce and plan disruptive tactics, collectively referred to as "Operation Spartacus" after the Kirk Douglas movie about the Greek slave rebellion. Their capers provide an escape from the narrowness of their parents' world. On this point Étienne Cherdlu quotes his father and so gives the rationale for the counterforce's pranksterism: "The only thing a machine *can't* do is play jokes. That's all they'll use people for, is jokes" (SI, p. 42). Étienne's father, in fact, seems to be the only parent immune to the bigotry that infects the adults when the Barringtons, a black couple, move into town. He runs the dump. In his spirit, or in the Simon Rodia tradition, the children take what the grown-up world has rejected and build an imaginary friend, Carl Barrington, gleefully speculating that such a friendship would cause "havoc" in the PTA.

As *The Crying of Lot 49* unfolds, the Tristero looks more and more like a positive counterforce to the prevalent grotesque and entropic forces that desecrate contemporary America. For Oedipa, who mimics Pynchon here in applying the laws of physics to social movements and psychological responses, the presence of such a counterforce is inevitable: since the alienated "could not have withdrawn into a vacuum (could they?), there had to exist a separate, silent, unsuspected world" (*49*, p. 92). Pynchon's suggested separate world offers as close an approximation to a norm as can be found in his work: the idealized anarchy of Jesús Arrabal in which "the soul's talent for consensus allows the masses to work together without effort, automatic as the body itself," automatic as the deaf-mute ball in which individual dancers have freedom and yet continuity with the other dancers (*49*, pp. 88 – 89).

In the present time of the novel, the Tristero seems to be a medium for such "miraculous" possibilities. Arrabal's *Regeneración* arrives through W.A.S.T.E., hinting at a salvation of religious magnitude. The Pentecostal power of miraculous communication is a social as well as a spiritual counterforce, for "Pentecost is a phenomenon of the preterite,"[16] an irrational experience that subverts routine and

---

[16]W. T. Lhamon, Jr., "Pentecost, Promiscuity, and Pynchon's *V*.: From the Scaffold to the Impulsive," in *Mindful Pleasures: Essays on Thomas Pynchon*, ed. George Levine and David Leverenz (Boston: Little, Brown and Co., 1976), p. 71.

hierarchy and promotes egalitarian immediacy. Through W.A.S.T.E., the human waste may become a unified and powerful anti-entropic concentration of political energy. Consequently, the Tristero is a revolutionary threat to the oppressive, stultifying Yoyodyne and the apparently "exitless" San Narciso. It poses a radical alternative to the "spiritual poverty" and "absence of surprise to life, that harrows the head of everybody American" (49, p. 128).

In the final section of *Gravity's Rainbow*, a number of the more sympathetic and preterite characters draw together and form a counterforce to oppose Their entropic and death-dealing regime. As Pirate Prentice the banana grower tells Roger Mexico the lover and "novice paranoid," "Creative paranoia means developing at least as thorough a We-system as a They-system" (GR, p. 638). Katje speculates that "dialectically, sooner or later, some counterforce would have had to arise [. . .] even with all the power on the other side" (GR, p. 536). Scientifically, she could be right, and Pynchon's very term *counterforce* points up again his predilection for describing psychological and sociological phenomena in terms of physics: David Hawkins, in his book on science and information, could be referring to Their intricate network of interlocks when he observes that "the informational cost of achieving and maintaining" a "pyramiding system of sophistications. . . . rises very steeply," and the more complex the system becomes, "the more its significance is destroyed by small chance fluctuations. The system becomes, at some point, just a noise amplifier."[17]

Here Hawkins identifies the counterforce's chief ally: accident, "real random [. . .] something beyond Their grasp" (GR, p. 586). The narrator posits "Murphy's law, where the salvation could be" (GR, p. 471). When Their racist gofer, Major Marvy, disappears, Tchitcherine reasons: "Marvy was a key man. There is a counterforce in the Zone" (GR, p. 611). Actually, like many Pynchon characters he is correct, but not in the way he thinks — Marvy was abducted and castrated in place of Slothrop *by accident*. The human members of the counterforce function somewhat like accident or chance; they violate the rules of etiquette and predictable behavior, creating

[17]David Hawkins, *The Language of Nature* (San Francisco: W.H. Freeman, 1964), p. 348.

"noise" in the system or at least producing disruptive surprise. Slothrop, who becomes a rallying point for the counterforce, learns that the next time he comes across a logging operation, he should "find one of their tractors that isn't being guarded, and take its oil filter" (GR, p. 553). Osbie Feel defends the group's disorganized pranksterism by proclaiming: "They're the rational ones. We piss on Their rational arrangements" (GR, p. 639). Roger does actually urinate on members of the Firm in Clive Mossmoon's office. Later he and Pig Bodine initiate a literally nauseating word game that ruins one of Their dinner parties.

Fausto II interprets "life's single lesson: that there is more accident to it than a man can ever admit to in a lifetime and stay sane" (V., p. 300). But as noted above, Pynchon often sees freedom and possibility in accident. As early as "Low-lands" he writes that "Geronimo Diaz was clearly insane; but it was a wonderful, random sort of madness which conformed to no known model or pattern, an irresponsible plasma of delusion he floated in" (L, p. 88). Diaz undercuts causality, claiming he is Paganini and has sold his soul to the devil, then proving it by being unable to play the priceless Stradivarius that he keeps in his desk. As Flange's therapist, he would "spend whole sessions reading aloud to himself out of random-number tables or the Ebbinghaus nonsense-syllable lists, ignoring everything that Flange would be trying to tell him" (L, p. 88). Pynchon also describes the sea as a "sustaining plasma" (L, p. 102); the madness, the sea, and the dump, another "low-land," all have the chaotic virtue of allowing surprise and fantasy that can exist nowhere in the rationalized world. In Gravity's Rainbow Pynchon continues to set the spontaneous and accidental against the programmed and routinized. Leni's "early dream" for Ilse "is coming true. She will not be used. There is change, and departure: but there is also help when least looked for from the strangers of the day, and hiding, out among the accidents of this drifting Humility, never quite to be extinguished, a few small chances for mercy" (GR, p. 610).

Wasted Possibilities

Pynchon does offer us possible solutions and grounds for hope. But we should not therefore overestimate his optimism: despite the real chances for salvation, very few of his characters are saved. In many cases they are just not strong, clever, honest, vital, or whole enough to take the opportunities and make the solutions work. For example, Pynchon considers purging violence to be one answer to decadence and benighted self-absorption. Siegel is fighting for his own survival when he lets the partyers be slaughtered, but he is not his own hero; he must use a preterite person, Irving Loon, to fight for him. He has not within him the rich, regenerative, apocalyptic force — he is only the arranger and manipulator who, as with his college panty raid, gleans his "sense of exhilaration" from "knowing it was he who had set it all in motion" (MMV, p. 213). The intelligent and troubled young American may escape immediate damnation or absorption into the sick society, but he cannot perform an effective action, partake of communion, and win salvation. In Pynchon's fiction, such a person never does. It is hard to imagine what Siegel's life will be like after he leaves the party. Where will he go, what will he do, and how will he regard himself? To the people of Watts, violence is not so much a solution as a lingering presence, "never far from you," or simply a condition of existence, like Newton's "equal and opposite reaction." It might also be a form of self-expression or a kind of therapeutic release, but not a long-term course of action: the rioting changed little and resolved nothing.

On Pynchon's spectrum of solutions, withdrawal and self-isolation stand at the other extreme from righteous violence. But these responses prove no more workable. The passive and introverted Dennis Flange retreats from his cold and domineering wife, seeking emotional security in the ambience of his house, an "almost organic mound" toward which he (if not his wife) "had come to feel attached . . . by an umbilical cord woven of lichen and sedge, furze and gorse; he called it his womb with a view" (L, p. 87). Pynchon, in addition to showing that he cannot resist a pun, least of all a bad one, demonstrates that an unhappy marriage drives Flange to pursue fetal shelter. As Dennis draws into himself, Pynchon first links solipsism with the tendency to confuse the animate and the inanimate. One night Flange finds himself sleeping in the fetal position, catches himself "red-handed at Molemanship . . . a state of mind in which . . . even the secret cadences of one's pulse become mere echoes of the house's heartbeat" (L, p.

88). But Dennis's withdrawal does not make him happy or save his marriage. At night in the dump, Nerissa leads Dennis underground through a "cast-off chaos" of refuse and into a womb of junk whose writhing, irregular tunnels recall the womb from which Cindy had ejected him. His new love and his new home might answer Dennis's "several wounds, needs, dark doubles" (49, p. 98); on the other hand, Flange may only be dreaming and about to wake up.

His retreat is no worse than Callisto's experiment with self-isolation. Hermetically sealed off on the floor above Meatball's party, somewhat as Cindy is above Dennis, Callisto has tried to create a closed system safe from the disintegrating forces at large in the cosmos and society. But the system has become a prison. Callisto and Aubade cannot "be omitted from that sanctuary; they had become necessary to its unity" (E, p. 279). Their attempt fails for a variety of reasons. First, Callisto and Aubade are no more in touch with each other for being shut away together: each is in a separate world. Second, each one has to burn up calories in a frantic and futile struggle to regulate that artificial realm, thus speeding up the heat death they try to avoid by the very intensity of their trying. They enact one of Pynchon's favorite ironies, adumbrating a host of other characters who also merely hasten some end in their efforts to escape it. Callisto's and Aubade's endeavor is self-defeating, for as the theorem of Clausius states, "the entropy of an isolated system always continually increases" (E, p. 282). Through Callisto's failure, Pynchon impugns the strategies of Dennis Flange and all those characters who seek to buffer themselves with hothouses, towers, siege parties, mathematical graphs, or work on the Rocket.

But if withdrawing from the world is a flawed solution, so is paranoia or any attempt to "project a world" — to assert a structure for possibly chaotic events and invest it with meaning. To begin with, this attempt can become an obsession, and "such an obsession is a hothouse: constant temperature, windless, too crowded with particolored sports, unnatural blooms" (V., p. 422). In *Gravity's Rainbow* the narrator notes that the paranoid seeks "to perfect methods of immobility" (GR, p. 572). But existence is a constant flux of emerging and dissolving forms in shifting relations; reality is mobile. Besides being inflexible, projected worlds are dangerous because they

become, like von Göll films, self-fulfilling prophecies.
Consequently, many critics see V. in particular as disparaging
the "modern tendency to allow the imagination to enthrall,
rather than to enlarge human capabilities."[18] As Richard
Lehan comments, the Vheissu episode shows "that all reality,
whether it be good or evil, is first a state of mind." Man, then,
has misused his imagination and "created the state of mind
that made a Vheissu an ultimate reality." In this way, "modern
man seems to be the victim of his dying [and death-dealing]
imagination," of his failure to create on a massive scale the
kind of life-sustaining fictions that the Maltese made.[19] His
fictions can even promote degradations such as imperialism
and war. Stencil, V.'s chief fabulator, works for no one's
"amusement" or salvation but his own. His solipsistic
obsession counters whatever good the quest does him, and
if he helps anyone else in the book, it does not show.

With characteristic ambivalence, Pynchon fears the
impotence as well as the destructive potence of the modern
imagination. He doubts that it can devise a new code of values
that will animate and give a sense of purpose to life. His
misgivings parallel Michael Harrington's definition of the
decadence of the Western tradition:

> The moment would be announced when there was no longer a
> basis within society for people to take new ideas passionately and
> to seek change. It ["the end of ideology"] would mean, not a
> decay from the past, but the rotting of the future. . . . [The] more
> serious idea of decadence is that the West no longer senses either
> a City of God or of man in the middle or long distance. It has lost
> its utopia to come rather than its golden age that was. . . . the
> present decadence is the corruption of a dream rather than of
> a reality.[20]

The strongest dream is now, in Hugh Godolphin's words, a
"dream of annihilation." Here we are past the modernist's
waste land, unable to look back for guidance to previous forms
of religion, economy, or social structure, as Eliot and Pound
did. The contemporary writer suspects that history and

---

[18]Stephen Koch, "Imagination in the Abstract," *Antioch Review* 24 (Summer 1964), 254.

[19]Richard Lehan, *A Dangerous Crossing: French Existentialism and the Modern American Novel* (Carbondale: Southern Illinois University Press, 1973), p. 162.

[20]Michael Harrington, *The Accidental Century* (New York: Macmillan, 1965), pp. 295, 17.

traditional myth may have exhausted their possibilities, except for parody (see chapter 7). Paola, as noted, does give her husband the comb she took from V., a comb that closely resembles an artifact of the White Goddess. But the scene is weak (as discussed below), and it is followed by other depictions of twentieth-century decadence; moreover, there is the suggestion that Pappy might lose the comb in a poker game.

In *Loss of the Self in Modern Literature and Art*, Wylie Sypher contends that despite all the disintegrating forces in the world "there seems to remain some existence, however minimal — some residue of a self that still causes us trouble, malaise, unhappiness. This minimal self, a nearly spectral identity that refuses to vanish, or that cannot vanish, is the cornerstone on which a new humanism must be based."[21] Although Sypher never treats Pynchon, his statement applies very well. One feels in reading the fiction that the characters could tap some "residue of a self" more assiduously than they do, that they are responsible for their lack of substance or dimension because they are lazy or weak; they resign themselves too easily to dehumanizing forces, choose to yo-yo rather than find the courage and energy "to arouse in one another their potentialities for love and hope."[22] Decadence and entropy can be fought, but only with "slow, frustrating and hard work" that few Pynchon characters are willing to undertake.

Free choice, opportunity, and avoidable failure speak most strongly through the many abortive attempts at love. Siegel is divided from Rachel (Owlglass?) as well as from his other selves, Dennis and Cindy break up, Callisto and Aubade are sealed off from each other along with the world. Benny Profane literally flees the kind of salvation from rootlessness and schlemihlhood that love affords. He cannot or will not read the signs with Fina Mendoza; with every possible door open and light green, he avoids the commitment her love would mean, refuses her, and in effect leaves her to the Playboys' gang-bang. He likewise retreats from Paola and fears a relationship with Rachel. When he loses his job at Anthroresearch Associates because of an alarm clock malfunction, he sees the chance to

[21]Wylie Sypher, *Loss of the Self in Modern Literature and Art* (New York: Random House, 1962), p. 68.
[22]Richard Poirier, "Cook's Tour," *New York Review of Books* 1, no. 2 (1963), p. 32.

resign himself fatalistically to schlemihlhood—an inability to
coexist with inanimate objects or give of himself to people. He
offers these supposed shortcomings to Rachel as excuses for
escaping to Valletta, but she counters, "You are scared of love
and all that means is somebody else. . . . People can change.
Couldn't you make the effort? . . . You've taken your own
flabby, clumsy soul and amplified it into a Universal Principle"
(V., p. 359). If alignment with the inanimate is the mark of a
villain in V., then Benny Profane's inability to manage
inanimate objects demonstrates a kernel of goodness; but he
does not develop it to the point where it could possibly benefit
anyone, himself included.

McClintic's prescription to "keep cool, but care" sounds like
a hip version of Eliot's "give, sympathize, control," but it
hardly speaks in thunder. Pynchon makes no attempt to codify
it into a unifying myth for society or even a structuring theme
for the novel. The "word" appears suddenly about two-thirds
of the way through the book and then gives way immediately to
more immersion in the same types of troubles that preceded it.
There are basic problems, Pynchon knows, with Sphere's
dictum as words to live by. First, it does not work for most
people most of the time, though not necessarily through any
fault of its own; the characters just don't make it work. Benny
has picked up on the creed somehow, because SHROUD, in one
of their imaginary conversations, warns him to "keep cool but
care" (V., p. 345). Of course the knowledge is wasted on
Profane: he begins almost immediately to withdraw from
Rachel. A number of critics have found the musician's advice
both platitudinous and unconvincing. But perhaps its
weakness is part of the point; Pynchon tenders it apologetically,
aware that it is unequal to the pessimism, social grotesquerie,
and existential nausea that he presents far more abundantly
and persuasively. McClintic's words constitute a flawed,
difficult, and individual means of coping with—not of
changing—twentieth-century conditions, the causes of which
transcend the individual, even though individuals may share a
collective guilt for "letting it happen" (49, p. 112).

For the efficacy of caring one is tempted to look past Benny
and the others to Paola, the woman McClintic loves. She was
born "just before the war and the building with her records

[was] destroyed" (as Pynchon's service records have been).[23]
Also, "American movies had given [everyone] stereotypes . . .
all but Paola" (*V.*, p. 6). Pynchon tells us that Paola is an
individual, that she defies the cultural typing and loss of
identity seen in Siegel's roommate or in Esther. We also hear
that as a Maltese she is all races and no race, and that she can
communicate in many languages. As mentioned, she gives her
husband V.'s comb, changing the emblem of decadence to a
pledge of faith. But several critics note that Paola remains too
sketchily drawn to make plausible such a momentous symbolic
reversal, even if it is just a tentative note of hope. At the outset
she seems a different character—dependent, scattered,
clinging to Benny Profane of all people for help and guidance.
She changes and grows, but the reader never sees or
understands how; Pynchon might want her transformation for
thematic statement, but he has not earned it dramatically. He
can profitably use two-dimensional characters to reveal human
ineptitude, but not to portray human efficacy in the face of
global or cosmic forces.

More than one reader has been troubled by what Tony
Tanner calls the brilliant hollowness of the book. For example,
Stephen Koch complains: "But that the moral ideal animating
this immense production is present only through conspicuous
absence suggests that Mr. Pynchon, like his characters, is
himself trapped in his own imagination, responsive though it
is to history and society."[24] "Trapped" may be too strong, for
Pynchon does offer a direction with "keep cool, but care." And
yet he does not seem to act on the advice himself: one senses
his coolness and detachment in the novel, but not his caring
and involvement—even with his own characters.

In *The Crying of Lot 49* he translates many of the abstractions
of *V.* into the immediate dilemmas of Oedipa Maas, a more
human, sympathetic, and multi-dimensional creation than any
of her predecessors. But even in Oedipa, a certain retrograde
impulse hinders the attempt to care, to make human contact.
Noticing a "sense of buffering, insulation" that robbed her life

[23]Mathew Winston, "The Quest for Pynchon," in *Mindful Pleasures*, p. 252. I
made the correlation between the destructions of Pynchon's and Paola's
records. Again, coincidence or conspiracy?
[24]Koch, "Imagination in the Abstract," p. 262.

of "intensity," Oedipa "gently conned herself into the curious, Rapunzel-like role of a pensive girl somehow, magically, prisoner among the pines and salt fogs of Kinneret, looking for somebody to say hey, let down your hair" (49, p. 10). She deludes herself. Having had numerous lovers before Pierce Inverarity, she is hardly a captive maiden, or is so only in the sense that nobody has penetrated her buffer, touched her, brought her to realize something outside of herself. Pierce tried, playing by her rules at first and climbing up Rapunzel's tresses, only when he "got maybe halfway up, her lovely hair turned, through some sinister sorcery, into a great unanchored wig, and down he fell, on his ass." Pierce's love could not deliver her from "the confinement of that tower" (49, p. 10). People generally choose to put on wigs, just as V. chose to substitute inanimate parts for her own. Consciously or not, Oedipa frequently buffers herself from others. Roseman tries to "play footsie" with her, but she is so "insulated" by her boots that she "couldn't feel much of anything" (49, p. 9). At the Echo Courts she apparently dons a padded bra before knowing that Metzger will arrive (49, p. 22). When he coaxes her into playing "Strip Botticelli," she first encases herself in an entire wardrobe of clothing. And with Mucho she finds herself "overcome by, call it a tenderness she'd never go quite to the back of lest she get bogged. . . . Like all their inabilities to communicate, this too had a virtuous motive" (49, p. 29). She never manages to communicate effectively with anyone.

Säure (acid) Bummer of *Gravity's Rainbow* maintains that despite everything, "isolation is overcome [. . .] that is the one great centripetal movement of the World [. . . .] *love occurs*" (GR, p. 440). But can it survive? The narrator says,

> There are two sorts of movement out here—as often as the chance displacements of strangers, across a clear skirmish-line from the Force, will bring together people who'll remain that way for a time, in love that can even make the oppression seem a failure, so too love, here in the street, can be taken centrifugally apart again. (GR, p. 219)

Here love is "subject to the laws of physics," not vice versa, as in "lucky" Bland's vision of Gravity (GR, p. 590). Unfortunately, nobody else in the novel, including the narrator, can share Bland's "enlightenment," and so love remains a fragile hope, contingent upon haphazard circumstance, the need for security, or the fear of death. When the rockets stop falling, Jessica drifts away, back to a safe and reassuringly routine life with Jeremy. Bianca Erdmann offers Slothrop a chance to have the transforming magic, but he turns his back on it after creating "a bureaucracy of departure, inoculations against forgetting, exit visas stamped with love bites." He loses salvation and "is to be counted, after all, among the Zone's lost" (GR, p. 470). As in his other fiction, Pynchon holds out love as a solution, but he holds it out to characters not strong, aware, or unselfish enough to resist the deadening, routinizing forces of Their world. He explicitly links Puritan descendant Tyrone Slothrop's failure to love with the loss of America — perhaps the West's last chance — to Them.

For Pynchon the inability to care, or to translate caring into behavior, means the inability to perform socially and politically significant action. Each novel centers on a quest for knowledge of some plot with national, global, or even cosmic implications — knowledge of something "that mattered to the world," as Oedipa says (49, p. 136). Yet no one completes the search; each protagonist falls short of revelation because of some spiritual weakness, some reluctance to risk and give of the self, some incapacity to love. Herbert Stencil's quest is a purely self-serving ploy to keep a "sense of animateness." Similarly, though less consciously, Oedipa may try to restore intensity to her life by immersing herself in the Inverarity estate and the Tristero mystery. She too approaches and avoids knowledge, just as she approaches and avoids human contact or caring. She guards herself against tenderness for Mucho "lest she get bogged" (49, p. 29), just as she is "anxious that her revelation [about the Tristero] not expand beyond a certain point. Lest possibly, it grow larger than she and assume her to itself" (49, p. 125). Her anxiety is a variation on Cleanth Siegel's fear, but it does not fully explain Oedipa's attitude toward the Tristero. She tries to return to Dr. Hilarius because she "wanted to know why the chance of its being real should menace her so" (49, p. 98). She never quite finds out.

Throughout the book, Oedipa senses that Answers are hiding just around the corner, and yet she fears their existence and tries to shy away from them. She will not ask Dr. Hilarius why he wants her for his experiment, "being afraid of all he might answer" (49, p. 7). On overlooking San Narciso, she feels that "words were being spoken"; on arriving in San Narciso, she worries that the Tristero will "bend to her alone . . . and begin to speak words she never wanted to hear" (49, pp. 13, 36). Consequently, she begins to avoid following up clues as early as her first visit to Zapf's, even though she continues to pursue other leads. She is "demoralized" by the "miracle" of the deaf-mute ball, by its "mysterious consensus" or suggestion of overriding design. As Tony Tanner observes, she is disturbed by both the presence and the absence of hieroglyphics on bathroom walls, by visions of a "plotted or a plotless universe."[25] Her response to the Tristero points up a peculiarly human dilemma: while feeling imprisoned by her tower, she fears that Nothing outside it exists to break down the walls— and simultaneously fears that Something does. She craves and yet cowers from freedom, choice, a new range of possibilities.

In the Remedios Varo painting, the frail embroiderers do not appear to create their tower: it is outside of the tapestry they make. But what about Oedipa's? She feels imprisoned not so much by the tower, which like her "ego" has a form that is "only incidental," but rather by "magic, anonymous and malignant" and completely gratuitous. Yet if this is the same "sinister sorcery" that transformed her Rapunzel's tresses into "a great unanchored wig," then at least some of the magic emmanates from herself, although she does not realize it. Several critics argue that the sorcery which solipsizes Oedipa is external, the same, says Charles Harris, that "incarcerates some in prisons of poverty and others in straightjackets of organizational 'efficiency': our absurd modern mass society."[26] Doubtless, the state of America is part of her problem—but by no means all of it. In "The World (This One), The Flesh (Mrs. Oedipa Maas), and The Testament of Pierce Inverarity" (Esquire, 1965), Pynchon wrote that Oedipa "was to have all manner of revelations. Hardly about Pierce Inverarity, or herself; but about what remained: this Republic. It had somehow, before this, stayed away." In publishing the novel, Pynchon revised the passage for greater ambiguity. It now reads: "about what remained yet had somehow, before this, stayed away" (49, p. 10). Here one has no grounds for assuming

[25]Tanner, City of Words, p. 180.
[26]Charles B. Harris, Contemporary American Novelists of the Absurd (New Haven: College and University Press, 1971), p. 95.

that Pynchon means specifically the Republic because the
Republic is clearly not the whole point. Whether Oedipa
recognizes her revelations to be "about herself" or not, her own
fearfulness and weakness are part of the magic's malignance
and power.

Like his predecessors Stencil and Oedipa, Slothrop has
"played" the game of questing because he has "nothing better
to do" (GR, p. 364). He too runs after and away from the big
revelations. His exploits often travesty those of Orpheus, but
this latter-day, double-minded version is not strong enough to
maintain his love — or his quest — for Eurydice/Bianca, for
enlightenment, for the world retrieved from Them:

> Of course Slothrop lost her, and kept losing her — it was
> an American requirement — out of the windows of the Greyhound,
> passing into beveled stonery, green and elm-folded on into a
> failure of perception, or, in a more sinister sense, of will (you
> used to know what these words mean), she has moved on,
> untroubled, too much Theirs [. . . .] Too much closer and it
> begins to hurt to bring her back. But there is this
> Eurydice-obsession, this *bringing back out of*
> . . . though how much easier just to leave her there, in fetid
> carbide and dead-canary soups of breath and come out and have
> comfort enough to try only for a reasonable fascimile [sic] —
> "Why bring her back? Why try? It's only the difference between
> the real boxtop and the one you draw for Them." (GR, p. 472)

The double mindedness overcomes the singleness of purpose,
the weakness conquers the will, and Sloth(as in laziness)rop —
part "spiritual medium," part "tanker and feeb" — is broken
down and scattered (GR, pp. 622, 738).

In Pynchon, all forms of failure — to risk self-loss, to face
uncertainty, to engage the moment and its possibilities, to care
or to quest — are related not only to each other as individual
shortcomings but also to the collapse of the counterforce.
Pynchon is optimistic in presenting the counterforce as a
possibility, even a dialectical necessity, but pessimistic in
showing how consistently it flops. Collectively as well as
singly, his characters just don't have the wherewithal to make
available solutions work. In V. the hint of collusion implies that
human beings are consciously abetting the entropic trend, or at
least are permitting it to run its course by lazily resigning the
control they should exert over machines and systems to the
machines and systems themselves. McClintic's middle of the

road program may work in personal relationships, if the related persons are both strong enough to live by it, but Sidney Stencil realized as early as 1919 that "the once-respectable Golden Mean" had become "obsolete" as a mass political solution. There will be only "Right and Left; the hothouse and the street. The Right can only live and work hermetically, in the hothouse of the past, while outside the Left prosecute their affairs in the streets by manipulated mob violence" (V., p. 440). The courses intersect in V., like the lines that form her letter, but not to advocate any middle way. The "men-of-no-politics" between the extremes will become, "at the very least, a highly 'alienated' populace," such as we see in Nueva York, San Narciso, and Their domain.

"The Secret Integration" portrays temporary resistance giving way to surrender and assimilation. The counterforce, here called "Operation Spartacus," fails year after year to secure its objectives. It is too weak or small to handle the Forces at Large, and its plots keep complicating themselves exponentially, somewhat as the Tristero does in Oedipa's perception of it. Perhaps, Tim wonders, there was "something basically wrong and self-defeating with the plot itself" (SI, p. 44). The counterforce becomes a group of ineffectual pranksters playing for "nothing, nothing but laughs" (SI, p. 46). It also loses its moral strength to continue the fight: fear, along with the desire for comfort and security, corrupt the soul. Tim thinks of confronting his parents with the evidence that they conspired to dump trash all over the Barrington's front yard, "but then figured all that would get him was spanked, and hard, so he forgot about it" (SI, p. 51). At the story's close, we see the counterforce splitting up as each member goes out of the rain and into "his own house, hot shower, dry towel, before-bed television, good night kiss, and dreams that could never again be entirely safe" (SI, p. 51). Joseph Slade writes that "Carl is being discarded, consigned to the junkheap of childish fantasies. And so is youthful rebellion."[27] With the loss of innocence, hope, or will, the junkheap becomes a place for dumping and rejecting rather than finding and salvaging. In Watts, individual artists may recycle debris into "fine, honest rebirths," but "next to the Towers, along the old Pacific Electric

[27]Joseph W. Slade, Thomas Pynchon (New York: Warner Paperback Library, 1974), p. 44.

tracks, kids are busy every day busting more bottles on the
steel rails. . . . Simon Rodia is dead, and now the junk just
accumulates" (W, p. 149).

Much of the hope in *The Crying of Lot 49* rests upon what
Maxwell's demon symbolizes: the ability to transfer and apply
information so as to retard or locally reverse entropy. Such
"communication," says John Nefastis, depends on "sensitivity."
In the Nefastis machine, for example, the demon supplies
intelligence and sorting ability, but it is impotent by itself—
a human will is also needed to violate the second law of
thermodynamics. A "sensitive" person must choose the
cylinder in which the demon is to raise the temperature.
Without deliberate choice and effort by a human being, entropy
continues to increase. A real demon may not exist, but real IBM
7094's do: modern cybernetics allows people to collect,
correlate, and store information as leading scientists of the
previous century believed only a supernatural being could. If
computers alienate instead of integrate, the fault lies with
human sensitivity.

Nefastis and Koteks are not absurd in arguing that
information can be used to challenge entropy. They are absurd,
like many Pynchon characters, because they try to make a
metaphor literal. Nonetheless, Pynchon often uses such
ridiculous figures to make serious points. America has failed
to exploit the potential hinted at in the Nefastis machine;
instead, as typified by San Narciso, it has levelled distinctions,
narrowed options, and enforced a conformity that paradoxically
leads to isolation, alienation, and inability to share experience.
Oedipa fails to make real contact with anyone or anything
important to her. Ironically, as Peter Abernathy notes, "our
human ability to communicate seems to decrease in proportion
to the increase in our technical ability to communicate."[28]
Recall Dennis Flange, the "competent communications officer"
who could not communicate with his wife, or Saul of
"Entropy," who breaks up with his wife after they get into a
terrible fight—over communication theory.

The Tristero system offers a nontechnical means of
communication, something like the Nefastis machine. But one
cannot be sure if it is much more effective. Bortz's history,

[28]Peter L. Abernathy, "Entropy in Pynchon's *The Crying of Lot 49*," *Critique* 14, no. 2 (1972), p. 18.

fictitious or not, reveals its inconsistency and fallibility. Arrabal's *Regeneración* arrives through W.A.S.T.E.—sixty years late. The crackpots, perverts, and alienated souls who use it remain cracked, perverted, and alienated. The old sailor seems no more happy or whole after he gives his letter to Oedipa; perhaps he senses that he does not have anything like sixty years to wait. If the letter finds his wife and if one of hers should find him in return, it will be as if by accident.

One can look to the counterforce, as to accident, and hope against probability for a disruption of entropy or of Their power, but one cannot rely on either accident or the counterforce for a predictable disruption. Sometimes, like the pinball players who cause "Malfunction" in Their machines, the counterforce members may be "forever strangers [....] a unity unaware of itself" (GR, p. 586). Spontaneous, uncoordinated, and occasional efforts—even if locally successful—will not affect mass behavior, in physics or in history. Speaking of the physical world, Sir William Dampier observes that a "determinate mechanism" seems to direct "macroscopic phenomena which depend on the statistical average action of multitudes of units, and to fail when the ultra-microscopic detail of individual atoms, electrons and quanta are considered." He adds that "it is impossible to miss the analogy" with living organisms: "According to present knowledge, mankind may be statistically the slaves of fate, but for the individual. . . . there may still be room for free will."[29]

Yet what is the force of a microscopic particle, or an individual, to a macroscopic system? On entering a gaming room at the Casino Hermann Goering, Slothrop suddenly intuits that much more goes on there that "games of chance"; he senses Their presence and shrinks from it instinctively: "'Fuck you,' whispers Slothrop. It's the only spell he knows." But it is pathetically powerless against Their complex edifice. In the hieroglyphic room, a symbol of Their interlocking system, "his whisper is baffled by the thousands of tiny rococo surfaces" (GR, p. 203). The impact is weak even if the "free will" is strong, but as noted, the will itself weakens in individuals. Then the counterforce fails: its members

[29]Sir William Dampier, *A History of Science and Its Relations with Philosophy and Religion* (New York: Macmillan, 1936), pp. 475, 473, 474.

are as schizoid, as double-minded in the massive presence of money, as any of the rest of us, and that's the hard fact. The Man has a branch office in each of our brains, his corporate emblem is a white albatross [which Pynchon has used to represent the self], each local rep has a cover known as the Ego. (GR, p. 713)

"They" are not only a group of people but also a state of mind that the Firm members embody most purely, although we are all tainted. After persecuting Them with rather juvenile and finally ineffectual pranks, such as urinating on Them and nauseating Them, the counterforce becomes rationalized and assimilated in the late sixties (GR, pp. 738–39).

The pessimism, however, is not absolute: even though the counterforce continues to fail, or to succeed only so far as disruptive, "Operation Spartacus"-like tricks will carry it, there will always be a chance: "in each of these streets, some vestige of humanity, of Earth, has to remain. No matter what has been done to it, no matter what it's been used for" (GR, p. 693). Also, Pynchon affirms a "kindness reflex [. . .] that now and then, also beyond the Zero, survives extinction" (GR, p. 714). Velleity and venality corrupt some, but there is a "defection rate" from Their side. And, most importantly, there are countless possibilities inherent in the moment — any moment — even if they go unrealized. Such possibilities will still exist if and when human beings become capable of seizing them.

Symbols of Randomness and Fright

"There is little ground for believing that the current world view
of science has directly influenced the development of modern
art or could have done so," wrote Werner Heisenberg.[1] Perhaps
these words were true when they were written in the spring of
1959, but that same year Thomas Pynchon published his first
short story in a national magazine and began a career that
renders Heisenberg's statement obsolete. Jacob Bronowski has
observed that transitional periods in literature have often
coincided with transitional periods in science. Pynchon's work
reveals a contemporary coincidence of transitional periods in
the two disciplines better than does the work of any other
writer. His fiction reformulates in human terms the questions
and discoveries that Maxwell, Planck, Heisenberg, and
Einstein formulated in their physics.

As will be discussed in subsequent chapters, Pynchon
not only bases his thematic analyses of human society and
psychology on the concepts or "themes" of today's science,
but he also renders into literature its most challenging
epistemological and methodological problems. David Cowart
rightly points out that the author is not essentially an engineer
or a scientist but an artist with much interest and learning
in the humanities.[2] This, however, does not distinguish
Pynchon from many other important novelists. Pynchon's use
of science is not analogous, as Cowart suggests, to Melville's

---

[1] Werner Heisenberg, "Nearer the Truth: The Representation of Nature in
Contemporary Physics," *Graduate Journal* 2 (Spring 1959), 61.
[2] David Cowart, *Thomas Pynchon: The Art of Allusion* (Carbondale: Southern
Illinois University Press, 1980).

use of whaling; whaling in itself does not urge a new understanding of the cosmos or a new aesthetic of fiction. Most of what is distinctive in Pynchon, even his radical ambivalence, reflects some development in modern physics. His profound and varied use of science may be his most important contribution to contemporary letters; it is what differentiates him most clearly from the other counterrealists and makes him seem esoteric or inaccessible to many readers.

Pynchon's views of the world's problems and possibilities (discussed in chapters 2 and 3) correspond to his view of the cosmos as contemporary science has led him to see it. Entropy and gravity, for example, provide him with emblematic grounds for sociological despair and hope. At the very least, science has been a source of metaphors, if not concepts, for "the way things are," to echo a title from physicist Percy Bridgman. But Pynchon's view of the cosmos has not *determined* his view of man and society, or vice versa; in fact, his understanding of the cosmos has steered him away from such determinism, away from the notion that "A could do B," and toward relativity, toward the notion that A and B "are names for parts that ought to be inseparable" (GR, p. 30). Similarly, Pynchon's scientific and sociological thought are really inseparable parts of the same mode of thought, a mode that reveals itself in paradoxes and ambivalences, signs and symptoms.

Pynchon believes that he cannot progress beyond these to apprehend or convey some final, unmediated truth. Perhaps this is the most profound lesson he has learned from a science that has been forced to recognize its own bounds: no system of knowledge can absolutely comprehend reality or deliver it in a definitive statement. Pynchon sees that science — like any means of explanation — is limited and flawed. Consequently, as Mark Siegel writes, he "invests the physical sciences with no more authority than he does the literary and mythological systems that he uses in a tentative manner. The narrator [of *Gravity's Rainbow*] sees science itself as composed of metaphorical conceptions of universal forces, and sees metaphorical structures in science, the arts, religion, and even casual figures of speech as all valid but tentative ways of imagining, investigating, and testing the structures of reality."[3]

[3]Mark Siegel, *Pynchon: Creative Paranoia in Gravity's Rainbow* (Port Washington, N.Y.: Kennikat Press, 1978), pp. 73–74.

Entropy and Its Reversal: The End of Cause and Effect

Pynchon employs the scientific concept of entropy in presenting his view of physical as well as social reality (for the latter see chapter 2). Actually, the author's use of entropy parallels to some extent the course of scientific understanding: early Pynchon and early thermodynamics are relatively unsophisticated and pessimistic in that they view entropy as an irreversible and irresistible constant *force*. The French astronomer Jean-Sylvain Bailly (1736–1793) was the first to speculate that "all bodies in the universe are cooling off and will eventually become too cold to support life." He predicted that "all bodies must eventually reach a final state of equilibrium in which all motion ceases."[4] Bailly's countryman, Jean Baptiste Joseph Fourier (1768–1830) put this theory on a quantitative basis by devising a heat conduction equation which, "unlike Newton's laws of motion, is *irreversible* with respect to time. It postulates that wherever temperature differences exist, they tend to be evened out by the flow of heat from high temperature to low."[5]

A young French engineer named Sadi Carnot applied these principles to the notion of work in *Reflections on the Motive Power of Fire* (1824). Carnot maintained that steam engines would always fail in practice to perform at maximum efficiency, that is, to provide the mechanical work theoretically derivable from a given amount of heat, because the heat imbalances or concentrations necessary for producing work would "dissipate" themselves; heat equalizes its distribution by flowing unstoppably from hot bodies to cold and so becomes unavailable for conversion into work. Moreover, this movement applies not just to steam engines but to all of nature. All forms of energy tend to degrade themselves into heat, which then tends to spread itself evenly throughout the system.

In 1852 William Thomson, later Lord Kelvin, "generalized the Second Law of Thermodynamics and asserted the existence

---

[4]Gerald James Holton, *Introduction to Concepts and Theories in Physical Science*, 2nd edition revised and with new material by Stephen G. Brush (Reading, Mass.: Addison-Wesley, 1973), p. 285.

[5]Ibid., pp. 286–87.

of 'a universal tendency in nature to the dissipation of mechanical energy.'"[6] Two years later, Hermann von Helmholtz

pointed out that Thomson's principle implied the cooling of the entire universe. All energy would eventually be transformed into heat at a uniform temperature, and all natural processes would cease; "the universe from that time forward would be condemned to a state of eternal rest." Thus was made explicit the concept of the *heat death* of the universe, as foreseen nearly a century earlier by Bailly, but now apparently based much more firmly on the new science of thermodynamics.[7]

In 1865 the German physicist Rudolf Clausius applied the name *entropy* to the law regulating the transfer of heat from one body to another, coining it from the Greek words for energy and transformation. Clausius then stated the first two laws of thermodynamics:

1) The energy of the universe is constant.
2) The entropy of the universe tends toward a maximum.[8]

As such, entropy has been called "time's arrow" and used in equations to designate the movement from past to future states.

Such conceptions of entropy correspond to Callisto's fatalism or to Mehemet's "cheerful" pronouncement that "the only change is toward death" (*V.,* p. 433). But science gradually developed a rather different notion of entropy as part of a whole new conception of the cosmos. As Norbert Wiener remarks, Newtonian physics "described a universe in which everything happened precisely according to law, a compact, tightly organized universe in which the whole future depends strictly upon the whole past." He adds that "this is now no longer the dominating attitude of physics, and the men who contributed most to its downfall were [Ludwig] Bolzmann [sic] in Germany and [Willard] Gibbs in the United States."[9] These two physicists convincingly applied the idea of statistically probable or "contingent" courses of a system: one certain past does not lead inevitably to one certain future, and "physics now no longer claims to deal with what will always happen,

[6]Stephen G. Brush, "Thermodynamics and History," *Graduate Journal* 7, no. 2 (1967), 494.
[7]Holton, *Introduction,* p. 290.
[8]Ibid., p. 291.
[9]See Norbert Wiener, *The Human Use of Human Beings: Cybernetics and Society* (New York: Avon Books, 1967), pp. 13, 14.

but rather with what will happen with an overwhelming probability."[10]

Gibbs maintained that not just one world but a growing number of worlds, or futures, are "possible answers to a limited set of questions concerning our environment."[11] By *entropy* he meant the tendency for the number of such contingent worlds to multiply, that is, for a given set of conditions to point toward an ever larger range of possible outcomes. Viewed in this way, entropy does not mean the narrowing of alternatives down to one inevitable doom, but just the opposite. Different worlds, or "closed systems," become similarly disorganized, but not identically constituted; for example, Tyrone Slothrop's desk and the San Narciso landscape are not identical but are alike in exhibiting random distribution of parts. The tendency is for the variety as well as the number of such "arrangements" to increase.

The later Pynchon refined his thinking on entropy along the same lines as did the later science. In 1878 the Austrian physicist Ludwig Boltzmann attempted a more general definition of the second law, one that "depends on the probabilities of molecular arrangements, and can change even when there is no heat flow, for example if a system becomes more random or disordered (when you scramble an egg or mix two pure substances)."[12] Here was a problem: physicists who studied molecular action had accepted Newtonian mechanics, the equations of which imply complete reversibility with respect to time. In other words, the laws would describe equally well the movement of bodies in a film run forwards or backwards. But entropy, time's arrow, seemed irreversible in practice. Boltzmann, Thomson, and James Clerk Maxwell proposed a solution which "involves two recognitions: the surprising admission that the principle of dissipation of energy ... is *not* an inviolable law of physics—it may occasionally, and for short time spans, be violated—and that in most ordinary circumstances the probability of such violations is extremely small."[13]

Thus the equation is in principle—and sometimes in practice—reversible. A random, mechanical shuffling *could*

[10]Ibid., p. 18.
[11]Ibid., p. 20.
[12]Holton, *Introduction*, p. 290.
[13]Ibid., p. 374.

produce a highly structured system, such as a perfectly
ordered deck of cards; it is possible but unlikely. Subsequent
reshufflings would very likely produce a less ordered
arrangement, and the more ordered the first arrangement, the
greater this likelihood. Number also influences probabilities. A
deck with fifty-two cards has a remote but reasonable chance of
being ordered accidentally, but a substance in nature, a gas, let
us say, has billions of molecules, and the countless possible
arrangements of them must affect the odds. The most probable
condition of the gas would be to have all the possible molecular
arrangements represented in such proportions as would be
produced by "shuffling." As each split second corresponds
to innumerable shufflings, the gas quickly moves toward
maximum disorder, randomness, and chaotic equilibrium.
Such shuffling could in principle produce a highly ordered,
complex structure by accident, but, in Sir Arthur Eddington's
analogy, the chances are about the same that an army of
monkeys hammering on typewriters could reproduce all the
books in the British Museum.

Pynchon offers his own analogy with the deaf-mute ball in
The Crying of Lot 49. The dancers cannot follow any kind of
music familiar to Oedipa: the random assortment of their
unrelated steps recalls the hodge-podge landscaping of San
Narciso or the bottom of the Fangoso Lagoons. Yet the dance
proceeds without collisions, seemingly in violation of physical
necessity. It is as if the molecules of a gas suddenly ceased their
collisions, reversed entropy, and spontaneously increased their
organization. Statistical thermodynamics allows for such a
possibility, but its chance of occurrence is so indescribably
remote that one might see in the "mysterious consensus" of
steps or gas molecules an "anarchist miracle" (*49*, p. 97). The
analogies of Eddington and Pynchon are illustrative but not
rigorous; nonetheless, they do allow for the miraculous
possibility of the very improbable event. Boltzmann went
beyond analogy to formulate a precise mathematical definition
of entropy in terms of probability.

As a result of the work of Gibbs and Boltzmann, entropy,
once thought irreversible, no longer appears to be necessarily
so. Physicist Stephen G. Brush writes:

> The regularity that is observed in the physical phenomena of the
> world is not due to any regularity in atomic motion, but results

from the laws of statistics applied to random events — much as the average death rate of a country is usually accurately predictable even though each individual death is not.[14]

The statement reveals not only an overriding regularity but an underlying irregularity. Largely foreseeable macro-events build from haphazard micro-events. Brush adds that although the basic laws of physics may be "reversible on a microscopic basis," they will always look irreversible to us in mass "because of the inherent nature of the observations we can make" and the limited time span in which we can make them. In fact, French mathematician Henri Poincaré devised a proof which asserts that with enough time

> every mechanical system must almost certainly return infinitely close to its starting position infinitely many times, [somewhat as Kekulé's Ouroboros promises eternal return]. If this theorem were applicable to gases, and Boltzmann conceded that it was, then . . . it implied that the entropy could not continually increase but must eventually decrease and return to its initial value.[15]

One cannot be sure just how much of this Pynchon has in mind; he does mention Gibbs, Boltzmann, Maxwell, and probability theory, though, and his understanding of statistical probability, individual indeterminism, and reversibility may explain the anxious hope for recycling that one sees in his work.

Especially after *V.*, Pynchon often resorts to the notion of reversibility. In *The Crying of Lot 49* he draws upon Maxwell, who first hinted at the relation between information and entropy in his *Theory of Heat* (1871). M. J. Klein quotes Maxwell on the second law of thermodynamics

> "[The second law] is undoubtedly true as long as we can deal with bodies only in mass, and have no power of perceiving or handling the separate molecules of which they are made up." The status of the second law would be very different if we had the powers of "a being whose faculties are so sharpened that he can follow every molecule in its course. [We cannot function so,] not being clever enough."[16]

The scientist here alludes to his "demon." As Stanley Koteks tells Oedipa, the demon could gather information on the

[14]Brush, "Thermodynamics and History," p. 481.
[15]Ibid., p. 516.
[16]M. J. Klein, "Maxwell, His Demon, and the Second Law of Thermodynamics," *American Scientist* 58 (1970), 90, 94.

molecules of a system and sort them so as to produce the heat
concentration necessary to drive a heat engine. Since it
expended mental but not thermodynamic work, "You would
be violating the Second Law of Thermodynamics, getting
something for nothing, causing perpetual motion" (49, p. 62).
Contemporary scientists like Norbert Wiener realize that
because it costs energy to get information, the demon cannot
work indefinitely in a closed system; yet it "may temporarily
reverse the usual direction of entropy."[17] Pynchon shows that
a limited and local reversal of the dominant trend is possible,
but that it must be accounted miraculous. The giddy hilarity of
the Nefastis episode or the deaf-mute ball may indicate the
intensity of relief with which Pynchon greets any sign of
deliverance from entropic doom. He seems to share Oedipa's
awe-struck horror in contemplating the "irreversible process,"
and so he clings to, ferrets out, or manufactures examples of
reversibility which show that there are—will always be—
exceptions to the general rule. His hope is desperate but real.

Reversals pervade *Gravity's Rainbow*. Argentinians flee to
Germany and rocket blasts precede the sound of approach. The
imagination can run backwards like film and make the blast
reconstruct the rocket, break the rocket into raw materials, and
melt raw materials back into the earth. Similarly, the Puritan
flotilla sails backwards to England and bullets fly out of dead
bodies, which return to life. "But the reality is not reversible,"
says the narrator (GR, p. 139). Film is, though, and the relation
of reality to film or to any imaginative creation is problematic.
The film maker can move events back and forth in time, the
fourth dimension of a relativistic universe, just as people in
actual life can move objects around in three-dimensional
space. Pynchon broaches the technological innovation of
film to undercut the notion of causality, or at least to blur
the categories of cause and effect rather badly. PISCES
(Psychological Intelligence Schemes for Expediting Surrender)
contracts Gerhardt von Göll (der Springer) to make a film about
black troops in Germany, a film that would play upon the
enemy's worst guilts and fears. After he learns that real
"Schwarzkommando" are at large in the Zone, "leading real,
paracinematic lives," he becomes convinced that his film
brought them into being: "'It is my mission [. . .] to sow in the

[17]Wiener, *The Human Use of Human Beings*, p. 44.

Zone seeds of reality [. . . .] My images, somehow, have been chosen for incarnation'" (GR, p. 388).

Actually, von Göll's presumption may not be so far fetched. Back in the Weimar depression, the film maker had directed Greta Erdmann in a pornographic horror classic, *Alpdrücken* (nightmare). Greta conceived her child, Bianca, while filming the sado-masochistic gang rape scene that she and Slothrop reenact years later, in "real" life. The movie proved so exciting that Franz Pökler went home after seeing it and impregnated Leni with their daughter, Ilse. "How many other men, shuffling out again into depression Berlin, carried the same image back from *Alpdrücken* to some drab fat excuse for a bride? How many shadow-children would be fathered on Erdmann that night?" (GR, p. 397). Film, like fiction or projected worlds, can bring about new realities.

But this process is reversible, too. Blicero uses Ilse to ensure Pökler's cooperation on the S-gerät construction, letting her visit her father for a few weeks every summer and keeping her for the rest of the year in what Pökler surmises is camp Dora, right next to his job at Mittelwerke. In this way, Ilse becomes for Pökler a film image again: "They" have made her "the moving image of a daughter, flashing him only these summertime frames of her, leaving him to build the illusion of a single child" (GR, p. 422). The reality does not always precede and engender the film, nor does the film always precede and engender the reality. As a medium says at a seance, A does not "do" B, but A and B happen together (GR, p. 30). The two relative motions define one another, like mirror images (recall the "real" and "mirror" time of Schoenmaker's office clock); neither has hegemony or favored ontological status, and each is equally capable of affecting the field.[18] Reversal, exception, accident, uncertainty, unpredictability— freedom, in a sense—are parts of the basic existential fabric, allowing sparks of hope "never quite to be extinguished" (GR, p. 610), somewhat as Planck's constant can never be

[18]David Cowart discusses Pynchon's use of film in chapter three of his *Thomas Pynchon: The Art of Allusion*. Cowart argues that in *Gravity's Rainbow* "life imitates film" and film calls itself "into three-dimensional existence" (p. 36). In fact, Pynchon has so established such notions that "we feel no sense of absurdity at having apocalypse presented as the falling of a rocket that has, in effect, *escaped from the movie in which it was fired*" (p. 57)—or, rather, escaped from the narrative that presents itself as a kind of movie.

dismissed as a measure of indeterminacy in subatomic observation. Oedipa assumes that something in particular "made" Randolph Driblette insert the Tristero lines into the play only on the night she happened to attend, but Emory Bortz counters: "Maybe . . . maybe not. You think a man's mind is a pool table?" (49, p. 115). The narrator of *Gravity's Rainbow* observes of Ludwig and Ursula, "So not all lemmings go over the cliff, and not all children are preserved against snuggling into the sin of profit. To expect any more, or less, of the Zone is to disagree with the terms of the Creation." (GR, p. 729).

As a corollary to this world view, "force" becomes a dated, misleading term for Pynchon and for science. Drawing upon physicist Ernst Mach, Wylie Sypher argues that the notion of force superimposes the human mind on nature, "projects into the universe, animistically, our own sense of effort or will." There is a growing conviction in the newer physics that "laws of force are merely a way of describing how things behave," or how they are "interdependent" in the space-time field they create about themselves. "The forces are not 'in' nature but rather are our way of rationalizing what goes on in nature. . . . Our present notion of force has been compared to the middle term of a syllogism that drops out when we reach a conclusion."[19] "Force" and "causal sequence" have been replaced by concepts such as "relation" and "seriality." Arthur Koestler explains biologist Paul Kammerer's principle of seriality:

> In some respects it is comparable to universal gravity—which, to the physicist, is also still a mystery; but unlike gravity which acts on all *mass* indiscriminately, [seriality] acts selectively on *form* and *function* to bring similar configurations together in space and time; it correlates by *affinity*. . . .
>
> Kammerer was particularly interested in temporal Series of recurrent events; these he regarded as cyclic processes which propagate themselves like waves along the time-axis of the time-space continuum. But we are aware only of the crests of the waves, which appear to us as isolated coincidences, while the troughs remain unnoticed.[20]

---

[19]Wylie Sypher, *Loss of the Self in Modern Literature and Art* (New York: Random House, 1962), pp. 79, 82.
[20]Arthur Koestler, *The Roots of Coincidence* (New York: Vintage, 1973), pp. 86–87. This excerpt is also quoted in Joseph Slade, *Thomas Pynchon* (New York: Warner Paperback Library, 1974), p. 237.

Somewhat in this vein, Eigenvalue sees caries, or serial
coincidences, where Stencil sees cabals, or causal connections:

> Perhaps history this century, thought Eigenvalue, is rippled
> with gathers in its fabric such that if we are situated, as Stencil
> seemed to be, at the bottom of a fold, it's impossible to
> determine warp, woof or pattern anywhere else. By virtue,
> however, of existing in one gather it is assumed there are others,
> compartmented off into sinuous cycles each of which come to
> assume greater importance than the weave itself and destroy any
> continuity. . . . We are accordingly lost to any sense of a
> continuous tradition. Perhaps if we lived on a crest, things would
> be different. We could at least see. (V., p. 141).

Seriality characterizes the cosmos and the form of *Gravity's
Rainbow*: analogous events or parallel developments follow
one another in loose, associational rather than logical sequence
and are linked to one another not mechanically but through
mutual participation in their field of gravity.

For both the scientist and the author, this distinction
between force and relation is more important than it may
appear at first glance. The older physics assumed that gravity
worked by "instantaneous action at a distance" — that objects
exerted forces on each other and that forces were *causes*.
As "force" fades to "relation," so determinism fades to
probability. This radical alteration in world view is at the heart
of Pynchon's fiction, especially the later work. Perhaps the
conversation between statistician Roger Mexico and behaviorist
Edward Pointsman best exemplifies the issue. Seeing Roger
successfully predict bomb strike patterns with the Poisson
equation, Pointsman wonders fearfully:

> How can Mexico play, so at his ease, with these symbols of
> randomness and fright? Innocent as a child, perhaps unaware
> — perhaps — that in his play he wrecks the elegant rooms of
> history, threatens the idea of cause and effect itself. What if
> Mexico's whole *generation* have turned out like this? Will
> Postwar be nothing but "events," newly created one moment
> to the next? No links? Is it the end of history? (GR, p. 56)

Pynchon might have coined the behaviorist's name from
the example James Clerk Maxwell made of a "pointsman"
working switches on a railway to send goods down either one
line or another. Indeed, such "either/or" thinking describes
the character Pointsman. In the "domain of zero to one,

not-something to something, Pointsman can only possess the
zero and the one. He cannot, like Mexico, survive anyplace in
between [. . . .] But to Mexico belongs the domain *between*
zero and one — the middle Pointsman has excluded from his
persuasion — the probabilities" (GR, p. 55). Oedipa Maas
recognized such "excluded middles" as "bad shit."

Pointsman, a Pavlovian, seeks "the true mechanical
explanation" for phenomena. "No effect without cause, and a
clear train of linkages" (GR, p. 89). Either 1 (always A → B) or 0
(never A → B). This is what bedevils him so about Slothrop: the
response (a sexual encounter) seems to precede the stimulus (a
rocket strike). Mexico, however, believes that "cause and effect
may have been taken as far as it will go. That for science to
carry on at all, it must look for a less narrow, a less . . . sterile
set of assumptions. The next great breakthrough may come
when we have the courage to junk cause-and-effect entirely,
and strike off at some other angle" (GR, p. 89). Contemporary
science and Pynchon stand with Mexico. Leon Brillouin
observes that in light of Heisenberg's uncertainty and Bohr's
complementarity, "absolute determinism does not apply any
more. Physical laws take on an essentially statistical value, but
do not apply to the detail of movements."[21] Mass behavior is
predictable, but individual behavior is not.

Pynchon makes clear through his imagery that such
a discrimination applies to human as well as physical
phenomena. Appropriating terms from subatomic physics, the
narrator speaks of the "trace, particle and wave, of the sixty
thousand who passed [. . .] once or twice this way" (GR, p. 398).
He describes station doors "with edges smudged browner in
bell-curves of farewell by the generation of hands" that belong
to a "wordless ratcheting queue . . . thousands going away . . .
only the stray freak particle, by accident, drifting against the
major flow. . . ." (GR, p. 51). Opposition to the major flow is
possible, though improbable. The characters, dwarfed to two
dimensionality by patterns of relation, retain a measure of
freedom from *force*. Randomness can be positive, allowing for
the spontaneous, the surprising, the undetermined. As Alan J.
Friedman and Manfred Puetz note, "the uncertainty principle
means that no possibility can be ruled out, and that there is

[21]Leon Brillouin, *Scientific Uncertainty, and Information* (New York:
Academic Press, 1964), p. 20.

hope that nature's constant reshuffling will produce desirable new opportunities."[22]

In probability theory Pointsman sees "symbols of randomness and fright"; he cannot live with "a contingent future," which Norbert Wiener asserts "is the true condition of human life."[23] But oppositions to the "major flow" offer some consolation in a world where the major flow is downward, entropic—where human beings are drawn, like objects responding to gravity, toward the void: Enzian's rivals, the Ombindi faction, seek the "Final Zero," Greta Erdmann and a host of other sadomasochists ride a trail of pain toward "Nothing," and Slothrop along with who knows how many others pursues the 00000.

Unique Points, Discrete Quanta, and the Uniform Field

Entropy, once considered the perfect example of physical necessity, actually helped to erode the old notions of causality and physical determinism, notions that quantum mechanics has all but overturned for good. Before quantum mechanics it was generally assumed that cause always led to effect. But now "cause" and "effect" are seen as "events" that usually "happen" in some space—time relation. Sometimes they don't. One can predict the relative frequencies with which they happen in sequence versus not, but to do so requires a very large number of events. For example, scientists considering radioactive decay can only estimate the probability that a nucleus will emit radiation; they cannot say when or how any particular nucleus will decay. As Gerald Holton points out, some scientists have argued that Newton's laws about motion and energy "might, in the atomic world, hold true only 'on the average,' but not necessarily" at any given instant.[24]

Similarly, Heisenberg's 1927 "Principle of Uncertainty" states that a physicist can accurately describe electron behavior only in the mass. The fewer the electrons he considers, the less precise his account becomes. When he tries to locate a particular electron, he can speak only of probable positions.

[22]Alan J. Friedman and Manfred Puetz, "Science as Metaphor: Thomas Pynchon and *Gravity's Rainbow*," *Contemporary Literature* 15 (Summer 1974), 353.
[23]Wiener, *The Human Use of Human Beings*, p. 71.
[24]Holton, *Introduction*, p. 492.

If he tries to assess the velocity of the electron, its position becomes less determinable, and vice versa. The physicist cannot say that the electron really *has* a definite position and velocity, that it is in a precise spot moving at a certain speed. Consequently, science has abandoned the mechanistic world view, which supposed that the mass, position, and velocity of all phenomena in the present could in theory be known and used to predict a completely determined future. The "Laplace demon" was considered to have the absolute and certain knowledge of present conditions that Heisenberg denies is possible; from its knowledge it could divine the entire history of the universe, past and future.

Pynchon showed an early willingness to evoke the uncertainty of quantum mechanics in his fiction. He alludes to Heisenberg's principles in "Low-Lands" (p. 100), and in V. he names the character Eigenvalue after an abstruse mathematical formula used to describe electron behavior. In *The Crying of Lot 49* he sports with the atavistic desire for a logical and orderly world: after Oedipa punctures a hairspray can that propells itself around the room, she cringes on the floor, unable to determine if and when it will strike and thinking that "something fast enough, God or a digital machine, might have computed in advance the complex web of its travel; but she wasn't fast enough" (49, p. 23). Most contemporary scientists would argue on Heisenbergian grounds that human beings will never attain the predictive power envisioned by Laplace and Oedipa, but that this admission becomes a new argument for free will.

Besides indeterminism, quantum mechanics points to another kind of cosmic irregularity that Pynchon mimics in his fiction. Quantum theory actually began with the discovery by Max Planck that electromagnetic radiation, including light, does not flow from heated bodies in a smooth, unbroken stream but rather bursts forth in discontinuous bits called "quanta." In 1905 Einstein hypothesized that all forms of radiant energy travel through space this way and that light itself is composed of such discrete quanta, which he termed "photons." Einstein proved his contention with an experiment demonstrating the "photoelectric effect," an effect that the old and respected wave theory of light could not explain. However, light exhibits some characteristics, like diffraction and interference, that belong to waves and not to particles. Einstein had helped uncover a troubling inconsistency in nature, or else an equally troubling impotence in our ability to envision what happens beyond the limits of our senses. Far from resolving the paradox, subsequent research and experimentation made it more perplexing. Lincoln Barnett observes that "the dual character of light is . . . only one aspect of a deeper and more remarkable duality which pervades all nature."[25] Submicroscopic particles, the basis of physical reality, turned out to be not only indeterminate in their actions but undefinable as entities. In some experiments, for example, electrons behave like waves and not particles; in other experiments the opposite is true. Apparently we need two mutually exclusive explanations to cover the range of activity that is the foundation of our universe.

A sense of inconsistency or contradiction runs throughout Pynchon and throughout the new science. Einstein felt disturbed by the irregularities that quantum mechanics revealed in nature, even though his experiments with light helped reveal them. Dismayed by the prospect of randomness, he said he could not believe "that God plays dice with the world." He also tried to resolve a goading discrepancy that frustrates the attempts of modern science to explain the world, a discrepancy that reappears in Pynchon: great and small systems appear to operate on different principles and encourage different interpretations of how the cosmos is organized. For three centuries, science has pursued "simplicities and harmonies," notes Gerald Holton. But now, when dealing with subatomic particles or limited instances, "the search has turned to a more direct confrontation of complexity and derangement, of sophisticated and astonishing relationships among strangely juxtaposed parts."[26] A scientist probing the micro world of isolated subatomic events sees not order and stability but rather displacement and indeterminacy, disintegration and duality, violence and discontinuity. So does the reader of a Pynchon novel. Yet a scientist viewing the macro world of fields and systems sees interrelation and

[25]Lincoln Barnett, The Universe and Dr. Einstein (New York: Bantam Books, 1968), p. 28.
[26]Gerald James Holton, "Not in Logic Alone: Science and New Styles of Thought," Graduate Journal 7, no. 2 (1967), 404.

reciprocity, integration and uniformity, order and continuity. So does the reader of a Pynchon novel.

This paradox of physical theory mirrors the central paradox that informs Pynchon's fiction and creates its distinctive tension: the world as Pynchon renders it seems to be running down into disintegration and disorder, but at the same time it seems to be run, integrated, and ordered by some master plot that controls and directs all. Similarly, the Pynchon novel seems to comprise a myriad of random events, haphazard digressions, chaotic congeries, and unpredictable characters who proliferate without logical necessity, but at the same time it seems to form a web of interrelated details, echoing clues, and parallel developments, thereby suggesting that "everything is connected, everything in the Creation"—fictional as well as cosmic (GR, p. 703). One can ask of each creation, are its parts mutually alien or somehow equivalent, discontinuous or continuous?

Pynchon's later work in particular follows relativity theory in pointing toward equivalence and continuity as underlying themes of nature. Unlike quantum theory, relativity theory tends to deal in macro perspectives and collapse divisions between categories formerly thought to be absolutely distinct. For example, Einstein maintained that the separation of space and time is entirely subjective; it reflects the habits of the human mind and not the form of reality. The universe is a four-dimensional "space-time continuum," and any description that aspires toward objectivity must consider it as such. To describe a star system, for example, the astronomer must give the temporal as well as the spatial coordinates that measure its distance from us: we see not what is "now" at some point in the sky but rather what was there light years ago—and may no longer be anywhere. Gazing into space is also gazing back in time, back to a reality that cannot be revealed in only three dimensions.

Similarly, Einstein eroded the categorical separation of matter and energy. He demonstrated that the law for the conservation of mass in a system was identical to that for energy. Moreover, he postulated that mass, resistance to change of motion, increases with velocity, that is, with kinetic energy. If an increase in energy can effect an exactly proportional increase in mass, then mass and energy are ultimately different manifestations of the same thing and hence interchangeable: $E = mc^2$. "In other words," writes Barnett, "matter is energy and energy is matter, and the distinction is simply one of temporary state."[27]

Einstein persisted in the quest for the overriding uniformity in nature by working out his General Theory of Relativity: all reference systems "are equivalent for the description of natural phenomena (formulation of the general laws of nature), whatever may be their state of motion."[28] To prove this theory valid for reference systems in nonuniform as well as uniform motion, he had to demonstrate that the effects of gravity are identical to those produced by inertial resistance to change of motion—in other words, the proportional fluctuations of mass and energy. Einstein had eroded another categorical division.

In pursuing his explanation of gravity, Einstein, in a sense, merged the continua of space—time and matter—energy to posit a space—time—matter—energy continuum. He rejected the Newtonian idea that objects exert gravitational "force" on one another by instantaneous action at a distance through empty space. Rather he believed that matter (a form of energy) curves space (inseparable from time) into a geometric field— the greater the mass, the greater the curvature. This formation of space—time is like a network of paths guiding the motion of matter and energy within the field; motion helps to shape the field that directs the motion that shapes the field, and so on. All matter warps the surrounding space—time (i.e., propagates a gravitational field) with the speed of light, and warped space— time acts uniformly on all matter: an iron ball and a feather fall at the same rate in a vacuum. Thus Einstein maintained that there is no such thing as "empty" space—time, nor is there a discrete time or space interval that is independent of the motion of its reference system—independent of its gravitational field. As a corollary, measurements of time, space, mass, energy, velocity, and gravity vary interdependently, suggesting that some all-encompassing unity grounds them, grounds everything.

Einstein spent his final years working on the Unified Field Theory. His goal, never achieved, was to formulate a single set

[27]Barnett, The Universe, p. 64.
[28]Albert Einstein, Relativity: The Special and the General Theory, trans. Robert W. Lawson (New York: Crown Publishers, 1961), p. 61.

of equations that would describe gravity and electromagnetism in mutually consistent terms, thus showing the two basic "forces" of creation to be at bottom equivalent, different aspects of the same omnipotent process. Lincoln Barnett observes that the Unified Field Theory would bridge

> the abyss between macrocosmos and microcosmos . . . and the whole complex of the universe [would] resolve into a homogeneous fabric in which matter and energy are indistinguishable and all forms of motion from the slow wheeling of the galaxies to the wild flight of electrons become simply changes in the structure and concentration of the primordial field.[29]

Einstein pursued, without final success, what Pynchon calls "the tremendous and secret Function whose name, like the permuted names of God, cannot be spoken" (GR, p. 590).

In Pynchon's early fiction, eroding distinctions usually signify some grotesquerie such as the man-eating subway. In *The Crying of Lot 49*, though, Pynchon demonstrates something like the equivalence of matter and energy: in Oedipa's view, at least, the sailor's mattress could translate into the man's life, but Oedipa sees no way to release that huge store of psychic energy (mattress c^2?), or to use it constructively. *Gravity's Rainbow* is a gargantuan exercise, analogous to Einstein's, in reducing apparently separate categories to seamless continua. As Lawrence C. Wolfley comments, "Dreams and dreaming pervade the narrative, to the extent that the line between various waking and sleeping, conscious and unconscious, states is instructively blurred."[30] But even the lines between the individual and external states begin to dissolve: witness the merging of Roger and Jessica (GR, p. 38). Pirate Prentice has the talent, which the Firm exploits, "for getting inside the fantasies of others" and managing them, taking them over (GR, p. 12). A host of spiritualists, as well as the narrator, will affirm that the borders between minds or souls can be crossed: they regularly pass the barrier between the living and the dead, recalling the von Braun epigraph. The Hereros see the world as a mystical union in which "all sets of opposites" are "brought together" (GR, p. 100), and Pynchon respects their philosophy (see

[29]Barnett, *The Universe*, p. 14.
[30]Lawrence C. Wolfley, "Repression's Rainbow: The Presence of Norman O. Brown in Pynchon's Big Novel," *PMLA* 92 (October 1977), 885.

chapter 3, note 4). Even the distinction between reality and imaginative versions of it, for example a von Göll film (or a Pynchon novel), can be hard to make, and von Göll looks forward to a time when technology will allow each person to walk around making films on the spot.

Boundaries and classifications are nowhere less tenable than in the Zone. Relations are fluid, shifting "arrangements" that form and dissolve spontaneously. Fixed borders are illusions. Geli Tripping tells Slothrop to "Forget frontiers now. Forget subdivisions. There aren't any" (GR, p. 294). Schnorp the balloonist concurs: "There are no zones [. . . .] No zones but the Zone" (GR, p. 333). The Zone, where nothing is determined and everything is to make, embodies the "new Uncertainty" (GR, p. 303). It suggests freedom, possibilities, chances, new starts. Slothrop speculates:

> maybe that anarchist he met in Zürich was right, maybe for a little while all the fences are down, one road as good as another, the whole space of the Zone cleared, depolarized, and somewhere inside the waste of it a single set of coordinates from which to proceed, without elect, without preterite, without even nationality to fuck it up. (GR, p. 556)

Slothrop's meditation uncovers the paradox of macroscopic unity, microscopic disunity discussed above. The ontological basis for making distinctions, drawing borders, and assuming that entities have an existence apart from their contexts apparently dissolves in the "unified field" and in relativity, yet one senses with Slothrop the reality of discrete, particular points in the space-time continuum, points that are singular and discontinuous, as quantum theory proclaims them to be. Likewise, probability theory declares that each event is unique, undetermined by others (see Roger Mexico's attempt to explain the "Monte Carlo Fallacy," GR, p. 56). Apart from his special set of coordinates, Slothrop worries over "the Radiant Hour" and the "one moment of passage" by which he or the world might find "some way back" to a life of plenitude (GR, pp. 674, 693). In the early work "Low-lands" Dennis Flange sought "a minimum and dimensionless point, a unique crossing of parallel and meridian, an assurance of perfect, passionless uniformity" (L, p. 96). Thirteen years later the narrator of *Gravity's Rainbow* affirms that such points and moments — such "vestiges" — always exist.

From a macrocosmic perspective, the special integrity of any single point or object is an illusion. The components of matter and energy that make it up will not always be arranged so. Moreover, the very distinction between components of matter and energy is "simply one of temporary state," for they are, ultimately, the same stuff—the *only* stuff. Ultimately, a uniform four-dimensional space-time continuum is all that exists. Discontinuous objects, and we who perceive them as such, are just unspeakably brief eddies in the uniformity. From a microcosmic perspective, the single point or object is mostly vacancy, given the appearance of fixed shape, solidity, and stable position by the limitations of our senses. But from the typical human perspective, sharp boundaries and unique coordinates can signify powerfully:

> How the penises of Western men have leapt, for a century, to the sight of this singular point at the top of a lady's stocking, this transition from silk to bare skin and suspender [. . . .] there is a cosmology: of nodes and cusps and points of osculation, mathematical kisses . . . singularities! [. . .] In each case, the change from point to no-point carries a luminosity and enigma at which something in us must leap and sing, or withdraw in fright. (*GR*, p. 396)

There is a fearful fascination with what—if anything—lies between $x_1, x_2 \ldots x_n$ as $\Delta x \to 0$.

Lance Ozier helps clarify how Pynchon uses mathematics to convey the anxious hopes based on the particular event, isolated moment, or "single set of coordinates": "The two most obvious (and related) differentiating mathematical characteristics of a single point are the indeterminacy of the function's first derivative at the point (a condition which is sometimes represented by the symbol for infinity, ∞) and the fact that an infinite number of tangents to the curve can be drawn at a singular point."[31] In other words, an infinite number of paths could lead in an infinite number of directions from such a point: like the singular event in probability theory, it is unlimited, "indeterminate" because unconnected—in human terms, "free." Leni comes to the same conclusion about points of time as she visualizes Δt approaching zero: "There is the moment, and its possibilities," she tries to tell Franz, the

[31]Lance W. Ozier, "The Calculus of Transformation: More Mathematical Imagery in *Gravity's Rainbow*," *Twentieth Century Literature* 21 (May 1975), 209.

"cause-and-effect" man who doesn't understand her (GR, p. 159). In a world of such points and moments, nothing is irrevocably determined. Even at the last Δt on the last page, there is still time.

These unique objects, moments, and points seem to be separate and undetermined although not, paradoxically, "independent" of the context they help to create. The continuity of point and context is not one of causal sequence. Rather it is one of boundless relations that extend beyond the limits of our perception and comprehension; it is one of pervasive process that enacts itself consistently on all the arbitrarily designated "levels" and so equates them. Thus Kevin Spectro, a scientist from *Gravity's Rainbow*, comes not to differentiate much between "Outside and Inside. He saw the cortex as an interface organ, mediating between the two, but *part of them both*" (GR, pp. 141 – 42). Classical symptoms of insanity, like confusion of what Pavlov called "ideas of the opposite," now characterize the outside world too, where sounds of the V-1 and V-2 reverse one another. Even Pointsman wonders in a moment of doubt, "Was Spectro right? Could Outside and Inside be part of the same field?" (GR, p. 144). Such considerations add a new dimension to Pynchon's characteristic theme: the impossibility of distinguishing clearly between patterns inside and outside the mind.

Quantum mechanics and relativity theory refer questions about the nature of reality back to the observer: his perspective, scope, and methods will affect the answers he finds. Yet he has no definitive reference points or unobtrusive methods; his very integrity as a whole and separate being is undermined. Aware of these troubling considerations, Pynchon builds his works around epistemological dilemmas.

5

Pynchon's Epistemology

An Eye That Reflects and An Eye That Receives

Recent developments in science have deepened Pynchon's concern with epistemological problems, the cachet of his work; they have even helped him form his rationale and aesthetic for fiction. He writes, says Max Schulz, "out of a philosophical sense of the indeterminate as being the only reality available to man today—'that imminence of a revelation that is not yet produced' (to use Jorge Luis Borges's words)."[1]

Twentieth-century science and technology have created a reality no longer accessible by means of our five senses or our common sense. In trying to explain the effects of the Rocket, the narrator of *Gravity's Rainbow* can draw only upon film, which also defies normal experience: "Imagine a missile one hears approaching only *after* it explodes. The reversal! A piece of time neatly snipped out . . . a few feet of film run backwards" (GR, p. 48). Contemporary theoretical physics, as well as film and the Rocket, can invert the world that common sense and familiar modes of perception have given us. Speaking in terms of myth criticism, John Somer declares that

> We are different from . . . primitive societies in that the world
> we are consciously aware of exceeds the vision of the naked eye.
> The world of primitive man was circumscribed by the horizon.
> Ours is microscopically small and telescopically large, and
> consequently useless to us at the moment for a basis of initiation.
> The world we are consciously aware of is too intangible, too
> frightening for us to surrender ourselves to it.[2]

[1] Max F. Schulz, *Black Humor Fiction of the Sixties: A Pluralistic Definition of Man and His World* (Athens, Ohio: Ohio University Press, 1973), p. 61.

[2] John Somer, "Geodesic Vonnegut: Or, If Buckminister Fuller Wrote Novels," in *The Vonnegut Statement*, ed. Jerome Klinkowitz and John Somer (New York: Dell, 1973), p. 241.

We cannot reconcile our earth-bound sense of reality with the reality described by the post-Einsteinian universe we now confront: a universe in which there are four dimensions although we perceive and manipulate three, a universe in which there are only curved lines although we see straight ones, a universe in which all motion is relative although we register it as absolute, a universe in which "the state of falling is the normal state of bodies"[3] although we feel our feet on stable ground, a universe in which the foundation is particle–wave, although we can hardly envision the merger of wave and particle.

Such developments in technology and science must make us doubt our senses, question what we think we know, and suspect the means by which we come to "know" it. Norbert Wiener remarks that according to Einstein's theory of relativity "it is impossible to introduce the observer without also introducing the idea of message."[4] In Pynchon's terms, where Oedipa stands will determine what "concealed meaning" she senses. Oedipa receives intimations of a hidden, sacred design, a higher order behind the chaotic jumble of the landscape. But this happens only when she is at a remove from things, looking at a map of the Fangoso lagoons or gazing down at the city from an elevation. When immersed in the scene, she finds herself lost, without moorings or familiar reference points. The very scale of things undiagrammed and up close precludes her comprehension. As she descends into the city from her "religious instant" on the mountain, her vision of the printed circuit and its "hieroglyphic sense" gives way to confusion among the grotesque assemblages of buildings "whose address numbers were in the 70 and then 80,000's" (49, p. 14).

Max Weber's concept of "rationalization" fits into Pynchon's epistemological plot devices here. The world of San Narciso provides excellent sociological and psychological grounds for a paranoid positing of Them, the tiny and oppressive elite. The common individual, no longer equal to the works in progress, can see no pattern and feel no personal influence in the direction of events; but an inscrutable power structure seems to exist, just as in the abstraction of a blueprint or physical

[3]Somer, "Geodesic Vonnegut," p. 239.
[4]Norbert Wiener, The Human Use of Human Beings: Cybernetics and Society (New York: Avon Books, 1967), p. 30.

distance one may sense a design in the suburban sprawl.
Without such abstractions, however, the cancerous growth of
the city and the company seem unguided and formless. Is the
controlling pattern real or illusory? If real, is it a blessing or a
blight? These questions lie at the heart of each Pynchon novel,
but the answers are complicated: they exist not objectively but
rather as functions of viewpoint and attitude—that is, as
functions of the observer.

Pynchon's fiction suggests that homogeneity, continuity, and
integrating patterns may all be illusions of perspective, but
then so may be heterogeneity, discontinuity, and disintegrating
wastescapes. San Narciso close up reveals something quite
different than does San Narciso far away. To use the example of
Lecomte du Nouy, one "shuffles" or randomly mixes black and
white powders to get a gray one. "This homogeneous grayness
. . . would not exist for a microscopic insect, which would find
itself crawling among black and white boulders."[5] Mucho's
"unvarying gray sickness" becomes, on closer inspection, a
pile of dissociated objects, randomly thrown together.
Similarly, "WASTE" proves to be "W.A.S.T.E." when Oedipa
gets near enough to the inscription to see the periods that
separate the letters and thereby hint at a wholly different,
subsurface meaning. Like the letters, the groups that patronize
the Tristero are discrete and distinguishable, often unaware of
one another's existence. And yet, from another point of view,
the periods vanish and the groups merge into a continuity of
human "waste," or preterition.

Vantage Point: The Problem of the Observer

Pynchon's novels, especially *The Crying of Lot 49* and
Gravity's Rainbow, offer both the macro and micro
perspectives, sometimes juxtaposing them to force the
question: which one is valid? As Eben Cooke of *The Sot-Weed
Factor* asks, "Who's to say which end of the glass is the right to
look through?" After watching Oedipa vacillate between the
insect's view and the aerial view, perhaps until her mental lens
warps, or after observing Stencil perform his impersonations,

---

[5]Quoted in Rudolf Arnheim, *Entropy and Art: An Essay on Order and
Disorder* (Berkeley: University of California Press, 1971), p. 21.

or the *Rainbow* narrator his permutations, one may better ask: *is* there a definitive vantage point in this relativistic universe, and if so, what are the standards for determining it? One solves little by choosing the "human" vantage point, even if one chooses arbitrarily and for no other reason than that one is human, for the human perspective entails imagination and so comprises every view from microscopic to telescopic. Where within that range should one position oneself, and why? Oedipa tries to project a world—"if not project then at least flash some arrow on the dome to skitter among constellations and trace out your Dragon, Whale, Southern Cross. Anything might help" (49, p. 59). But constellations are figments of perspective:

> There's a Brennschluss point for every firing sight. They still hang up there, all of them, a constellation waiting to have a 13th sign of the Zodiac named for it . . . but they lie so close to Earth that from many places they can't be seen at all, and from different places inside the zone where they can be seen, they fall into completely different patterns. (*GR*, p. 302)

The myriad human perspectives raise deep epistemological problems, but then each perspective contributes more of its own. The macro perspective dissolves the integrity of the observer—the distinction, as Kevin Spectro says, between Inside and Outside—and makes him part of the same continuum he investigates: "He is, in the final analysis, merely an ephemeral conformation of the primordial space—time field" he would examine.[6] Far from being an independent observer of the system around him, he must recognize that even the time and space intervals he employs are variables of the system to which he applies them. No free and absolute reference points or criteria exist.

The micro perspective incurs rather different but equally insurmountable difficulties. Quantum mechanics confronts the relation between subject and object, observer and observed. Heisenberg's "indeterminacy principle" (see chapter 4) states that complete descriptive knowledge of an event, much less of the participants, is impossible, even though the event—like the Situation—cannot be said to exist apart from our observation of it. As Sidney Stencil laments, ". . . what hope has anyone of

---

[6]Lincoln Barnett, *The Universe and Dr. Einstein* (New York: Bantam Books, 1968), p. 118.

understanding a Situation?" (v., p. 443). Heisenberg explains the new attitude of contemporary physics in terms that apply to Pynchon:

> The familiar classification of the world into subject and object, inner and outer world, body and soul, somehow no longer quite applies, and indeed leads to difficulties. . . . the object of research is no longer nature in itself but rather nature exposed to man's questioning, and to this extent man here also meets himself.[7]

—just as Stencil finds himself reflected in his search for V. Heisenberg adds that the contemporary scientist will "have to renounce all thought . . . of objective events in time and space independent of observations of them."[8] "The question whether . . . [subatomic] particles [or V., or the Tristero] exist in space and time 'in themselves' can thus no longer be posed in this form. We can only talk about the processes that occur when, through the interaction [of observer and observed] . . . the behavior of the particle [or V., or the Tristero] is said to be disclosed."[9]

But this interaction creates more problems, for "every process of observation causes a major disturbance" in the behavior of the phenomena being observed.[10] While observing the electron, for example, the scientist cannot help but alter its path, the track of its energy in Henry Adams' terms. Dennis Flange justifies his passivity on this basis: "as long as you are passive you can remain aware of the truth's extent but the minute you become active you are somehow . . . screwing up the perspective of things, much as anyone observing subatomic particles changes the works, data, and odds, by the very act of observing" (L, p. 100). Furthermore, one cannot determine the degree of subjective influence because one can never know what objective reality was before the attempt to observe it. In short, one cannot see the object by itself or even learn where the subject leaves off and the object begins. With small systems, as Spectro said of large systems, one cannot tell inside from outside. The relevance of these admissions to the quests of

[7]Werner Heisenberg, "Nearer the Truth: The Representation of Nature in Contemporary Physics," *Graduate Journal* 2 (Spring 1959), 70–71.
[8]Quoted in A. E. E. McKenzie, *The Major Achievements of Science* (Cambridge: Cambridge University Press, 1960), II, 164.
[9]Heisenberg, "Nearer the Truth," p. 66.
[10]Ibid. p. 65.

Stencil, Oedipa, and even Slothrop comes clear with this suggestive remark from Heisenberg: we can speak of the orbit of the electron (or the career of V., the Tristero, etc.) just so long as we admit that this "path comes into existence only when we observe it."[11]

The object depends upon interaction with the subject. For example, Kurt Mondaugen wonders, "if no one has seen me then am I really here at all" (V., p. 240)? And Sidney Stencil avers that "no Situation had any objective reality: it only existed in the minds of those who happened to be in on it at any specific moment." But these minds "tended to form a sum total or complex more mongrel than homogeneous," one that would look four dimensional to any single observer (V., p. 174). Somewhat as in Borges's Tlön, perception is "creative" in the sense that it partially forms its object. Such perception is especially strong in paranoid fabrications, like Old Godolphin's Vheissu, and in aesthetic responses, like von Göll's Alpdrücken. Both "fantasies" affect "reality" by occasioning real, concrete events. Pynchon writes not only about the lines of force (or "patterns of relation") that shape the world but also about the attempts of the conscious mind to perceive them. Yet the perceiving mind, he tells us, is part of the system, itself one of the lines of force that is shaped, molded, and limited by the others, which it shapes, molds, and limits in return. The act of observing alters the field of which the observer is a part; consequently he, defined by his relation to elements in the field, is altered himself, and so the reciprocal process continues.

Pynchon's subject is the interconnectedness of the world, especially of the observer and the observed. Addressing similar concerns in The Quest for Certainty, John Dewey defines the "spectator" theory of knowledge prior to undermining it: it is "the assumption that the true and valid object of knowledge is that which has being prior to and independent of the operations of knowing. . . . that knowledge is a grasp or beholding of reality without anything being done to modify its antecedent state."[12] Pynchon characters have no independent criteria for

---

[11]Gerald James Holton, Introduction to Concepts and Theories in Physical Science, 2nd edition revised and with new material by Stephen G. Brush (Reading, Mass.: Addison-Wesley, 1973), p. 498.

[12]John Dewey, The Quest for Certainty, A Study of the Relation of Knowledge and Action (London: George Allen and Unwin, 1930), p. 196.

judging their discoveries: as David Hawkins notes in his book on scientific epistemology, "the very knowledge by which we can justify our inductive procedures must itself be a product of those procedures." If one is working through a maze, "there is no supra-maze knowledge."[13] Subjective influences and limitations are impossible to control, measure, or transcend. Pynchon several times complicates the problem of interpreting and assessing one's interpretation by citing Goedel's theorem, a mathematical demonstration that one cannot prove any logical system free from contradictions by using only corollaries derived from the premises; one must get outside the system. In human terms, one can verify one's own perceptions only by perceiving some validation outside them. This, of course, cannot be done. Uncertainty is inescapable. For modern thinkers like Kurt Goedel in mathematics, Percy Bridgman in science, Ludwig Wittgenstein in language, or Thomas Pynchon in literature, systems of knowledge and expression will always be unable to get beyond themselves and define their own grounds, and as such they are confining as well as limited. James Clerk Maxwell said nearly as much in 1873 when he wrote to Herbert Spencer: "It is very seldom that any man who tries to form a system can prevent his system from forming round him, and closing him in."[14]

Changefulness: The Problem of Multiple Vantage Points

Not only is perspective arbitrary and limited, subjective influence unavoidable and uncorrectable, but the object itself remains mysterious. Even the basic particle—or is it wave?—of contemporary physics appears "changeful." One faces such problems even with the best and least confining of investigative systems, but Pynchon characters deal not with physical objects, which might conform in some degree, at least macroscopically, to laws of cause and effect: they work with human beings, and this, as Emory Bortz tells Oedipa, adds to the uncertainty. Mr. Thoth could supply the crucial link between the U.S. mail

[13]David Hawkins, The Language of Nature (San Francisco: W.H. Freeman, 1964), p. 244.
[14]Stephen G. Brush, "Thermodynamics and History," Graduate Journal, 7, no. 2 (1967), 513.

system, the mysterious assassins in *The Courier's Tragedy*, and the symbolic posthorn, but his memory of the Pony Express adversary in black is "all mixed in with a Porky Pig cartoon" (*49*, p. 66). Pynchon makes his protagonists contend with characters far more changeful than the basic particle/wave: the behavior of these weird, fragmentary figures is inconsistent; their motivation is often inexplicable or absurd and seems to defy causal logic.

Naturally, changefulness is central to the epistemological problem, especially as it characterizes the observer as well as the observed. In "Mortality and Mercy in Vienna," Cleanth Siegel must sift, interpret, and weigh numerous observations in coming to a decision upon which hang the fates of the partyers. But Siegel appears mentally disturbed: we receive hints that he is prone to hysteria or at least a hyperactive imagination. Like Benny Profane of *V.*, Siegel is half Jewish and half Roman Catholic; but whereas Profane's "house-dividedness" comically ensures his schlemihl-like incapacity, Siegel's contributes to a serious psychological and moral quandary in which one side of his nature seeks to help people while the other, Machiavellian side seeks to gain power over their destinies.

Siegel seems to be the type of person who must consciously play a role to have a sure sense of self. His current favorite is that of the agent, the key cog in the machinery; the reader first sees him "clutching the fifth of scotch he was carrying as if it were a state secret." During the party, he plays a Nivenesque British staff officer as well as a father confessor, telling himself at one point to "bite the jolly old bullet and make the best of a bad job" (MMV, pp. 195, 205). But this, in the psycho-jargon Pynchon often parodies, creates a role conflict. Another part of Siegel feels that he has betrayed himself by becoming a functionary and working through routines. For this side of his nature, "there is no question of balance sheets or legal complexity, and the minute you become involved with anything like that you are something less" than a "healer—a prophet" (MMV, p. 196). Only immediate, instinctive, total action will do; hence the appeal for him of Irving Loon.

Both sides of Siegel's nature—the Machiavellian schemer and the sympathetic Jewish boy sitting *shivah* and saying *kaddish* for the dead—finally agree on the proper course of action: to loose Irving on the party. But rarely can the divided observer in Pynchon resolve his dilemma so conclusively. Dennis Flange, the basic particle of "Low-lands," is split between his public self—"something not so rare or strange" (L, p. 102)—and the *doppelgänger* he developed on naval tour of the Pacific, an imaginary and ideal Dennis Flange who has somehow been preserved from the corrosions of time, "fortune's elf child and disinherited darling, young and randy and more a Jolly Jack Tar than anyone human could conceivably be" (L, p. 90). This house-dividedness helps make Dennis passive and withdrawn; he is dissatisfied with his drab life, and his wife is dissatisfied with him. She kicks him out and he holes up in the dump, a psychological equivalent to the "low-land" of the sea which allows the *doppelgänger* to surface again.

Dennis falls asleep while his head swims with wine and happy visions of gypsies, better selves, and "sustaining plasmas." What follows then, may be some sort of delusion or dreamt wish fulfillment. We are never told this, though; we just hear that Flange is awakened by "a girl's voice, riding on the wind" (L, p. 103). Realizing that the voice is calling not him but his *doppelgänger*, he decides to leave the shack and investigate. If he was awake then, he does not remain so for long: he sets off one of Bolingbroke's booby traps and brings a huge stack of snow tires crashing down on top of himself. Perhaps he awakens after a blow on the head as Dorothy does in *The Wizard of Oz* (referred to in *Gravity's Rainbow*), perhaps not. We never really know. He regains consciousness, he thinks, to find himself being ministered to by a beautiful gypsy girl, elfin to match his *doppelgänger* and the answer to his various daydreams and needs. She was found in the low-land of the dump; she sees or loves only his ideal self-image; she has a pet rat named Hyacinth, whom she treats like the child that might have held Cindy and him together; and she presents herself as a sea woman. Her name, Nerissa, may be a play on *Nereids*, the nymphs of the sea.[15] And when Dennis consents to stay with her, he sees that "Whitecaps danced across her eyes; sea creatures, he knew, would be cruising about in the

[15]Joseph W. Slade, *Thomas Pynchon* (New York: Warner Paperback Library, 1974), p. 30.

submarine green of her heart" (L, p. 108). She is lover,
mother, womb, and sustaining plasma for fantasy.

But is she real? Or is Flange dreaming, or perhaps crazy? The
multiple choices recur throughout Pynchon's fiction, and here,
as usual, the question remains unsettled. Nerissa calls to
Dennis's fantasy self, but how could she ever have known it if
she had not also come from inside his head? This, her oneiric
appearance, Flange's drifting off to sleep, and the numerous
references to Flange's complexes all suggest that the girl is
a wishful projection, but not so strongly as to force the
interpretation. In portraying solipsistic and changeful
individuals, Pynchon poses his reader an insoluble and rather
Heisenbergian problem: to what extent does the character
perceive and respond to objective reality and to what extent
subjective reality—the processes of his or her own mind?

Such questions arise again in "Entropy." Callisto tries to
interpret the ominous logic of the second law, but his own
sense of personal change may affect what he sees. Like Siegel,
Flange, Stencil, and Oedipa, Callisto is aware of the passing of
his life; hence the "spindly mass of equations" he learned at
Princeton as a young man becomes "a vision of ultimate,
cosmic heat-death" when he reaches "the sad dying fall of
middle age": he is fifty-four (E, pp. 282, 283). Callisto's
melancholy raises the possibility so common in Pynchon that
neurotic (sometimes psychotic) self-projections account for
some of the character's observations and conclusions.
Despondent Callisto sees probability as inevitability, an
ominous force presaging helpless decline, overshadowing
human agency. In his youth, Callisto had sported "a vigorous,
Italian sort of pessimism: like Machiavelli [and V.'s Gaucho], he
allowed the forces of *virtù* and *fortuna* to be about 50/50; but
the equations [of Boltzmann and Gibbs] now introduced a
random factor which pushed the odds to some unutterable and
indeterminate ratio which he found himself afraid to calculate"
(E, p. 283).

Herbert Stencil demonstrates more than any other Pynchon
character how the mutability—perhaps insubstantiality—of
the observer leads to epistemological difficulties. Stencil, as
noted, does not really want to resolve his mystery, for he would
then lose his *raison d'etre*. In his aim of missing the target,
Stencil makes great strides when he comes to think of "Herbert
Stencil" (referring to himself in the third person) "as only

one among a repertoire of identities," any of which he can
"impersonate" through a "forcible dislocation of personality"
(*V.*, p. 51). None has hegemony; there is no real center or
consistency here, yet all are bound by the common pursuit of
simultaneously approaching and avoiding V. Stencil, then, is
a self-made *reductio ad absurdum* of a bit of avant-garde
philosophy bantered about by the Whole Sick Crew: Sartre's
thesis that "we are all impersonating an identity" (*V.*, p. 118).
But at least in this way he is not wholly at the mercy of external
forces; unlike the Crew members, he is the source of his own
dislocation, which he seems able to use consciously for his
own peculiar ends.

For example, "Stencil" can approach and avoid at once by
impersonating an indeterminate number of points of view
between V. and—for lack of a better word—"himself." The
problem becomes complicated beyond the hope of resolution,
Stencil might hope, when his impersonations themselves
develop multiple identities. About one seventh of the way
through the novel, the reader realizes that the "truth" about V.
or *V.* hides in the unreliable versions and reconstructions of an
impersonation (with multiple identities) of an impersonation
(with multiple identities) of an impersonation (with multiple
identities). This last is Stencil, an impersonation of the author.

The human particle is changeful and incomplete. Fausto
Maijstral, who also refers to himself in the third person and
works through four such selves in his "confessions," decries
"the false assumption that identity is single, soul continuous"
(*V.*, p. 287). But the matter is even more complicated. In
addition to being multiple, identity is reciprocal and relative
rather than independent and absolute. Herbert Stencil, for
example, defines himself as that which pursues V. But he
defines V. as that which Stencil pursues. Both Stencil and V.
become "remarkably scattered" concepts, existing as a range of
possible conjunctions in a centerless field. Whatever Stencil
perceives in this context is a reflection of his role, or—to say
the same thing—his identity.

Paranoia or Perception?

Pynchon associates changefulness such as that of Stencil or
Mondaugen with unreliable vision, pattern detection with
pathology and projection. One hears, for example, that in

tracking down "leads" our Stencil is "quite mysterious, and Dashiell Hammettlike" (V., p. 114). But Hammett made up plots—he didn't uncover them. Stencil's name suggests the dubiety of his perceptions. Splash a shapeless wash of color over a stencil and you will not discover a pattern that is latent in the paint; rather you will project a design that takes its shape precisely from the emptiness in the cut-out. Analogously, Stencil may create his own plots when history washes over him, fashion from chaos designs that conform to the admitted void in himself. And when combined with the comic context, Pynchon's nonmimetic act of name-labelling the character makes one see Stencil more as a two-dimensional cardboard or cartoon figure than as a serious person whose observations one should weigh carefully.

Other characters in the novel reflect unkindly on Stencil's pursuit through V. of the master conspiracy. Fausto Maijstral, who believes that much of life is accident, suspects the sanity of Stencil, for whom nothing is an accident, and concludes that "V. was an obsession after all, and that such an obsession is a hothouse" (V., p. 421 – 22). This, of course, recalls Callisto's ill-fated attempt to escape entropy by living in a closed and artificially sustained world. Pynchon shows ironically that the methods used to cure or prevent a condition will often hasten it. In seeking to evade "half-consciousness," decadence, and ennui, Stencil has become decadent, at least by Itague's definition: he has isolated himself in his monomaniacal quest and foisted off the humanity he has lost on inanimate objects and abstractions. Patterns of events or "the recurrence of an initial and a few dead objects" can take on lives of their own. Sidney Stencil appears better able than his son Herbert to cope with this incipient paranoia. He thinks to himself:

> Don't act as if it were a conscious plot against you. Who knows how many thousand accidents—a variation in the weather, the availability of a ship, the failure of a crop—brought all these people, with their separate dreams and worries, here to this island and arranged them into this alignment? Any Situation takes shape from events much lower than the merely human. (V., p. 455)

The spectre of "a conscious plot against you" is the plot device for all of Pynchon's novels, and in each case it gives rise to an epistemological dilemma. Oedipa Maas, like Herbert

Stencil before her and Tyrone Slothrop after her, senses
"another mode of meaning behind the obvious" (*49*, p.137),
and she struggles to discover whether the "Situation takes
shape from events much lower than the merely human," much
higher, or somewhere in between. But Pynchon makes the
reader ask whether the character's *perception* of the Situation
takes shape from a general human propensity to draw
connections, a private psychosis, both of the above, or neither.
The sense of imminent revelation could arise from immanent
psychological needs and pressures. Mucho, for example,
flounders about desperately trying to "believe" in something
besides the car lot, his nightmare of *nada*.

As discussed in chapter 3, Oedipa has a similar need. And
she, like earlier Pynchon characters, is changeful—internally
divided between "dark doubles" and deep ambivalences of
which she may not be aware. Oedipa Maas is one of the most
fully developed, realistic, human characters in Pynchon's
work, but that does not prevent the author from practicing his
custom of name-labelling on her. Catherine Davidson notes
that *maas* is the Afrikaans word for *web* or *net*, and as such it
"perfectly describes her [Oedipa's] situation—someone
trapped in various intermingling mazes and meshes."[16]
"Oedipa," as many critics have explained, recalls Sophocles's
Oedipus, who attempts to resolve a problem that involves a
dead man, first considering himself "an almost detached
observer, only to discover how deeply implicated he is in what
he finds."[17] He is "tormented by the question of man's place in
a universe he does not understand. The problems he faces are
religious, metaphysical, political, and epistemological. He is
forced to make choices, but he never achieves control over his
destiny; with none of the problems resolved at the play's end
he must go on seeking."[18]

One would never mistake Oedipa for a figure from Greek
tragedy, however. Points too obvious to need elaboration make
her a decidedly modern character: Pynchon's genre, tone, use

[16]Catherine N. Davidson, "Oedipa as Androgyne in Thomas Pynchon's *The
Crying of Lot 49*," *Contemporary Literature* 18, no. 1 (1977), 43.

[17]Edward Mendelson, "The Sacred, the Profane, and *The Crying of Lot 49*," in
Individual and Community: Variations on a Theme in American Fiction, ed.
Kenneth H. Baldwin and David K. Kirby (Durham, N.C. Duke University Press,
1975), p. 188.

[18]Slade, *Pynchon*, pp. 126–27.

of science; Oedipa's peculiar variations on the old problems, and so forth. But she is like Oedipus in the ways mentioned — particularly in that she sees ominous patterns around her and tries to interpret them. "It apparently is built into the brain itself," declares Norbert Wiener, "that we are to have a preoccupation with codes [and with decoding them]."[19] The world of the novel, as seen through Oedipa's eyes, abounds in suggestive designs and networks: a "laboratory maze" of facial lines, a grid of "fate furrows" on the palm, hieroglyphic maps and aerial views.

Oedipa tends to see not only designs but also a design in the designs, a "meaning" that is paradoxically "concealed" and yet "intended" to communicate something (49, p. 13). What is more, as her "religious instant" shows, she has this habit of mind before coming into contact with the estate that furnishes all her leads to the Tristero. In fact, only *before* the Tristero begins to preoccupy her does she intuit hieroglyphic *patterns* in their totality. The downhill view of San Narciso and the map of the Fangoso Lagoons promise her "hierophany" at the beginning of her adventure, introducing her to the idea of some hidden, integrating order of Meaning; but when she descends from the overview of the mountain or the blueprint into the grotesque jumble of immediate events, she senses only hieroglyphic *objects* — not patterns — which she then tries to synthesize into a coherent picture, perhaps driven by the gap between the possibility of order and the actuality of chaos.

Oedipa's tendency to respond so is understandable, but also undercut. She has a penchant for seeing conspiracies, as when she first meets Metzger. "He turned out to be so good-looking that Oedipa thought at first They, somebody up there, were putting her on." Later, when the Baby Igor movie comes on television, she assumes that he "bribed the engineer over at the local station" to run it as "part of a plot, an elaborate, seduction, *plot*" (49, pp. 16, 18).

Even earlier in the novel, Pynchon hints that Oedipa might herself be creating the "plots" she perceives. In Mexico City, she and Pierce had

somehow wandered into an exhibition of paintings by the beautiful Spanish exile Remedios Varo: in the central painting of

[19]Wiener, *The Human Use of Human Beings*, p. 114.

a triptych, titled "Bordando el Manto Terrestre," were a number
of frail girls with heart-shaped faces, huge eyes, spun-gold hair,
prisoners in the top room of a circular tower, embroidering a kind
of tapestry which spilled out the slit windows and into a void,
seeking hopelessly to fill the void: for all the other buildings and
creatures, all the waves, ships, and forests of the earth were
contained in this tapestry, and the tapestry was the world.
Oedipa, perverse, had stood in front of the painting and cried.
. . . She had looked down at her feet and known, then, because of
a painting, that what she stood on had only been woven together
a couple thousand miles away in her own tower . . . there'd been
no escape. What did she so desire to escape from? Such a captive
maiden, having plenty of time to think, soon realizes that her
tower, its height and architecture, are like her ego only
incidental: that what really keeps her where she is is magic,
anonymous and malignant, visited on her from outside and for no
reason at all. Having no apparatus except gut fear and female
cunning to examine this formless magic, to understand how it
works, how to measure its field strength, count its lines of force,
she may fall back on superstition, or take up a useful hobby like
embroidery, or go mad, or marry a disk jockey. If the tower is
everywhere and the knight of deliverance no proof against its
magic, what else? (49, pp. 10–11)

She does marry a disc jockey. Perhaps she also goes mad and
takes up embroidery, a metaphor for the paranoiac weaving
together of diverse strands to fill the void with a fabricated
design. The pattern of events that ensnarls Oedipus exists
objectively; of Oedipa's pattern one cannot be sure.

As the novel progresses, Oedipa's perceptions seem less
and less under control. In *V.*, clues slip away and hide; they
must be pursued or even desperately contrived; but here, for
a time at least, they force themselves on Oedipa whichever
way she turns, "crowding in exponentially" (49, p. 58). The
mathematical adverb is felicitous because it implies that an
underlying formula links the separate integers, just as Oedipa
suspects that one links her "revelations." Soon "everything she
saw, smelled, dreamed, remembered, would somehow come
to be woven into the Tristero" (49, p. 58). *Woven* recalls the
embroidered tapestry, and the phrase "somehow come to be" is
sufficiently vague and passive to show that Oedipa does not
know for certain who is doing the weaving. Her Tristero begins
to sound a little like the sinister sorcery: "They knew her
pressure points, and the ganglia of her optimism, and one by
one, pinch by precision pinch, they were immobilizing her"
(49, pp. 91–92). She does recognize, though, her desire to

"project a world" or "create constellations" (which Gravity's Rainbow shows to be figments of perspective), and she comes herself to wonder if the Tristero exists as anything more than a paranoid fantasy.

Tony Tanner has written that "one form of narcissism is to regard one's particular fantasy of the world as the definitive reality, and it is part of Oedipa's growing agony that she cannot be sure to what extent she herself is guilty of this."[20] Tanner might have added here that Oedipa is even uncertain of whether she is guilty, for as Marshal McLuhan notes, "the wisdom of the Narcissus myth does not convey any idea that Narcissus fell in love with anything he regarded as himself": he does not know for certain that he sees a reflection of himself, and neither does Oedipa.[21]

Pynchon sharpens these issues with his use of place names. Most of the action occurs in San Narciso, and although Oedipa seems to miss the connection, St. Narcissus figures in the plot of the play that introduces her to the Tristero. To continue the motif, Oedipa resides in the Echo Courts motel, managed by a sixteen-year-old who is an echo of his three chums and they of the mid-sixties English "mods"; also, the wonderfully grotesque thirty foot painted sheet metal nymph outside has a face "much like Oedipa's" (49, p. 14).

Main reference patterns of the novel build around shadows, echoes, and mirrors, all of which R. D. Laing calls common schizophrenic images.[22] In Berkeley, Oedipa sleeps under a Remedios Varo reproduction and has "a nightmare about something in the mirror" (49, p. 74). Based on the nature of the episode, David Cowart surmises that

> the painting in the room is one entitled Encuentro, in which a woman opens one of a number of small caskets in a room, only to find her own face inside staring back at her. Of this painting the artist wrote: "This poor woman, full of curiosity and hope at the opening of the little casket encounters only herself ... and who knows if when she opens them [the others] she will encounter anything new."[23]

[20]Tony Tanner, City of Words: American Fiction, 1950–1970 (New York: Harper and Row, 1971), p. 175.

[21]McLuhan is quoted in Peter L. Abernathy, "Entropy in Pynchon's The Crying of Lot 49," Critique 14, no. 2 (1972), 29.

[22]John Vernon, The Garden and the Map: Schizophrenia in Twentieth-Century Literature and Culture (Urbana: University of Illinois Press, 1973), p. 53.

[23]David Cowart, "Pynchon's The Crying of Lot 49 and the Paintings of Remedios Varo," Critique 18, no. 3 (1977), 24.

Moreover, the additional reference to Varo recalls the captive maidens and reinforces the suspicion that Oedipa grapples with self-projections. John Vernon speaks generally of schizophrenia in terms that are relevant here. The victim encounters the paradox of the "either-or" condition—what Oedipa calls "excluded middles": "aspects of experience are so polarized that they are at bottom the same."[24] In schizophrenia, solipsistic isolation from the world can lead to "merging," an inability to tell where one's self leaves off and the world begins.

But however conscious she becomes of her possible instability, Oedipa seems to have only marginal insight into *why* she might project fantasies. Stencil's motives are spelled out quite clearly and visibly on his two-dimensional surface, but Oedipa has hidden depths—hidden even from herself. Jung writes that projection is a measure of man's lack of self-awareness. The less conscious man is of his own psychological processes, "the more numerous the psychic contents (imagos) which meet him as quasi-external apparitions, either in the form of spirits, or as *magical potencies* projected upon living people" (italics mine).[25]

Perhaps Oedipa's personal experiences stand behind the Tristero—if it *is* a fantasy. "Despair" comes over Oedipa, as it does in the Greek Way—"when nobody around has any sexual relevance" to her (49, p. 86). The gay bar merely exaggerates the quotidian lot of unfulfillment that might be fueling her fantasies. We hear that "if she hadn't been set up or sensitized ... by her peculiar seduction," she might well not have stumbled onto the Tristero at all (49, p. 29). Her affair apparently triggers a complex reaction to the already-discovered possibility of an Other outside the tower. Oedipa's conception of the Tristero draws heavily upon her first sexual encounter with Metzger, except that the Tristero, in conformity with the narcissus motif, represents both her lover and herself: like the image she envisions of the Tristero, Metzger pinned her with a luminous and menacing smile, and she associates the "historical figuration" of the conspiracy with the clothes she used in a futile attempt to buffer herself from him. She wonders if, as with her own unravelling from the clothes, "a plunge toward dawn indefinite black hours long would indeed

---

[24]Vernon, *The Garden and the Map*, p. 27.
[25]Jerry H. Bryant, *The Open Decision: The Contemporary American Novel and Its Intellectual Background* (New York: Free Press, 1970), p. 95.

be necessary before the Tristero could be revealed in its terrible nakedness" (49, p. 36).

The Tristero manifests other ties with Oedipa's sex life. "Much of the revelation [of the system] was to come through the stamp collection Pierce had left, his substitute often for her . . . he could spend hours peering into each . . . [stamp], ignoring her" (49, p. 28), a habit that suggests that Pierce knew about the forgeries and perhaps the conspiracy. One gauges the degree of Oedipa's sexual frustration by noting the number of men with whom she tries and fails to communicate on various levels: Mucho, Metzger, Randolph Driblette (dead as well as alive), Mike Fallopian—even Maxwell's demon! Tony Tanner notes that while she is losing all her men in one way or another, "the stimulus to fantasy, or synthesizing perception, grows in the form of proliferating clues. . . . it may be a conspiracy of the imagination, which cannot stand too much nothingness or loneliness."[26] It may be. As the Tristero comes to us it is, to some extent, embroidered by Oedipa—but to what extent? Her bizarre perceptions can be doubted, particularly with respect to details, but they cannot be categorically dismissed as paranoid fabrications, for there seems to be some justification in physical, tangible reality for her suspicions of a conspiracy. As with Stencil, the reader has much trouble discerning that "nearly imperceptible line between an eye that reflects and an eye that receives" (V., p. 82).

None of Oedipa's fears is finally proved justified, as she never learns for sure if the Tristero is a real conspiracy, a hallucination, an elaborate hoax directed at her, or a paranoid fantasy. Neither does the reader. But in view of Pynchon's caveat about excluded middles, one should perhaps settle for a both/and rather than an either/or interpretation. Something out there does exist, probably as more than a practical joke. Oedipa does respond to it, though, according to "her several wounds, needs, dark doubles" (49, p. 98). Oedipa's subjective processes, like those of a scientist examining submicroscopic behavior, distort to an indeterminable degree the phenomena she is trying to observe; she partially creates the patterns she sees.

In Gravity's Rainbow, the startling, endless multiplicity of the world elicits what Pynchon apparently views as an

[26]Tanner, City of Words, p. 176.

involuntary human habit: the attempt to organize perceptions into some kind of system. Characters and narrative voices overlay patterns of experience and find parallels between sexual escapades, rocket strikes, and mosaics on the cerebral cortex. Most of the characters assume that they can draw conclusions from such parallels. To them, as W. T. Lhamon, Jr. writes, "everything announces, testifies, instructs, and spells itself out: Pensiero reads shivers, Bummer reads reefers, Thanatz reads whip scars, and Slothrop reads mandalas, trout guts, graffiti, paper scraps. . . . Pynchon asks, 'how can they not speak to Slothrop?' "[27]

That they speak is certain. Compared to *V.* and *The Crying of Lot 49*, there is relatively little suggestion that plots and patterns are merely tapestries woven by a solipsist to fill the void. Their interlocking conspiracies exist verifiably, apart from the mind of Slothrop the observer. And much of the world really *is* in code, concealed and yet intended to communicate. Katje finds her way to the counterforce because she reads the weirdly allegorical film left at the White Visitation by Osbie Feel.

That they speak is certain; what they speak and whether the characters interpret correctly is not. One finds few such clear successes as Katje's. The impulse to read signs is often undercut by the crudity of the situation or the playfulness of the language: as he falls down the Roseland toilet in his sodium amytal vision, Slothrop passes "shit nothing can flush away, mixed with hard-water minerals into a deliberate brown barnacling of his route, patterns thick with meaning, Burma-Shave signs of the toilet world, icky and sticky, cryptic and glyptic" (GR, p. 65). Startled and perhaps repelled by Slothrop's (and Pynchon's) passage, the reader may overlook *deliberate*, which raises the almost hidden but familiar spectre of ulterior motive and sinister intent behind the pattern.

Since the spectre arises from Slothrop's drugged mind, one can argue—inconclusively—that it is either a paranoid fabrication or a dream symbol of Their control. But there may be no other means through which to work. They are so good

[27]W. T. Lhamon, Jr., "Pentecost, Promiscuity, and Pynchon's V.: From the Scaffold to the Impulsive," in *Mindful Pleasures: Essays on Thomas Pynchon*, ed. George Levine and David Leverenz (Boston: Little, Brown and Co., 1976), p. 78.

at effacing Their tracks, says the narrator, that "those like
Slothrop, with the greatest interest in discovering the truth,
were thrown back on dreams, psychic flashes, omens,
cryptographies, drug-epistemologies, all dancing on a ground
of terror, contradiction, absurdity" (GR, p. 582). While this
hardly validates the results or the methods of the search, it does
approve the attempt. Besides sodium amytal and dope of all
kinds, the author injects a fictitious drug into his novel. Laszlo
Jamf's Oneirine perfectly reproduces the epistemological
dilemma around which Pynchon constructs his novels: it
affects all senses equally to produce hallucinations so
all-consuming, internally consistent, and plausible (even
"ordinary") that the user has hardly any way to distinguish
them from reality (GR, pp. 702–703). Moreover, Oneirine is a
product of Their cartel, which leads to the frightening thought
that They may be controlling "reality" in undetectable ways.

Even if one disregards such problems, Slothrop's
changefulness makes him another of Pynchon's unreliable
observers: "Slothrop, as noted, at least as early as the *Anubis*
era, has begun to thin, to scatter" (GR, p. 509). Instead of being
"present at his own assembly," he is "being broken down
instead, and scattered" (GR, p. 738). Soon even Pig Bodine (like
the narrator) is unable to see him "as any sort of integral
creature [. . .] to hold him together, even as a concept" (GR, p.
740). As Slothrop's temporal bandwidth shrinks, he loses a
sense of himself as well as of past and present; he cannot see
patterns develop, much less interpret them.

Approach and Avoid

In addition to the epistemological problems discussed so
far, perception itself is discontinuous. At different times, the
various "Stencils" find separate, fragmentary clues that point
to the quarry. Oedipa has only occasional, unconnected flashes
that promise "hierophany." Franz Pökler impregnated Leni
because he had been sexually aroused by the film *Alpdrücken*.
Ironically, his daughter Ilse becomes a "film child" for him:
Blicero allows her to visit Pökler once a year. The father
wonders if he sees his real daughter or a series of imposters.
Pökler transforms these separate "frames" into the "moving
image"—the "illusion"—of a single child, an illusion which

he accepts as real: he asks, "what would the time scale matter, a 24th of a second or a year?" (GR, p. 422). Here Pökler generalizes beyond his relationship with Ilse to acknowledge the epistemological problem that everyone must face to some degree. The apparent nature of reality depends upon the vantage point and time scale of the observer. Yet there is no ultimate vantage point and time scale, nor are there any absolute and independent criteria for choosing ones between the macro and micro extremes. Each entails its own special drawbacks. Moreover, the object is changeful and insubstantial — but then so is the subject. Even if they were not so, the subject still perceives discontinuously, quanta-like frame by frame, and so he cannot grasp the whole pattern at once, see it "blindingly One," as the mystic can; at best he can take the isolated frames and "string them all together," consciously or compulsively, into a cinematic illusion of coherence (GR, pp. 703, 590).

In addition, whatever "meanest sharp sliver of truth" might manage to slip in despite these problems could still be too hot to handle. Oedipa feels on several occasions that she approaches a sacred knowledge. But the approach is all she achieves — or remembers. At any rate, it is all the reader sees. As John May observes, "The mood of [the] novel is one of intense expectation; yet Pynchon, like life, reserves the final revelation."[28] Like Oedipa, the reader encounters "a secret richness and concealed density of dream" but nothing much more concrete and verifiable. Consequently, one may begin to suspect that the miraculous intrusions and otherworldly communications are unreal. Even if the clues do proceed to revelation, this Pentecostal moment may be impossible to hold. In this way, Oedipa, or anyone hovering at the threshold of such knowledge, is totally adrift, without compass or quadrant: "the central truth itself . . . must somehow each time be too bright for her memory to hold; . . . must always blaze out, destroying its own message irreversibly. . . . she would never know how many times such a seizure may already have visited, or how to grasp it should it visit again. Perhaps even in this last second — but there was no way to tell" (49, p. 69).

[28]John R. May, Toward a New Earth: Apocalypse in the American Novel (Notre Dame: University of Notre Dame Press, 1972), p. 218.

Similarly, the narrator of *Gravity's Rainbow* affirms that in critical moments, "what passes is a truth so terrible that history—at best a conspiracy, not always among gentlemen, to defraud—will never admit it" (GR, p. 164). And medium Ronald Cherrycoke fears that "the sheer volume of information pouring in through his fingers will saturate, burn him out" (GR, p. 150). Like the sailor's mattress for Oedipa or the used cars for Mucho, the world of objects for Cherrycoke (and perhaps Pynchon) is imbued somehow with the human lives that have touched it, ready to deluge the "sensitive" with unmanageable quantities of data, memory, and pain. Who can bear such sensitivity? Hardly anyone, says Pynchon—at least hardly any of his characters. Presumably, he finds this final and most discouraging obstacle reflected not so much in scientific research as in human nature: the fear of Answers, the failure of courage or will that causes one to "approach and avoid"—to retreat from knowing.

6

Metaphor, Model Building, and Paranoia

A Thrust at Truth and a Lie

In light of the epistemological pitfalls discussed in the previous chapter, it is no longer possible to believe that any mode of perception or explanation will ever fully disclose objective reality. Observation is not only deficient but actually disruptive, and yet some version of reality must be fabricated to fill the yawning void of the unknown, even though there is nothing but flawed observations on which to draw. As noted in chapter 4, the dominant scientific world views of this age arise from thermodynamic and quantum mechanics and from relativity theory. Norbert Wiener notes that these conceptions "are in sharp contrast" over issues such as discontinuity versus continuity or probability versus uniform law. However, statistical mechanics and relativity theory do concur on one thing: "both directions of work represent a shift in the point of view of physics in which the world as it actually exists is replaced in some sense or other by the world as it happens to be observed."[1]

Pynchon takes an attitude something like Wiener's: he grudgingly accepts the inevitable and decides to "bite the jolly old bullet and make the best of a bad job" (MMV, p. 205). He realizes that attempts to interpret and represent the world will misrepresent it, will be an "act of metaphor . . . a thrust at truth and a lie" (49, p. 95). A person needs such metaphors, or models of reality, to impose some kind of controlling design or limit on the overwhelming flow of information. A metaphorical

---

[1]Norbert Weiner, *The Human Use of Human Beings: Cybernetics and Society* (New York: Avon Books, 1967), p. 30.

structure lends him a sense of security; it shapes not only the outside world but also his response to it. For example, besides his analyst, Dennis Flange "had only one other consolation: the sea. . . . He had read or heard somewhere in his pre-adolescence that the sea was a woman, and the metaphor had enslaved him and largely determined what he became from that moment" (L, p. 89). Flange becomes the first in a long line of Pynchon characters whose lives are formed by a sometimes pathological susceptibility to metaphor.

But Pynchon does not merely dismiss Flange or his successors. Dennis's metaphor satisfies several psychological needs and so gives parts of his multiple and changeful self the outlets they must have if he is to carry on. The sea is not only a woman but, as Geronimo Diaz "pointed out, rather pedantically," a mother image that allows Flange to sublimate his fetal complex (L, p. 89). It is also the home of his *doppelgänger*, his metaphor for all that he finds vital and exciting in himself. Metaphor can put a person "into a curious contiguity" with "the truth of a true lie" (L, p. 100). Such sentiments are echoed by Fausto Maijstral, Oedipa Maas, and Enzian in their more lucid moments. Of course metaphor does not define what a thing or Situation "really" is but rather states — and misstates — that reality in other terms. Metaphor can, however, provide an experiential truth by defining how something is perceived, or an operational truth by allowing one to act in some accord with a pattern of events, even if one cannot know the details of that pattern or the substantive nature of its elements. Metaphor thus offers much of what a contemporary scientist hopes for in a theory.

Pynchon's artistic relationship with science extends beyond his appropriation of concepts or hypotheses to include his self-consciousness about the act of description. The new science has revised expectations about the limits of knowledge and disclosure. Lincoln Barnett writes,

> Science cannot yet really 'explain' electricity, magnetism, and gravitation; their effects can be measured and predicted, but of their ultimate nature no more is known to the modern scientist than to Thales of Miletus, who first speculated on the electrification of amber around 585 B.C. Most contemporary physicists reject the notion that man can ever discover what these mysterious forces 'really' are. Electricity, Bertrand Russell says,

'is not a thing, like St. Paul's Cathedral; it is a way in which things behave.'[2]

Science still applies names to these "forces" to enable discussion of them, but Leon Brillouin notes that "Wise men know where and how to use these figures of language, and they are aware of their complete lack of reality."[3] These "unreal" metaphors or theoretical symbols are liaisons with "an outside world independent of us . . . not directly accessible to us"; our relations with it are mediated, by our senses if nothing else. Scientists, using "unreal" figures of language, "imagine simplified models which serve us as . . . *representations* of this inaccessible world."[4] Gerald Holton explains further:

> First, the 'facts' of observation . . . impress themselves on our senses. Next, we find here a puzzling mixture of complexity and order which triggers the curiosity. . . . And finally we resolve the apparent puzzle by the imaginative construction of an analogon.
> . . . [which] is successful if it correlates convincingly the puzzling element in the observation with the consequences . . . of the postulated structure of the analogon.[5]

Such an "imaginative construction" well describes the responses, successful or not, that a Herbert Stencil or an Oedipa Maas will make when confronted with the ominous logic that an order is lurking in complex phenomena. For Pynchon as for the scientist, *defining* "reality" is not so important as achieving metaphoric validity or tracing patterns of events faithfully.

For example, science cannot say what electrons really are: they could be elementary particles of matter, quanta of electrical energy, waves, probability distributions, eddies in the four-dimensional space—time continuum, or some forms of being we cannot imagine from familiar models. "Thus in a sense electrons are not 'real' but merely theoretical symbols."[6] Nonetheless, such unknowable entities do exist and figure in actual "events," which the model helps describe: two electrons

[2]Lincoln Barnett, *The Universe and Dr. Einstein* (New York: Bantam Books, 1968), pp. 14–15.
[3]Leon Brillouin, *Scientific Uncertainty, and Information* (New York: Academic Press, 1964), p. 100.
[4]Ibid., p. 50.
[5]Gerald James Holton, "Not in Logic Alone: Science and New Styles of Thought," *Graduate Journal* 7, no. 2 (1967), 400.
[6]Barnett, *The Universe*, p. 116.

could meet, for instance. Although knowing that every attempt to name the entity "leads only deeper into a misty realm of symbolism and abstraction," science still applies names for convenience.[7] In fact, Niels Bohr with his principle of "complementarity" advises scientists to switch names freely when it is expedient to do so: call an electron a wave when investigating its wave-like behavior and a particle when investigating its particle-like behavior. Science has thus given up the attempt for a definitive, qualitative description of objective reality and recognized that it must, aside from mathematics, speak in metaphors, metaphors which it can replace but not transcend. Modern physicists, who may find a pleasurable release in this admission, speak of "charm" as helping to hold the atomic nucleus together. A scientist of the previous century, still striving for ultimate definition and mechanical explanation of nature, never would have dared. As long as the model or metaphor helps the modern researcher describe and predict the design of events, he wisely forgives it (as one may forgive Pynchon characters) for not being able to define what those events really are. "In the abstract lexicon of quantum physics there is no such word as 'really.' "[8]

Sir William Dampier adds: "While we must accept provisionally and with caution the mental models which are made from time to time to represent the *relata* . . . we can use freely and feel growing confidence in the ever-increasing knowledge of those relations which science gives us. . . . It is quite good enough to act upon; the truth of the relations does not depend on the reality of the *relata*."[9] Because science deals in such models and metaphors, it is, in a sense, literary. In fact, A. E. E. McKenzie declares that a "model in science is like a metaphor in language,"[10] and Gerald Holton has raised the question of whether "themes" in science — for example the concept of *force* in its various manifestations — may not be bound in some way to archetypal imagery and myth.[11] The

[7]Ibid., p. 116.

[8]Ibid., p. 32.

[9]Sir William Dampier, *A History of Science and Its Relations with Philosophy and Religion* (New York: Macmillan, 1936), p. 468.

[10]A. E. E. McKenzie, *The Major Achievements of Science* (Cambridge: Cambridge University Press, 1960), I, 190.

[11]Gerald James Holton, "The Thematic Dimension: Presupposition in the Construction of Theories," *Graduate Journal* 7, no. 1 (1966), 87–109.

problem with Pynchon characters is not that they make
"mental models," just that they forget to accept them
"provisionally and with caution," to recognize that they
do not disclose "the reality of the *relata*."

Consequently, Dennis Flange's "metaphor had enslaved
him." Callisto takes thermodynamic entropy as "an adequate
metaphor" by which to understand American society, but he
does not take it provisionally: he sees an ominous logic of
coded messages wherever he looks, and so he becomes
imprisoned by his metaphor as much as by the hothouse into
which he tries, self-defeatingly, to escape. Pynchon guardedly
affirms that one has to trace patterns in the chaotic welter of
appearances — also that "a pattern is a message, and may be
interpreted as a message"[12] or even construed as "a
hieroglyphic sense of concealed meaning, of an intent to
communicate" (49, p. 13). But he also sees the limitations and
dangers; the ambivalence remains at the heart of the
epistemological dilemma that dominates each book.

Many readers miss the depth of that ambivalence and,
thereby, Pynchon's complexity in handling the dilemma.
Because Herbert Stencil is eccentric, clownish, and driven —
and because his quest is expedient, arbitrary, and unnaturally
prolonged — most critics reject too complacently the
"revelations" he achieves. Max Schulz, for example, sees him
as "modeled in the contemporary mode of a Quixote aware that
his search is an adventure of the mind, an intellectual gesture
of order flung out against the illogic and patternlessness of
events."[13] Although admitting Stencil to be aware of his own
contrivance, Schulz joins many other readers in assuming that
the investigator fabricates transparently unreal plots merely to
cover the void. George Levine and David Leverenz agree that
"V. mocks the synthetic minds that insist on making shapes
out of the meaningless variety and colorfulness of
experience."[14] In addition to denying any reality to his
discoveries, numerous critics also see Stencil as purely the

[12]Weiner, *The Human Use of Human Beings*, p. 131.

[13]Max F. Schulz, *Black Humor Fiction of the Sixties: A Pluralistic Definition
of Man and His World* (Athens, Ohio: Ohio University Press, 1973), p. 144.

[14]George Levine and David Leverenz, "Introduction: Mindful Pleasures," in
Mindful Pleasures: Essays on Thomas Pynchon, ed. George Levine and David
Leverenz (Boston: Little, Brown and Co., 1976), p. 3.

object of Pynchon's satire, a character with no real insight into himself. Richard Wasson maintains that Pynchon's "immediate targets are of course the conspiracy theories of history which dominated the cold-war mentality."[15] Similarly, Raymond Olderman sees Stencil's belief in conspiracies as a demented response to life in the waste land, as the inversion of man's impulse to believe in a superior being, and as the "need to replace a lost mythology":

> When a man of the sixties feels he has lost control of his own life, when he thinks no single individual can influence large public events, when he feels he can no longer cope with the irrationality of public and private affairs, when he yearns for some transcendent explanation and meaning, he begins to find patterns in the accidents of fortune — mysteries in the indifference of fact.

"Plots and conspiracies," the critic asserts, "are illusions."[16]

Perhaps Tony Tanner argues most cogently against the validity of Stencil's discoveries: while Pynchon's novel "is certainly about a world succumbing to entropy, it is also about the subtler human phenomena — the need to see patterns which may easily turn into the tendency to suspect plots."[17] To prove that Stencil's great need gives way to this tendency, Tanner quotes a key passage from V.: "Cavities in the teeth occur for good reason, Eigenvalue reflected. But even if there are several per tooth, there's no conscious organization there against the life of the pulp, no conspiracy. Yet we have men like Stencil, who must go about grouping the world's random caries into cabals" (V., p. 139).

Tanner finds further proof that Stencil's "plots" are illusory when he examines the story of Kurt Mondaugen, a young engineering student who returns twenty years older in Gravity's Rainbow. In 1922, Mondaugen was sent to the South-West Protectorate to investigate atmospheric radio disturbances, or "sferics." His adventures, rife with voyeurism, delirium, and confusing mirror images, suggest the epistemological themes of the whole novel. As his health

[15]Richard Wasson, "Notes on a New Sensibility," Partisan Review 36, no. 3 (1969), 474.

[16]Raymond M. Olderman, Beyond the Waste Land: A Study of the American Novel in the Nineteen-Sixties (New Haven, Conn.: Yale University Press, 1972), pp. 124, 119, 138.

[17]Tony Tanner, City of Words: American Fiction, 1950–1970 (New York: Harper and Row, 1971), p. 153.

begins to wane and his voyeuristic tendencies to wax, Mondaugen starts to think that he detects in his presumably random sferics "a regularity or patterning which might almost have been a kind of code." He decides that "the only way to see if it were a code was to try to break it," and so he fashions an oscillograph to record the signals (*V.,* p. 228).

From "might almost have been a kind of," Mondaugen's belief in cosmic cryptography grows, seemingly in proportion to his failing health, lapsing mental clarity, and swelling paranoia. Finally the German officer Weissmann (who also returns in *Gravity's Rainbow*) claims to have broken the code. By removing every third letter he obtains "GODMEAN-TNUURK," which rearranged spells "Kurt Mondaugen." The remaining letters read "DIEWELTISTALLESWASDERFALLIST" (*V,* p. 258 – 59). This, of course, is the opening proposition from Wittgenstein's *Tractatus,* burlesqued elsewhere in *V.* by Charisma's logical positivist lovesong, "Let P Equal Me." Tanner argues that

> As a coded message it would be the supreme irony, like discovering that the secret is that there is no secret. The assertion that the world is everything that is the case repudiates the very notion of plots. . . . As the book shows, human instinct pulls in the other direction: towards cabalism, or demonism, or projected fantasies. . . . People would rather detect an 'ominous logic' in things than no omens at all.[18]

Positivism or no, one should not reject Stencil's (or Mondaugen's) account of events; rather, one should accept it provisionally. On the one hand, V. does become an obsession; her apparent movements may be the result of countless accidents. But on the other hand, underlying randomness will add up to overriding regularity. Macro events build from accidental, haphazard micro events, but this does not mean that the macro events are accidental and haphazard themselves. The course of a system can be perfectly regular and predictable even though its individual components are not. It can also be mythologized or metaphorically explained in a way that does not misrepresent the nature and degree of its regularity. The perception of pattern or chaos will depend purely on vantage point, but no one vantage point is definitive. Who can say that the micro view is more accurate, valid, or real than the macro

[18]Ibid., pp. 168 – 69.

view? Each has its own validity, depending on what one is viewing. Herbert Stencil observes not the micro underpinnings of one Situation so much as the macro motion of Western civilization. The question is not whether he fabricates, but whether his fabrications allow for some insight.

Pynchon did not make Stencil such a complete fool or paranoiac as many readers find him, for to destroy entirely his credibility or threat of discovery would eviscerate the fiction. The crucial and characteristic tension between order and disorder could not exist if Pynchon debunked one possibility altogether. Coincidence, echo, and *déjà vu* are part of the fictional texture, leading characters and reader alike to feel more than know that malicious design may camouflage itself as chance. Commentators responding to *V.* after reading *Gravity's Rainbow* can see in Herbert Stencil some partially redeeming features that might otherwise be missed. For example, W. T. Lhamon, Jr. writes in 1975 that

> Paranoia is another indication in Pynchon's work of an alternative world beyond the customary one, for paranoids read signs of mystery and force that philistines never suspect. Paranoids are on to something, some sub rosa and unedifying connectedness that no philistine's grammar can accommodate.[19]

With each novel, paranoia becomes more and more "operational" and They become more and more plausible, but even in *V.* one senses that Something beyond the control of ordinary people is happening and that Someone invisible and higher up is making it happen. One minor character quips: "History, the proverb says, is made at night. The European civil servant normally sleeps at night. What waits in his IN basket to confront him at nine in the morning is history. He doesn't fight it, he tries to coexist with it" (*V.,* p. 215).

One might profitably imagine history as a quasi-animate being whose motive power and consciousness are hidden; in fact, such a view helps Van Wijk realize that he must coexist with history rather than fight it if he is to survive. Eigenvalue would find Van Wijk's attitude a lesser version of Stencil's demonism and reflect on the error of "grouping the world's

---

[19]W. T. Lhamon, Jr., "Pentecost, Promiscuity, and Pynchon's V.: From the Scaffold to the Impulsive," in *Mindful Pleasures: Essays on Thomas Pynchon,* ed. George Levine and David Leverenz (Boston: Little, Brown and Co., 1976), p. 74.

random caries into cabals." Eigenvalue's point has some
validity when applied as a check to Stencil's excesses, but
one should not take it, as many do, for Pynchon's definitive
statement on cabalism. After all, the "psychodontist" is a
dubious figure who has a fascination for prosthetics —
especially artificial teeth — and a penchant for seeing the
animate in terms of the inanimate, an evil in the context of the
book. By equating emotional problems with dental ones, he
bases his professional life on the absurd metaphor that the
human psyche is a tooth. Obviously Eigenvalue, whose name
evokes the uncertainty of quantum mechanics, is part of
Pynchon's ongoing satire against psychiatry, that "priesthood"
of "father confessors" he debunks in "Mortality and Mercy in
Vienna," "Low-lands," "A Journey into the Mind of Watts,"
and *The Crying of Lot 49*. In short, Eigenvalue is no oracle.

The human soul is not a tooth; will, consciousness, and
intention figure somehow in the decay. *V.* does not offer clear
internal evidence of an evil and manipulative cabal, as will
Gravity's Rainbow, but it does adduce grounds for suspicion:
the subways, the photographs of Auschwitz. . . . a cabal can
occur if a group of human beings gains power over others by
jumping on entropy's bandwagon — by acquiescing to the
malevolent trends of history, appropriating them, employing
them to subjugate others rather than trying to resist them. The
cabal members may rule by accelerating the movement of
society along a set course that They appropriate, even if They
had no hand in setting it. They may not create a Situation, but
They know that a Situation will arise which They can shape to
Their purposes. Probability guarantees that materials will be
available to Them. Chance, not design, may bring a given
person to a certain place at a certain time, but statistically valid
laws determine that *somebody* will be present to fill, perhaps
unwittingly, the slot in Their scheme. Mass behavior follows
a pattern, even if the behavior of individuals does not.

Stencil uses *V.*'s career as a map for the pattern of mass
behavior and asks, in studying the map, to what extent has
twentieth-century man — perverse and self-destructive,
conscious and organized — participated deliberately in his
own degradation? Stencil's pursuit may be mad, foolish, and
ridiculously exaggerated, but his basic question and
methodology are not. He is not wrong in connecting *V.* with
apocalyptic mass violence and conspiracy, or even in viewing

her as an emblem of an ongoing force, the "particular shape" of which is "governed only by the surface accidents of history at the time" (V., p. 141). He is wrong in trying to make his metaphor literal, to make V. a shaper of precise historical events rather than a sign and symptom of the general texture of modern life. Near the end of the book, when faced with having to end the quest that sustains him, Stencil refuses to believe that his quarry died on Malta. Grasping for any "frayed end" of a clue that will keep him in motion, he exists for Stockholm in pursuit of one Viola, "oneiromancer and hypnotist" (V., p. 425).

But Stencil's excesses do not prove that no ominous patterns or plots are lurking beneath "the surface accidents of history." Tony Tanner sees "the supreme irony" when Mondaugen's code resolves itself into Wittgenstein's thesis, for this assertion in effect denies that "plots" exist. But the *presence* of the thesis in the sferic monitorings hints otherwise. What are the odds that a randomly produced set of sounds would generate so powerful a statement as Wittgenstein's—in the formulator's language—with an anagram of the monitor's name thrown in for good measure? Because it is so unlikely that these patterns were created by accident, information theorists would argue that the sferics form a "message." There seems to be "an intent to communicate" (49, p. 13).

As Pynchon will show again in his later novels, excluded middles belie the truth of the situation. Apparently, something is going on, but just as apparently, those who try to observe it and account for it have both succeeded and failed to an uncertain degree. In making this point, Pynchon demonstrates the validity of Ortega y Gasset's assertion that "a fundamental revision of man's attitude towards life is apt to find its first expression in artistic creation and scientific theory."[20] Science, of course, does not deal purely in projections and subjectivity, nor does Stencil. Something is there to be investigated and described, but one must adopt a new attitude toward investigation and description. "The aim of science," announced Henri Poincaré in 1905, "is not things themselves, as the dogmatists in their simplicity imagine, but the relations between things; outside these relations there is no reality knowable."[21] Bertrand Russell adds that physics "is quite

[20]Jose Ortega y Gasset, *The Dehumanization of Art: And Other Writings on Art and Culture* (Gordon City, N.Y.: Doubleday Anchor Books, n.d.), p. 39.
[21]McKenzie, *Achievements of Science*, I, 341.

unable to tell us what . . . things are like in themselves,"
although it may describe *patterns* of events with great
fidelity.[22] To the limits suggested by Heisenberg, Bohr,
Poincaré, Russell, and company, science can use mathematics
and "unreal" metaphors to describe, measure, and predict the
behavior and relations of the unknowable entities as they
interact with subjective influences. Herbert Stencil's obsession
is a sloppy, misshapen effigy of such a mathematics; it too
should be judged not by how well it defines what things
"really are" apart from his observation of them, but by how
well it describes symbolically our experience of the
contemporary world.

That description is rather good, if one can judge by the
number of parallels, recurring themes, and major concerns it
shares with the Profane subplot. Also, Stencil's method boasts
some predictive validity: the five-figured comb Victoria wore
in Stencil's impersonation shows up on Malta when Paola
gives it to Pappy Hod. More importantly, the Bad Priest
assumes in Fausto's experience the same traits she had in
Stencil's reconstructions: she opposes the Virgin in the
children's "Manichaean" dualism, she is "ubiquitous as
night," a "sinister uncertainty surrounded" her, and she
proselytizes for inanimation (V., pp. 317, 318, 319).

Moreover, Stencil is aware of the limitations of his
investigative method, as is a modern scientist. For example,
in chapter three a barmaid named Hanne thinks she sees a
triangular (V-shaped) stain on a plate she is washing. Tony
Tanner nicely points out that

> She is experiencing as a temporary puzzle what for Stencil is
> a lifelong dilemma. . . . "Was the stain real? She didn't like its
> color. The color of her headache . . ." The problem of the book
> is here in miniature. Perhaps the changing shapes we see on
> the external blankness are the shifting projections of our own
> "headaches" or subjective pressures; on the other hand there
> might actually be a stain on the plate.[23]

But Tanner does not consider that Hanne is Stencil's seventh
impersonation and that Stencil must therefore know the
epistemological pitfalls of his type of quest so well that he can
objectify them artistically here. Also to debunk Stencil's

[22]Jerry H. Bryant, *The Open Decision: The Contemporary American Novel
and Its Intellectual Background* (New York: Free Press, 1970), p. 23.
[23]Tanner, *City of Words*, p. 169.

cabalism, Tanner quotes a key line from the novel: "'There must be a nearly imperceptible line between an eye that reflects and an eye that receives'. . . . this is related to the narcissistic habit of turning people into reflectors of one's own fantasies and obsessions."[24] The quotation capsulizes the whole question of whether plots are perceived or projected. But again, Tanner does not note that Stencil himself must recognize the difficulty of the issue: these words came from Stencil's own mouth (V., p. 82).

In general, critics make nothing of the fact that Stencil the fabulator has fashioned the episodes and spoken the lines that call his quest into question.[25] For example, Stencil relates the Florentine disturbances to Eigenvalue through "impersonation": Stencil — not his father — declares that "no Situation had any objective reality" (V., p. 174); Stencil — not old Godolphin — realizes that Vheissu has only subjective reality and metaphorical relevance; Stencil — not any of the F.O. men, spies, or consular agents — perceives that the ridiculous conspiracy paranoia, V-word phobia, and bureaucratic snafus are mostly misguided responses to an old man's fantasy. By the same token, it is really Stencil, not Itague, who explains that "Because we are less human, we foist off the humanity we have lost on inanimate objects and abstract theories" (V., p. 380). Perhaps he also planted Wittgenstein in the sferics!

Even if Stencil's metaphorical description of recent Western history is inaccurate, even if he has no insight into the dangers of his method, and even if he works "for no one's amusement [or salvation] but his own," his type of endeavor is still necessary (V., p. 50). We must construct models of reality, for as Jerry Bryant notes, "models help us find things in reality that we could not find without them." Bryant quotes a scientist as arguing that "if we were forbidden to talk in terms of models at all, we should have no expectations at all, and we should then be imprisoned forever inside the range of our existing experiments,"[26] unable to learn a damn thing, like Benny

[24]Ibid. p. 159.
[25]Speaking of chapter three in V., for example, William Plater declares that "various natives reveal their recognition of the illusions imposed on them." He does not observe that these natives are Stencil's impersonations. The Grim Phoenix: Reconstructing Thomas Pynchon (Bloomington: Indiana University Press, 1978), p. 110.
[26]Bryant, Open Decision, pp. 35, 33.

Profane, or Tyrone Slothrop in his "anti-paranoia" phase.
Gerald Holton quotes fellow physicist Martin Deutsch in
making this point: "it is possible to understand and use
observations in physics today only if the scientist has, from
the very beginning, a 'well-structured image of the actual
connections between the events taking place.' This is indeed
far from the conventional idea that the scientist keeps a
completely open mind."[27] Heisenberg recalls how Einstein
criticized him for claiming that "physicists must consider none
but observable magnitudes." Einstein countered, "It is the
theory which decides what we can observe. . . . Only theory . . .
enables us to deduce the underlying phenomena from our
sense impressions."[28] The world may be all that is the case, but
we must go beyond that and hypothesize if we are to have any
hope of learning what the case is.

Models, metaphors, and preconceptions may be necessary
to make any sense of events, but they involve us in projection.
Science, says Leon Brillouin, will always be plagued with the
question: "how can we distinguish these creations of our
imagination from factual observations?"[29] Pynchon's novels
portray a similar problem: imagination and language, to some
uncertain degree, distort "reality" in trying to define it, yet man
cannot give up these tools or his compulsive quest to know.

Nor can woman. With more convincing and human
motivation, Oedipa goes on a quest much like Stencil's and
faces essentially the same epistemological problems. She
realizes that in her conception of the Tristero she faced "a
metaphor of God knew how many parts," and she also sees that
even a simple "act of metaphor" is "a thrust at truth and a lie,
depending where you were: inside, safe, or outside, lost,"
taking the macro or micro vantage point, the mountain top or
the valley basin view (49, pp. 80, 95). Oedipa's problem is that
she "did not know where she was," nor does she have any
stable, nonrelative reference point to help her find out. Seeing
"how far it might be possible to get lost in this," she concludes
that she must steer by the Tristero metaphor to orient herself,
even if it is a projected world or constellation, a figment of
perspective: "For there either was some Tristero beyond the

[27]Holton, "Logic," p. 414.
[28]Werner Heisenberg, *Physics and Beyond: Encounters and Conversations*,
trans. Arnold J. Pomerans (New York: Harper Torchbooks, 1972), pp. 60, 63.
[29]Brillouin, *Scientific Uncertainty*, p. 103.

appearance of the legacy America, or there was just America and if there was just America then it seemed the only way she could continue, and manage to be at all relevant to it, was as an alien, unfurrowed, assumed full circle into some paranoia" (49, pp. 69, 137). Her Tristero may be delusion, but on the strength of delusion Fausto's Malta survived (V., p. 305); Oedipa cannot hold out for a better guarantee of truth.

The whole novel undercuts the possibility of finally knowing anything, and if nothing can really be known, what can be communicated? Richard Patteson states:

> Pynchon's fictional territory might be said to lie along the perimeter which divides knowledge from non-knowledge. As long as the perimeter itself cannot be clearly defined, one cannot possibly distinguish between what is known and what is not known, since Pynchon clearly implies that we fill the void beyond the perimeter with illusions that pass for truth.[30]

But Pynchon does not "clearly imply" a stand on these "illusions"; the author has shown that such mental constructs, while imperfect and even dangerous, are also necessary, functional, and in their own way true.

Model building, paranoid or not, offers an alternative to the "either 1 or 0" mode of knowledge that Pynchon rejects as inhuman both in Lot 49 and Gravity's Rainbow. Norbert Wiener explains that digital machines are "all or none": they either register or transmit a unit of information (1) or they don't (0). But not all machines work this way. "Analogy machines . . . operate on the basis of analogous connections between the measured quantities and the numerical quantities supposed to represent them."[31] In human terms, one must approach the world through analogies and metaphorical constructs that define the patterns if not the particulars of reality. Metaphor is flawed: it fictionalizes reality in tracing it. It is "a thrust at truth and a lie," not either truth or lie. (49, p. 95, my italics).

In "The Secret Integration," the constant struggle against a superior force conduces to paranoia, a special kind of model building. Grover, an only-sometimes-successful inventor, develops a jealous hatred of Tom Swift. He keeps coming across the books "by apparent accident, though he had

---

[30]Richard Patteson, "What Stencil Knew: Structure and Certitude in Pynchon's V.," Critique 16, no. 2 (1974), 42.
[31]Wiener, The Human Use of Human Beings p. 89.

developed a theory lately that it was by design; that the books were coming across *him*, and that his parents and/or the school were deeply involved" (SI, p. 39.). Grover hates Tom Swift because he is "a racist" who treats his black servant with smug condescension. "Do they want me to read that stuff so I'll be like that?" Grover asks his friend, Tim. The answer, undoubtedly, is yes. Perhaps Grover's paranoia is operational. Certainly the adults, even if they are not planting the books, would want to mold Grover after Tom into a racially exclusive citizen who makes a lot of money on inventions and investments. The paranoid perception may misconstrue details but register an underlying truth.

The paranoid model builder must make a rather daring leap of faith in asserting a continuity between events.[32] Does he delude himself in doing so, entrap himself in a structure of his own making? The pattern tracer thus opens himself up to the dangers of solipsism. Pynchon seems to say that we must take the risk. We cannot help but enclose ourselves within our own perceptions anyway, regardless of how discontinuous they are; moreover, we cannot help but fabricate to some uncertain degree what we perceive, if for no other reason than that our act of observing alters what we observe. At worst, the paranoid only alters what he observes more radically than the average person does. "Anti-paranoia" can be even harder to bear than paranoia. As Slothrop slides into anti-paranoia, he "feels the whole city around him going back roofless, vulnerable, uncentered as he is, and only pasteboard images now" (GR, p. 434).

Paranoia rather than anti-paranoia lends the more accurate vision of a world in which interlocking economic, political, and military interests persecute the likes of Slothrop. There *is* a plot directed at him, and paranoia at least alerts him to it. "Reality" may appear in discrete quanta, frames of film, or fragmentary clues, but the paranoid makes them continuous. He traces the lines between the dots to reveal the pattern. He could be totally wrong about journalistic particulars such as who, what, when, and where, and still provide an accurate analogue of events; his model could be metaphorically apt,

[32]Mark Siegel has also compared this act to the existentialist's leap of faith in *Pynchon: Creative Paranoia in Gravity's Rainbow* (Port Washington, N.Y.: Kennikat Press, 1978), pp. 50–51.

illuminating the interconnectedness of the world and the cosmos. William Plater speaks here of Slothrop's "projected world": "Relative, arbitrary, and changing, his fantasy is as real as anything. Slothrop's four dimensional Raketen-Stadt may be closer to a true description of the world than [is] any map of occupation, especially for the state of mind."[33] Recall Wiener's assertion that science now describes not "the world as it actually exists" but rather "the world as it happens to be observed." When Slothrop slips from these habits of mind into anti-paranoia, the narrator laments: "Forgive the fist that doesn't tighten in his chest, the heart that can't stiffen in any greeting. . . . Forgive him as you forgave Tchitcherine at the Kirghiz Light"—another missed opportunity for revelation (GR, p. 510). Paranoia is a defective mode of vision (see chapter 3), a thrust at truth and a lie, but the sin of delusion is exceeded by the sin of obtuseness.

By tracing out a pattern, the paranoid to some unknowable extent creates what he perceives. Such creative perception is inescapable even in scientific observation, Heisenberg tells us, and yet not everyone knows this or adjusts to it. To perceive and affirm some continuity, one must make a leap of faith over uncertainty, subjectivism, and apparent discontinuity—a leap that many are too terrified or unaware to make. Franz Pökler best characterizes such a man. He is afraid, in George Levine's phrase, to "risk" the moment and its possibilities. Pynchon associates "penetration" of the moment with approach toward an awful continuity: "Δt approaching zero, eternally approaching, the slices of time growing thinner and thinner, a succession of rooms each with walls more silver, transparent, as the pure light of the zero comes nearer. . . ." (GR, p. 159). As Δt approaches zero on a graph with time as one of the coordinates, the isolated points merge into the continuity of a line, of an unbroken present, metaphorically speaking.

Oedipa realizes that in an unbroken present "change had to be confronted at last for what it was, where it could no longer disguise itself as something innocuous like an average rate; where velocity dwelled in the projectile though the projectile be frozen in midflight, where death dwelled in the cell though the cell be looked in on at its most quick" (49, pp. 95–96). Pökler lacks the courage to make such a confrontation—to live

[33]Plater, *The Grim Phoenix*, p. 61.

in the moment, on the continuity of the line. In a brilliant passage, Pynchon uses mathematical symbolism to explain Pökler's fear of the Street, Pynchon's favorite metaphor for the modern world:

> He couldn't go out in the street. Later he thought about its texture, the network of grooves between the paving stones. The only safety there was ant-scaled, down and running the streets of Ant City, bootsoles crashing overhead like black thunder, you and your crawling neighbors in traffic all silent, jostling, heading down the gray darkening streets. . . . Pökler knew how to find safety among the indoor abscissas and ordinates of graphs: finding the points he needed not by running the curve itself, not up on high stone and vulnerability, but instead tracing patiently the xs and ys, P (atü), W (m/sec), T_i (°K), moving always by safe right angles along the faint lines. . . . (GR, p. 399).

Pökler tries to dismantle the continuity of the curve or the moment through analysis, fragmenting both into many separate combinations of x and y designates. Like Pökler's calculus, a sign of "impotence and abstraction," film fragments continuous process into still frames (GR, p. 567). In a cruel form of poetic justice, Pökler must encounter his daughter Ilse as he has lived his life: frame by isolated frame. The mode of life he retreated to for security has only delivered him into a terrible uncertainty: how can he be sure than Blicero sends him the same girl every summer? He decides that the "time scale" is irrelevant. How does he know anything if he doesn't live on the curve, in the continuous moment? Pökler finally abandons his "abstraction" and makes the leap of faith, accepting Ilse as his own child, even though "the only continuity has been her name [inessential], and Zwölfkinder [decaying], and Pökler's love—love something like the persistence of vision" (GR, p. 422). Love is possible in Pynchon's world, but only for a person brave enough to "risk the moment" and forgo the buffering security of withdrawal from life's immediacy. Knowledge and the "persistence of vision" depend on courage, will, and effort. For Pynchon, epistemology involves ethics.

Tragically, Franz Pökler does not learn to make his leap until he has lost his wife and, in a way, his daughter. But Leni Pökler was a different sort of person from the outset. She has always had the will to "penetrate the moment," the courage to love, the endurance to make a vision persist. She has shortcomings, for example a tendency to make racial generalizations, but in her ethical ideals and her epistemology she may speak for

Pynchon more faithfully than does any other character in his works. Generally, Pynchon's men do not measure up to his women. Positive male characters such as McClintic Sphere or Pirate Prentice are not fully developed or given main roles in the action, and Roger Mexico tends to be "somber," "selfish," dependent, and immature (GR, p. 126). Heroines such as Rachel Owlglass, Paola Maijstral, Geli Tripping, and Oedipa Maas have admirable traits, especially the ability to care, but not to the degree that Leni does. Moreover, the others each suffer from some lack, either of character or of artistic treatment.

Rachel, for example, participates a little in the decadence and fetishism regnant in V.: she cultivates an emotional attachment for her MG. The reader never really sees inside her head. Paola's interior space is even less visible; as discussed in chapter 3, she undergoes an unconvincing offstage transformation from weak girl to strong woman. Nor is Geli rendered in much depth. She demonstrates the virtue and the power of love, but in general she is less a vehicle for serious themes than a device for engaging Slothrop in comic misadventures. Moreover, she is concerned almost entirely with her own limited affairs. She makes Tchitcherine "blind now to all but" her (GR, p. 734), as she has been to all but him. We last see them lying beside a stream, spellbound and oblivious to whatever is happening outside their own private realm. Leni has transpersonal as well as personal passions; she is committed to fight for political ideals and against the dehumanizing forces of the Street (GR, p. 158). Unlike Geli, she cares, as Oedipa would say, about things "that mattered to the world" (49, p. 136). But Oedipa does not have quite the bravery, honesty, or insight into herself that Leni does: she is afraid of self-loss — she cannot quite risk the moment or go "to the back of" her tenderness. She "cons" herself and buffers herself. She fears what happens when $\Delta t \to 0$. Leni embraces it. Consequently, Oedipa never experiences or understands as much as Leni does. In pursuing hierophany, Oedipa remains something of a novice; she speaks of projecting worlds and tracing constellations, but unlike Leni she never takes her thinking a step further to discuss the methodology or the moral and philosophical justification of such activity. In doing so, Leni is not just a vehicle for Pynchon's ideas, but a voice.

Despite his scientific sophistication, Pynchon seems to

vindicate Leni's astrology as a means of knowledge. Franz belittles the sciosophy, proclaiming that "'there is no way for changes out there to produce changes here.' 'Not produce,' she tried, 'not cause. It all goes along together. Parallel, not series. Metaphor. Signs and symptoms. Mapping on to different coordinate systems'" (GR, p. 159). A pattern of stars does not *cause* a pattern of events on the earth or in the mind. Rather, Inside and Outside could be "part of the same field" (GR, p. 144). The same process that unfolds itself in the mind, on the earth, or under the ground unfolds itself, in parallel fashion, in the sky — a larger map, perhaps more legible because distance strips away the confusing details and minor, chance fluctuations to leave only the general outline. If "the process follows the same form, the same structure" on all levels, why not "follow the signs" in the heavens as well as on or under the earth (GR, p. 167)?

Pynchon has belittled "cause-and-effect" thinking; his view of the cosmos, generally shared by contemporary science, validates Leni's line of argument. Ironically, Leni understands the new scientific thought better than her formally trained husband does. Her version of astrology reminds one of what Gerald Holton calls the enduring principle of relativity from Galileo through Einstein: "All laws of physics observed in one coordinate system are equally valid in any other coordinate system moving with a constant velocity relative to the first."[34] Actually, Einstein's General Theory of Relativity goes beyond the "special" case of constant relative velocity to state that the laws of nature are identical for all space– time coordinate systems, whether or not they move uniformly in relation to one another.

In Pynchon's terms, metaphorical constructs, paranoid visions, or projected worlds are really just fabricated coordinate systems; when taken "provisionally," they offer a valid means of understanding the "real" world. If the same laws apply in the same way to patterns of events in each coordinate system, then a person can infer the general structure and operation of any world from the structure and operation of any other. Because all systems are equivalent in this sense, and because

[34]Gerald James Holton, *Introduction to Concepts and Theories in Physical Science*, 2nd edition, revised and with new material by Stephen G. Brush (Reading, Mass.: Addison-Wesley, 1973), p. 423.

there is no fixed and absolute system by which to make definitive measurements, Leni can choose for reference whatever coordinate system she likes. She likes the celestial. Although its constellations are illusions of perspective, they bear constant relation to earthly cycles and so allow her to understand her world not through 1 or 0 thinking but through analogy and parallel. Leni's mode of perception is validated not only by echoes from contemporary science but also by its resemblance to the mystical vision of simultaneity. Kabbalist spokesman Steve Edelman informs us that "although the Rocket countdown appears to be serial [like Franz's "cause-and-effect"], it actually conceals the Tree of Life [the ten part Sephiroth], which must be apprehended all at once, together, in parallel" (GR, p. 753). Franz can see only the Rocket countdown. Leni might be able to glimpse the Tree of Life behind it.

Pirate Prentice explains "creative paranoia" in terms that recall Leni's epistemology: "We don't have to worry about questions of real or unreal [. . . .] It's the *system* that matters. How the data arrange themselves inside it. Some are consistent, others fall apart" (GR, p. 638). In reading the world metaphorically, one worries less about defining reality than about describing it consistently, or as a modern scientist might say, "isomorphically": opaque, "unreal" symbols, whether verbal metaphors or mathematical signs, stand for real events but disclose nothing of the intrinsic nature of those events; and yet one can relate the symbols to each other in a way that traces the pattern of relations between the phenomena. One can thus describe the form if not the elements of the ineffable process. Lincoln Barnett speaks for science in declaring that such a "consistent isomorphic representation of these relationships and events is the maximal possibility of . . . [man's] knowledge. Beyond that point he stares into the void."[35]

It is because of this boundary that scientists such as A. E. E. McKenzie and Gerald Holton see connections between science and metaphor or myth. Each "merely depicts structure and represents . . . functional relations between phenomena. . . . [The] validity [of each] rests upon its success in making predictions about future phenomena."[36] The ancient Herero

[35]Barnett, The Universe, p. 117.
[36]McKenzie, Achievements of Science, I, 190.

myth which designates north as "death's region" helps Enzian to realize that the Rocket took its final shape at Nordhausen (GR, p. 322). Myth reveals a design in events that endures, even though the particulars do not: the "form of reality" persists even though the "content" changes. The narrator speculates, for example, that the Zone might supplant Spring Equinox festivals with the celebration of Wernher von Braun's birthday, which falls on nearly the same day: "the same German impulse that once rolled flower-boats through the towns and staged mock battles between young Spring and deathwhite old Winter will be erecting strange floral towers out in the clearings and meadows, and the young scientist-surrogate will be going round and round with old Gravity or some such buffoon, and the children will be tickled, and laugh" (GR, p. 361).

An overriding process that reveals itself in myriad, shifting signs and various coordinate systems is frequently suggested in *Gravity's Rainbow.* Even if it exists, though, it cannot be isolated and explained by means of language; to try for such precision is to fall into "the insanely, endlessly diddling play of a chemist whose molecules are words" (GR, p. 391). And yet linguistic combinations, like chemical reactions, can reflect the process in conforming to it. Enzian thinks, "There may be no gods, but there is a pattern: names by themselves have no magic, but the *act* of naming, the physical utterance, obeys the pattern" (GR, p. 322). One cannot "name" the pattern, but one can reveal or embody its form in the act of naming. This is similar to Wittgenstein's point that a sentence can represent but not "say" the "form of reality." The names work not by precise, objective reference but by a sort of parallelism, "a sympathetic magic, a repetition high and low of some prevailing form" which they can never directly articulate (GR, p. 232). Pynchon characters from Dennis Flange through Fausto Maijstral, Oedipa Maas, and Enzian have always had to settle for this "truth of a true lie." Pynchon has settled for it, too. He writes fiction.

*Assertion Through
Structure*

Because uncertainty is inescapable, Pynchon views fictional versions of reality as deficient, or even dangerous, but necessary. He mocks characters who fail to accept their perceptions and beliefs provisionally, and yet he ultimately sanctions the attempt to "project a world." In writing a story or a novel, he is himself projecting a world, although he is a more self-conscious artificer than his characters. He weaves together plots in which his characters weave together plots; their endeavors comment on the problems and possibilities of his own. Pynchon's fiction is his own model of the world and the cosmos, revealed through his methods as well as his materials. Uncertainty, for example, is not just a theme: it is also a technique, or rather an ultimate effect that Pynchon achieves through all of his fictional techniques.

Fact as Fiction; Reader as Character

A favorite stratagem is to build a weird story that strains the reader's "willing suspension of disbelief," but to build it around a real phenomenon, an actual scientific experiment, or a verifiable bit of history that itself seems weirder than the fiction. As a result, the surreal proves real, and the real becomes surreal. Pynchon first plays this trick in "Mortality and Mercy in Vienna," and he keeps playing it through *Gravity's Rainbow*. In "Mortality," the Windigo psychosis is real—so real that Siegel had learned about it in college. Maxwell's demon is the brainchild not of the loony Nefastis but of a great scientist. Many of the presumably fictitious elements in

Pynchon are scarcely less credible than actual events or facts. As Christopher Ricks observes, "Mr. Pynchon has a remarkable talent for exploiting the fact that fiction is stranger if possibly truth."[1]

Thus the disquieting or even sinister uncertainty experienced by the characters extends to envelop the reader. The reader then tries to corroborate his sense of reality, or at least to orient himself within the fictional world, by finding some meaningful pattern in events. In this way, Pynchon makes the reader imitate the protagonist and live through a similar epistemological ordeal. For example, Pynchon skillfully arranges his materials to display correspondences between Stencil's historical episodes, especially the sieges, and the escapades of the Whole Sick Crew. But he does not draw the pattern tightly at all; rather he leaves it to Herbert Stencil — and to his readers — to make the connections. Tony Tanner, for example, has concluded that "the juxtaposition of the historical and the personal dimensions is vital" because the novel seeks to explore "what common process" links the lethargy and dementia of individuals with "remote imperialist incidents . . . contemporary automation, tourism, Hitler, and the Whole Sick Crew."[2] And R. W. B. Lewis infers that "the lady V. and her career enact in far-reaching historical terms the sickness with which the crew is afflicted."[3] These critics are correct, and yet they mimic Herbert Stencil in their very attempts to uncover a pattern of correspondences between V.'s career and the "subplots."

Pynchon continues this ploy without the aid of subplots in *The Crying of Lot 49.* Unlike Remedios Varo's captive maidens, he weaves into his fabulous tapestry bits and pieces of the "real" world, such as Maxwell's demon, which seem on first glance more bizarre than the inventions. Most of the postal service history is accurate, and Pierce Inverarity appears to be a "compound of a quite famous, real-life stamp collector named Pierce, and of the fact that if you should go to Mr. Pierce for the kind of flawed and peculiar stamps so important in *The Crying*

[1]Christopher Ricks, "Voluminous," *New Statesman* 66 (11 October 1963), 492.

[2]Tony Tanner, *City of Words: American Fiction, 1950–1970* (New York: Harper and Row, 1971), pp. 159, 158.

[3]R. W. B. Lewis, *Trials of the Word: Essays in American Literature and the Humanities* (New Haven: Yale University Press, 1965), p. 229.

of *Lot 49* you would ask him for an 'inverse rarity.' "[4] Cases
have been made for a number of other plausible meanings
behind the name. Like a microcosmic Tristero, it can apparently
support a variety of interpretations.

The reader rarely brings a knowledge of all such bits of
actuality to his first reading; rather he stumbles upon them
accidentally, while reading unrelated material, much as
Oedipa stumbles on her clues, and this reinforces his suspicion,
as it does hers, of a hidden network that intends to communicate
and yet hides beneath the surface. Paradoxically, recognition of
such real materials heightens the reader's sense of the novel's
unreality, its artifice; Pynchon's verbal tapestry announces
itself as a fiction, a fabrication, an intellectual game on the
writer's part, a self-contained world with self-reflecting parts, a
San Narciso (and a better formed one).

Yet the self-reflecting patterns somehow recall the patterns
of this world and bring the reader back out of the fiction to
contemplate public concerns such as the contemporary
sociological problems Pynchon broaches. The author
interweaves the real world and his fictional one, but where
does one leave off and the other begin? We may as well ask
when observing subatomic particles where objective reality
leaves off and subjective influence begins. Pynchon's
technique is to make us always uncertain, always unable to say,
and yet to seduce us into drawing connections just as the
characters do — connections which never illuminate or exhaust
the mystery.

It is only fitting that the reader should come to mimic the
characters in this novel about the problems of reading signs,
imperfect metaphors, and dubious texts. The subject of the
book — our inevitable and always frustrated attempt to read
meanings — is the experience of the book. As Frank Kermode
writes, the work "imitates the texts of the world, and also
imitates their problematical quality,"[5] although it amplifies the
sense of mystery surrounding the problems. Like Oedipa, the
reader gets the teasing sense that something yet undiscovered

[4]Richard Poirier, "The Importance of Thomas Pynchon," in *Mindful
Pleasures: Essays on Thomas Pynchon*, ed. George Levine and David Leverenz
(Boston: Little, Brown and Co., 1976), p. 22.

[5]Frank Kermode, "Decoding the Trystero," in *Pynchon: A Collection of
Critical Essays*, ed. Edward Mendelson for Twentieth Century Views
(Englewood Cliffs, N.J.: Prentice-Hall, 1978), p. 166.

is going on by the very way the details click together. Randolph Driblette says that his version of the play, the "unique performance," would vanish if he "washed down the drain into the Pacific" (49, p. 56). He does and it does. The tiniest, seemingly most insignificant details come back to haunt in the most unexpected places. For example, Mucho whistles "I Want to Kiss Your Feet" (no doubt a takeoff on "I Want to Hold Your Hand") as Oedipa leaves for San Narciso; the rightful Duke of Squamuglia dies when he kisses the feet of Saint Narcissus in the play.

Such a web of echoes conduces to an eerie feeling of perpetual *déjà vu*, a sense of some pattern revealing itself just beyond our conceptual horizons. In this way, *The Crying of Lot 49* is not "about" the ominous logic but rather conveys the attitudes, fears, and needs surrounding it. The book delivers not revelation but rather the *mood* of revelation, of the dawning perception that *"everything is connected, everything in the Creation,"* woven into a plot that could be miraculous or malign depending on the perceiver who partially constructs it. One feels the almost sublime terror of awareness touched by the otherworldly, forced to expand beyond its familiar scope and assimilate the knowledge that nothing is real or significant in itself: significance lies only in relations that reverberate endlessly into the distance, over the edge of perception and understanding, beyond the ability of any one mind to register them and reliably interpret their meaning.

Gravity's Rainbow plays havoc with readers who demand certainty and factual verification. Scanning the criticism, one finds a wide assortment of loosely related assertions as to why Tyrone Slothrop was given sodium amytal, how They are using him and to what purpose, what connection there is between his sexual adventures and the rocket strikes (this recalling the variety of explanations by "White Visitation" researchers), why Enzian and Blicero are building rockets (I offer mine anyway), whether Enzian goes up in his, and so on. Such questions are crucial to full understanding of the plot—Theirs or Pynchon's—but the narrator does not often give clear, unequivocal answers, such as characters or critics seek. Rather the novel, like Mexico's equations, will define a range of possibilities. It emulates the new "contingent" method of science as opposed to the old mechanistic attempt to establish cause and effect, a clear train of linkages — that is, a determinate and determinable reality.

I have argued that von Göll films blur the distinction between cause and effect, or between the fictional and the real, by seeming to create actual events through cinematic representation of them. One may counter that these films are only parts of the fiction, so Pynchon can make them do whatever he wishes. But Pynchon mixes in actual cinema, too — Fritz Lang's *Die Frau im Mond* (1929), for example — just as he mixes in actual Windigo psychoses, sorting demons, and postal monopolies. Fittingly, the real film has the same effect as the fictitious ones: to confuse the relation between fiction and reality. William Plater notes that Lang's movie stimulated the imaginations and energies of numerous young German engineers, including von Braun; it may even have influenced the body design of the A4.[6] The illusion helped call the reality into being, or accompanied it: Leni thinks, "Real flight and dreams of flight go together. Both are part of the same movement. Not A before B, but all together" (GR, p. 159). By refusing to distinguish between the actual and the imaginary, Pynchon makes the reader feel unable to distinguish what is real from what is not. Apart from films, the author intertwines real scientists like von Braun with imaginary ones like Jamf, actual companies and cartels with invented ones, genuine high-level intrigues with pure fabrications (?). The reader may be daunted by the complex patterns of relations that outstrip his powers of perception and contradict his expectations about reality. Again, he is made to feel like the character, for Pynchon's plots in their immensity and intricacy can overwhelm those who read them as well as those who people them.

Pynchon's Characterization

The mass and gravity of Pynchon's plots often work to minimize, to flatten the characters caught in them. These figures seem bizarre, grotesque. They add to the reader's sense of uncertainty in an alien world. Pynchon has been faulted more than once for not making "real" characters, but he writes

[6]William M. Plater, *The Grim Phoenix: Reconstructing Thomas Pynchon* (Bloomington: Indiana University Press, 1978), p. 104.

to undermine our complacent, familiar assumptions about reality. Why would he want to reinforce them through traditional methods of characterization? E. M. Forster defined a "real" character as one who seems explicable even if he or she has not been fully explained, but Pynchon purposely creates worlds that are inexplicable, defiantly mysterious. Thus he makes us question our powers to know and explain any world, his or ours. Explicable characters would subvert his plan and clash with all of his other fictional methods.

This does not mean that Pynchon's flat, "unreal" characters always work. Richard Poirier writes that the moral heroines of *V.*, Paola and Rachel, were not meant to be as flat as they are, but they are "presented with a satiric extravagance that puts an excessive limit on the possible development of the figures in the book." Pynchon's "comic inventions are always so active, his caricature so eager, that he cannot effectively allow his characters the seriousness and delicacy his thematic ambitions require of them."[7] Poirier may be right about Paola and Rachel, who are meant to signify the redeeming potential of the human spirit. But in other cases, the inferiority of character to thematic development might objectify the point. Pynchon sees the integrity of the individual as socially and cosmically undermined.

In *V.*, somewhat as in *Catch-22*, the forces, trends, and conditions of the twentieth century seem more real than the people, singly or collectively. Decadence, the Street, technology, bureaucracy, and paranoia overwhelm the individual, erase his personality, and grind him into insubstantiality. Although Pynchon often keeps them mysteriously vague, he chooses to focus on larger-than-life, impersonal forces, rather than on those ridiculously helpless and insignificant stage props, his characters. In "Under the Rose," for example, Porpentine was a human being with an inner life; when Pynchon revised this short story for his third chapter of *V.*, he made the spy a bizarre, depthless puppet in Stencil's "impersonations." The baroquely complex plots detract attention further from the characters. It seems that the overall pattern of related events is more important than the objects (people?) being related. And in his prose, as Poirier

[7]Richard Poirier, "Cook's Tour," *New York Review of Books* 1, no. 2 (1963), p. 32.

himself notes, Pynchon creates "a style that renders similar states of being in which separate identities can barely be located and, when they are, seem merely accidental."[8] Pynchon describes Esther's nose job with a technical virtuosity and professional detachment that exceed even the skill and detachment of Schoenmaker. For Pynchon as for Schoenmaker, Esther becomes an object on which to practice his art; she loses human significance as even the reader stops considering her feelings and becomes absorbed in the precision with which the surgeon or the writer works.[9] Pynchon could not do justice to his theme of social entropy without reducing the human figure, for "traditional character is an imagination of order and structure that belies the pervasiveness of change, variety, aimlessness, waste" — conditions that dominate the landscape of V.[10]

In the creation of Oedipa Maas, Pynchon comes closest to traditional characterization. The Crying of Lot 49 focuses consistently on her thoughts and her responses to the mystery. Yet even she can seem, to herself as well as the reader, less substantial than the suprapersonal forces and organizations that confront her. If she is not fully dimensional and realistic, it may be that on the one hand she is rather allegorical, an everypersonish seeker after knowledge of "the case," and on the other typically human, inexplicable even in her own eyes (E. M. Forster notes that actual persons cannot be as "real" as characters, if we require full understanding of psychology and motivation for a sense of reality). The other characters in the novel are more like caricatures; their inexplicability and inconsistency heighten the sense of mystery, for Oedipa and for us, and their lack of substance underscores Pynchon's point about modern decadence, the "falling-away from what is human" (V., p. 380).

In Gravity's Rainbow such methods of characterization, far from being artistic flaws, could be devices for enforcing

[8]Richard Poirier, The Performing Self: Compositions and Decompositions in the Languages of Contemporary Life (New York: Oxford University Press, 1971), p. 26.

[9]The idea was suggested by George Levine in "Risking the Moment: Anarchy and Possibility in Pynchon's Fiction," in Mindful Pleasures: Essays on Thomas Pynchon, ed. George Levine and David Leverenz (Boston: Little, Brown and Co., 1976), p. 22.

[10]Ibid., p. 123.

Pynchon's point that individuals are macerated by "thematic" forces such as entropy, routinization, and the cyclical motions of decay and regeneration, corruption and defection; such forces and motions reduce the individual to a tiny datum in mass phenomena, or they eclipse him altogether. Pynchon's concept of the self and hence his delineations of character reveal the impermanence of being. Enzian, leader of the Zone-Hereros, tells Slothrop:

> Well, I think we're here, but only in a statistical way. Something like that rock over there is just about 100% certain — it knows it's there, so does everybody else. But our own chances of being right here right now are only a little better than even — the slightest shift in the probabilities and we're gone — schnapp! like that. (*GR*, p. 362)

The self is unfixed, insubstantial, contingent. It varies with the different identities one adopts like comic book roles (consider Rocketman) or even with interchangeable material possessions (recall Mucho's car owners). Often individuals lose their definitions entirely as they blend into bizarre and, for all practical purposes, homogeneous groups. William Faulkner and Flannery O'Connor created human grotesques; Pynchon more typically creates bands or associations like Marvy's Mothers, the *Anubis* party, or the homosexual inmates who fabricate their own prison camp after being liberated. Weird proto-individuals or groups can suddenly materialize or disappear without warning, a device that Pynchon exploits to enhance the air of sinister unpredictability and imminence in his novels. Alfred Kazin's remark about *V.* applies even better to *Gravity's Rainbow*: "What is also striking . . . is the proliferation of dummy characters who come up from anywhere and may be anything."[11]

The simpler characters recall comic book figures. Even those who don't dissolve into a group or assume different guises have ridiculous names that "often suggest specific attitudes or ideas," as Charles Harris notes. With the use of "two-dimensional, 'comic strip' characters . . . normal processes of life and death, not to mention of pain and sorrow, are temporarily suspended" — as they would be, for example, in a Roadrunner cartoon. Such disengagement accounts for

[11] Alfred Kazin, *Bright Book of Life: American Novelists and Storytellers from Hemingway to Mailer* (Boston: Little, Brown and Co., 1973), p. 277.

much of the "black humor" in this and other contemporary American novels: "Often we find ourselves laughing at the various cruel and violent events that fill their pages."[12] But Pynchon will also shift suddenly back to "real" history or straightforward depiction of horrors to prevent his reader from settling to rest in this or any other perspective on events.

Even a more developed character such as Franz Pökler comes to the reader not so much as a person with a solid form but as a locus of emotions — guilt, fear, timidity — refracted as they pass through remembered or fantasized events. Such characters are no more integrally cohesive or ontologically sound for being complex. Joseph Slade notes that in Pynchon the self is "predicated on shifting multiple states of consciousness, endlessly fluctuating, as if frames of film were sprocketing through a field of view."[13]

Critics like Harris and Raymond Olderman are correct in pointing out that this "two-dimensional characterization is used specifically to prevent sympathetic identification with a character's tortured pursuit of a unified identity."[14] Pynchon, like many other post-1950s writers, has shifted the focus of his novel away from the individual's search for authenticity or quest for existential self-creation and has fixed it on the larger social or cosmic forces within whose confines the reduced characters try to move. Consequently, Gravity's Rainbow seems at times like a gargantuan X-rated comic book filled with puny forms randomly colliding like subatomic particles — two-dimensional figures racing about chaotically against a four-dimensional backdrop. The third dimension, home of traditional representational art, the middle ground, has been dropped.

Tony Tanner puts the argument quite well in talking about the contemporary American novel in general:

> There is a feeling that the true reality is whatever it is that works through the characters and conventions of the social foreground; an evil waiting in the land, the attractions of occult power, the

---

[12]Charles B. Harris, Contemporary American Novelists of the Absurd (New Haven, Conn.: College and University Press, 1971), pp. 26, 27, 28.

[13]Joseph W. Slade, "Escaping Rationalization: Options for the Self in Gravity's Rainbow," Critique 18, no. 3 (1977), p. 28.

[14]Raymond M. Olderman, Beyond the Wasteland: A Study of the American Novel in the Nineteen-Sixties (New Haven, Conn.: Yale University Press, 1972), p. 16.

coming triumph of entropy. Reality is ultimately made up of
those mysterious forces which are so vast, so elemental, and
perhaps so timeless, that any prolonged sense of them, or quest
for them, inevitably has a reductive effect on the human image,
and for some writers a trivializing one. It can make man appear
such a futile and pathetic speck, participating in such
desperately transient episodes, that some writers now avail
themselves of formal devices like the cartoon-strip to project
their vision. It is an appropriate form for a fiction which does not
consider the presence and appearance of people to constitute a
primary level of reality.[15]

Such changes in characterization may correspond to changes
in the conception of physical reality: Sir William Dampier
observes that "the hard, massy, ultimate particles of Lucretius
and Newton have been resolved into complex systems of
protons and whirling electrons, non-material, perhaps only to
be represented by wave-equations. . . . in the light of relativity,
matter has ceased to be something which persists in time and
moves in space, and has become a mere system of interrelated
events."[16] No longer "hard, massy, ultimate particles," the
characters — the matter of fiction — may seem less like whole,
comprehensible, and consistent entities than like brief
"interrelated events" or quanta of energy in undetermined flux.
Sometimes, as with Nora Dodson-Truck (GR, p. 149), Pynchon
presents the energy — the thought, action, or sensation — before
identifying the matter.

Wylie Sypher could be a representative Pynchon character
indicting his author when he says: "Our *situation* — the
field in which our experiences happen to us, if they be our
experiences at all — seems to be more actual than the self on
which these experiences are imposed."[17] Commenting on a
Robert Musil character, he could be referring to Tyrone
Slothrop: "the value of his actions depends not upon himself
but upon 'the whole complex to which they belonged.'" Each
figure does not *live* so much as he "belongs to a system of
relationships where everything that happens is a symbol for
other happenings to be felt only as they bear upon still more
remote happenings." His life "is merely a function dependent

[15]Tanner, *City of Words*, p. 151.
[16]Sir William Dampier, *A History of Science and Its Relations with
Philosophy and Religion* (New York: Macmillan, 1936), p. 216.
[17]Wylie Sypher, *Loss of the Self in Modern Literature and Art* (New York:
Random House, 1962), p. 67.

on other functions whose significance levels off into distances and circumstances quite beyond his comprehension or [finally] concern." He becomes "a trivial item in some vast equation of forces" that tend "to run down into an average condition, a compromise, and inertia."[18]

Pynchon's Fictional Worlds: Symbols of Multiplicity

Pynchon's techniques for handling context are also important means of creating uncertainty. The human figure is trivialized by an equation of forces that is vast and complex not only because of the magnitudes involved but also because there are so few constants and so many variables. For example, a character trying to solve the equation can see an object or event as symbolic—"hieroglyphic," as Oedipa thinks. But instead of signifying one consistent meaning, the symbol can have an indefinite range of meanings; these vary with its relation to other objects or events in the changing field and with the shifting vantage point of the diminished human observer. Dennis Flange sees the dump first as a symbol of proliferating waste and entropy. But then even more unsettlingly, the bizarre image begins to assume symbolic relevance to his own life:

> Whenever he was away from Cindy and could think he would picture his life as a surface in the process of change, much as the floor of the dump was in transition: from concavity or inclosure to perhaps a flatness like the one he stood in now. What he worried about was any eventual convexity, a shrinking, it might be, of the planet itself to some palpable curvature of whatever he would be standing on, so that he would be left sticking out like a projected radius, unsheltered and reeling across the empty lunes of his tiny sphere. (L, p. 96)

In addition to this fetal nightmare of isolation and exposure, Flange is "haunted" by other "correspondences" that lead to more pleasant visions. For him,

> any arrival at sea level was like finding a minimum and dimensionless point, a unique crossing of parallel and meridian, an assurance of perfect, passionless uniformity; just as in the spiraling descent of Rocco's truck he had felt that this spot at which they finally came to rest was the dead center, the single point which implied an entire low country. (L, p. 96)

[18]Ibid., p. 71.

Because of this "weird irrational association," the dump becomes for Flange a sort of surrogate sea as well as an emblem for the condition of his life and a symbol of what Fausto Maijstral calls the "slow apocalypse." Like other dominant metaphors in Pynchon, the dump begins to appear not so much as a symbol of something in particular but rather as a symbolic potential that can support a variety of meanings, much as a Bohr atom with its different electron shells can form a wide variety of chemical bonds.

Similarly, V. gives rise to multiple interpretations, even concerning Pynchon's choice of letter. As noted in chapter 3, the "Right and Left; the hothouse and the street" intersect in her and form her initial, but not so as to encompass any Golden Mean (*V.*, p. 440). The V-shape, like the waterspout at the end of the novel, suggests entropy: when gas is emitted from a nozzle, diffusion of the molecules increases with distance and time. The first V. reference in the book raises a number of possibilities, all of which fit the major themes of urban blight, apocalypse, decadence, dispersal, and distorted perception: "overhead, turning everybody's face green and ugly, shone mercury-vapor lamps, receding in an asymmetric V to the east where it's dark and there are no more bars" (*V.*, p. 2). V. becomes a "remarkably scattered concept," even in the mind of the single observer, because that observer can adopt an unlimited number of viewpoints. And as Sidney Stencil notes, the Situation observed becomes more varied and complex with each new observer.

The Tristero, therefore, has more than one face or symbolic valence. Just as the question of its objective existence becomes unanswerable, so does the question of its objective value. At times it looks like anonymous and malignant magic, especially when Oedipa's contacts mysteriously begin to disappear. *The Courier's Tragedy* presents the Tristero as a kind of evil, superhuman scourge that destroys lines of communication and also kills the good Niccoló, leaving his remains "in a condition too awful to talk about" (*49*, p. 51). Yet the Tristero also appears as a salvation, a counterforce, an alternative to the "lies, recitations of routine, arid betrayals of spiritual poverty" that the disaffected are saving "for the official government delivery system" (*49*, p. 128). If it were to prove a real means of communicating and of recycling human "waste," it could counter social entropy.

But one cannot conclude that the Tristero *is* positive, that positivity inheres as an integral and objective part of its makeup. It only appears so in the context of the novel and the setting of San Narciso. It is something like Stencil's V., a potential or force, "its particular shape governed only by the surface accidents of history at the time" (*V.,* p. 141). In Wharfinger's day, one invoked "the protection of God and Saint Narcissus" against it (49, p. 50); in Oedipa's day, one sees it as a possible antidote to narcissism (see, for example, the opening paragraph of the novel's third chapter). To a certain age and point of view, it represented death, destruction, and chaos — a "blind, automatic anti-God" (49, p. 124); to another, it becomes an emblem for miracles, sacred communication, and regeneration. Even within the same era, it has different and seemingly irreconcilable meanings. It compels Oedipa to consider the fate of others, and yet the posthorn is also the symbol of the Inamorati Anonymous, who isolate themselves. The Tristero not only recalls Stencil's V. and Dennis Flange's dump, it anticipates the Rocket in *Gravity's Rainbow*. All can sustain a wide range of symbolic interpretation. Richard Kostelanetz's words on *V.* apply here: "Pynchon's special achievement . . . is devising a symbol for metaphysical reality that suggests not ambiguity as, say, *Moby Dick* does, but unbounded multiplicity."[19] *The Crying of Lot 49*, with its two-dimensional characters, label names, and quest motif, is like an allegory in which the significance of characters and events is partially hidden and totally mutable, dependent on shifting relations and perspectives.

The Rocket also inspires an "unbounded multiplicity" of interpretations by characters and readers as well. To Blicero it is a means of transcendence, to the Hereros an ultimate destiny (as to which destiny the Hereros themselves cannot agree), to Katje a "clear allusion" to the world's death-lust, to Pökler a quasi-erotic subjugation, to Thanatz a "baby Jesus" with Weberian charisma, to Pointsman a means for establishing behavioral theory, to Mexico a confirmation of the statistical method, to Tchitcherine a sign of the post-war cartelized state, to Slothrop a key to understanding "his own assembly — perhaps, heavily paranoid voices have whispered, *his time's*

---

[19]Richard Kostelanetz, "The Point Is That Life Doesn't Have Any Point," *New York Times Book Review*, 6 June 1965, p. 3.

assembly" (GR, p. 738). What is the Rocket to Pynchon? No single answer will suffice. The narrator, our best facsimile of the author, says that

> the Rocket has to be many things, it must answer to a number of different shapes in the dreams of those who touch it—in combat, in tunnel, on paper—it must survive heresies shining, unconfoundable . . . and heretics there will be: Gnostics who have been taken in a rush of wind and fire to chambers of the Rocket-throne . . . Kabbalists who study the Rocket as Torah, letter by letter—rivets, burner cup and brass rose, its text is theirs to permute and combine into new revelations, always unfolding . . . Manichaeans who see two Rockets, good and evil, who speak together in the sacred idiolalia of the Primal Twins (some say their names are Enzian and Blicero) of a good Rocket to take us to the stars, an evil Rocket for the World's suicide, the two perpetually in struggle.
>
> But these heretics will be sought and the dominion of silence will enlarge as each one goes down . . . they will *all* be sought out. Each will have his personal Rocket. (GR, p. 727)

The Rocket is symbolic to the narrator himself; obviously he does not mean one literal missile per person. But what does it symbolize? Each new interpretation becomes a heresy, perhaps not because it is *wrong* but because it is only partial—because it tries to define the indefinite, reduce the unlimited possibilities to one, even "with the chances . . . so good for diversity" (49, p. 136). Something unreachable, unrevealed by any one statement, survives. In critical readings, too, "excluded middles" are "bad shit, to be avoided." Pynchon's uses of symbolism promote uncertainty. As Mark Siegel writes, the author "is purposely undercutting the reader's attempts to confirm a positivistic fictional world in which choices must either be one or zero."[20]

This handling of symbolism derives from the author's epistemology. Because the nature of reality depends on the vantage point of the viewer, because the "magic" is in the *act* of naming, not in the names, and because one can apply an indefinite number of apt metaphors to any one object or event, the narrator and the characters show a playful, almost unrestricted ingenuity in their coinages. Any object or event in Pynchon's world, the peripheral as well as the central,

---

[20]Mark Siegel, *Pynchon: Creative Paranoia in Gravity's Rainbow* (Port Washington, N.Y.: Kennikat Press, 1978), p. 17.

will have not one meaning but the potential to support multiple meanings. For example, the double "S" shape of the Mittelwerke tunnels is seen as "the SS emblem." It could be the double integral used in rocket engineering "to find volumes under surfaces whose equations were known — masses, moments, centers of gravity," or more commonly "to operate on a rate of change so that time falls away: change is still." It "may be the ancient rune that stands for the yew tree, or Death." It also suggests, "the shape of lovers curled asleep" (GR, pp. 300, 301, 302).

Since the novel draws connections between fascism, mathematical analysis, death, and love, a common resonance binds the interpretations of the double "S". In addition, each reveals something of the meaning of the underground rocket factory; each could be as "correct" as any other. The superimposing of multiple interpretations could suggest an overarching Process, just as stringing together the terms of a power series could suggest the "tremendous and secret Function" which cannot be named or perceived directly (GR, p. 590). But the non-mystic observer with a finite "temporal bandwidth" can sense the Function or the Process only mediately — as it appears from the limited perspective he holds at any given moment, as it organizes elements of "reality" that are perceptible from his peculiar vantage point.

Perception of the Process will never by complete or unified, for the endless possible perspectives can never be exhausted or held simultaneously. The mediating elements of "reality" that conform to the Process are not set symbols of some definable thing; they are bases for as many acts of symbol making as there are viewpoints. A character or a reader perceives V., the Tristero, the double S, or the Rocket in much the same way as a stargazer perceives a constellation. The configuration of each depends on one's position. From another solar system, a familiar grouping of stars would fall into different patterns, or perhaps its members would appear totally unrelated. But from our own system, they *are* related. Even though figments of perspective, the constellations that take shape from any given place define reality there by establishing relative positions, by embodying or tracing the Process as it manifests itself at that particular vantage point. Faced with boundless possibilities, Pynchon says, we have no choice but to navigate by our tentative impressions and symbolic readings of the world. We

can guard ourselves a little by accepting them provisionally—
by remembering how terribly partial, arbitrary, and dependent
on viewpoint they are.

Perspective: Voice and Point of View

For an author with an epistemology such as Pynchon's, point
of view becomes the crucial narrative technique; it creates as
well as conveys whatever meanings the fiction has, and it
ensures that they will be multiple—potentially inexhaustible—
for there are infinite points of view possible for even one
Situation. The meanings derived from the various points of
view are all uncertain, their transmissions unreliable. If reality
and its symbolic representations vary with position, and if the
act of metaphor is "a thrust at truth and a lie, depending where
you were," then all depends on knowing where you are—
that is, what your relative position or point of view is. The
characters rarely know, and Pynchon manipulates point of
view so that the reader may experience similar confusion. He
plays this trick in his first story. Siegel listens to one girl
rambling on about her problems, "laying bare. . . . the anatomy
of a disease more serious than he had suspected. . . . that
heightened hysterical edginess of the sort of nightmare it is
possible to have where your eyes are open and everything in
the scene is familiar" (MMV, p. 205). As in so much of
Pynchon, ambiguity dominates. "Hysterical" could refer to
the girl's tendencies or to Siegel's, already so termed by the
narrator; moreover, the switch to second person is puzzling,
although again characteristic of the author's technique. Which
person is neurotic and which is having the waking nightmare?
As in the novels, especially *Gravity's Rainbow*, individuating
contours melt away.

   In *V.*, Pynchon manipulates narrative structure, giving
Stencil alone a cluster of fragmentary points of view to suggest
both the diversity of possible perspectives and the limitations
of any given one. As Richard Patteson comments, Pynchon
also "underscores the difficulty of piecing together historical
truth and of separating it from the purely subjective."[21] By
fragmenting "Under the Rose" into the eight impersonations

[21]Richard Patteson, "What Stencil Knew: Structure and Certitude in
Pynchon's *V.*," *Critique* 16, no. 2 (1974), 32.

of chapter three, Pynchon represents not only the multiplicity of reality but also its inaccessibility, except as personal reconstruction. For his eighth impersonation, Stencil dons the third person objective, showing that it, like the third person Stencil, is only one of a repertoire of possible perspectives — not the last word. In fact, his whole tale of Florence in chapter seven is an impersonation of the third person omniscient, and so it undercuts any notion of the authoritative vantage point and definitive account.

"Mondaugen's Story" illustrates another quirk of perspective: there are multiple points of view, as in chapters three and seven, but they now lie inside rather than beside one another. Stencil relates to Eigenvalue his version of Mondaugen's version of Foppl's version of the past. One has here what might be called unreliability to the nth power, for insofar as we can believe Stencil, Mondaugen ("moon eyes") is subject to sickness, delirium, voyeurism, and self-questioning. Nor is Foppl without his aberrations. Patteson remarks, "Chapters Three and Seven question whether a Situation can be known by piecing together various accounts of it; Mondaugen's story questions the validity of those accounts themselves."[22] Similar problems beset chapter fourteen, "V. in Love," which Stencil either impersonates or "Stencilizes" from strange sources. Perhaps Stencil even sublimates his own compulsions by inventing the scene in which Melanie and V. multiply themselves in the mirror so as to become voyeurs of their own activity. Certainly their reported behavior reflects his trick in chapter three of multiplying himself into various observers of V. These allow him to stand back and be an observer of his own pursuit, to experience the voyeur's titillating frustration at approaching and avoiding. We never know what or how much Stencil spins.

Pynchon takes on a third person omniscient voice of his own in the last two chapters of the book to provide us with "knowledge" not available to Stencil. For example, Patteson says, the narrator reveals what Stencil can never know — the "absurdly accidental, ridiculously random way" in which his father died.[23] Indeed, many critics see the sudden waterspout as an emblem for both the gratuitous dangers man faces and the

[22]Ibid., p. 36.   [23]Ibid., p. 43.

patternless, chaotic reality that belies his paranoid belief in organized plots; as such, it would refute Stencil's notion of a master conspiracy. But this may oversimplify. As noted, a random universe does not preclude conscious or unconscious human plots to serve death and decadence. Also, the omniscient point of view continues to call itself into question: the author teases his readers by leaving them with another disastrous V shape, a remarkable coincidence meant to seem uncanny and minatory, intended to prolong doubt, tension, and irresolution. Moreover, the ostentatiously rational and mathematical language of the last paragraph cannot explain away these uncertainties; consequently it points up the insufficiency of our modes of knowledge, reveals the unsettling and unsettled schism between seen and unseen. The language, tool of discovery and communication, is the language of "surface phenomena," and like the whitecaps and kelp islands that close over the sunken ship, it shows "nothing at all of what came to lie beneath, that quiet June day" (*V.*, p. 463). The novel ends not with a clear resolution of the pattern/chaos question but with a symbol of provocative obscurity.

The very presence of a third person omniscient narrator assumes that possibility of knowledge which the book undercuts. Stencil's impersonations of it and the language of the conclusion show it as another imperfect viewpoint on the Situation. This raises the problem of Pynchon's third person narration in general. In his novels, each built around an epistemological dilemma, an authoritative voice will suddenly come out of nowhere, as it does in *V.*, for example, to remark upon the ridiculousness of the "Bird lives" cult. When the reader first meets Stencil, such a narrator speculates on the character's conversation with a woman named Margravine di Chiave Lowenstein: "Perhaps they may have felt like the last two gods—the last inhabitants—of a watery earth; or perhaps—but it would be unfair to infer. Whatever the reason, the scene played as follows: . . ." (*V.*, p. 42). This raises some questions. Who is speaking? How has he acquired the knowledge that he implicitly opposes to inference? And why is it unfair to infer, when Stencil makes an occupation of it? The statement reveals a perspective and a set of values distinct from the characters', but does it ever reappear in the same form?

Another voice, less scrupulous about invading Stencil's

mind, seems to take over the narration of "V. in Love" midway
through the chapter, although it is sometimes hard to tell
because Stencil habitually refers to himself in the third person.
Nonetheless, it is unlikely that he would say: "If we've not
already guessed, 'the woman' is, again, the lady V. of Stencil's
mad time-search. . . . Herbert Stencil was willing to let the key
to his conspiracy have a few of the human passions" (V., p.
382). A few pages later, whoever it is quips, "Stencil even
departed from his usual ploddings to daydream a vision of her
now, at age seventy-six. . . . Stencil on occasion could have as
vile a mind as any of the Crew" (V., pp. 386–87).

Such intrusions suggest that Stencil the impersonator is
the impersonation of someone who is himself multiple. The
boundaries between different voices and perspectives blur
to make the reader doubtful of any single one. These many
confusions in point of view between impersonators and
impersonations happen as suddenly and mysteriously as the
eruption of the waterspout, but again the reader gets the
feeling, never quite ratified, that some all-encompassing
consciousness stands just behind the shifting surface
phenomena, just beyond his ability to assimilate all the clues.
The narrator(s), then, are each "changeful" and incomplete, as
are the realities and symbolic representations that take shape
from their multiple perspectives.

The very act of fiction implies a point of view, but Pynchon
shows his ambivalence about fiction in The Crying of Lot 49, as
he does in V., by robbing point of view of its integrity and the
reader of basic certainties. Here point of view shifts even when
the narrator seems to remain the same person. The novel
focuses on a single figure, but hardly from a single vantage
point. For example, the novel opens:

> One summer afternoon Mrs. Oedipa Maas came home from a
> Tupperware party whose hostess had put perhaps too much
> kirsch in the fondue to find that she, Oedipa, had been named
> executor, or she supposed executrix, of the estate of one Pierce
> Inverarity, a California real estate mogul who had once lost
> two million dollars in his spare time but still had assets
> numerous and tangled enough to make the job of sorting it
> all out more than honorary. (49, p. 1)

The sentence begins with a deliberately vague phrase; the
indefinite time may recall a fairy tale or perhaps the openings

of "The Metamorphosis" and *The Trial*. But from this
purposely generalized, dim, never-never-landish start, things
get very particular and specific: witness the complexity and
the tripping, painstaking self-qualification of the rest of the
sentence. The narrative stylistically anticipates Oedipa's
vacillation between the aerial and insect view. The camera has
zoomed from a long shot with a wide-angle setting to a high
shutter speed close-up, leaving the reader without much sense
of stable perspective.

By exploiting such rhetorical distancing and zooming
tactics, Pynchon forces the reader to alternate between what
Wayne Booth calls an identification of reader and character and
a collusion of author and reader behind the character's back;
the reader can so shift from sympathy to irony and back again.
This is not the least subtle of the book's ambiguities. At times,
as in the opening sentence, the reader senses that he is seeing
things through a shaping consciousness very different from
Oedipa's: it orders perceptions and clauses hypotactically, as a
tipsy housewife probably would not. That consciousness, by
virtue of the style in which it expresses itself, often sounds
better informed than Oedipa, and condescending to her.

But sometimes, especially later in the novel, the reader is
made to identify with Oedipa by being made to share her
vantage point and her confused attempt to make sense out of
things. The rhetoric of this situation appears even early in the
novel. Following the first sentence:

> Oedipa stood in the living room, stared at by the greenish
> dead eye of the TV tube, spoke the name of God, tried to feel as
> drunk as possible. But this did not work. She thought of a
> hotel room in Mazatlán whose door had just been slammed, it
> seemed forever, waking up two hundred birds down in the
> lobby; a sunrise over the library slope at Cornell University
> that nobody out on it had seen because the slope faces west; a
> dry, disconsolate tune from the fourth movement of the Bartók
> Concerto for Orchestra; a whitewashed bust of Jay Gould that
> Pierce kept over the bed on a shelf so narrow for it she'd
> always had the hovering fear it would someday topple on
> them. (49, pp. 1–2)

In the second sentence of the novel, the narrator simulates the
protagonist's view of events. The actions are coordinated and
therefore given approximately equal weight, as they probably
are by the inebriated Oedipa, who simply registers one

sensation as it follows the other without organizing or valuing them. The fourth sentence, recounting Oedipa's memories, follows the same pattern: a list, a coordinate series, bonded by associational rather than logical connections, not ordered according to any apparent rational scheme or overview.

Through such rhetorical devices, Pynchon forces the reader to switch back and forth from outside to inside, and perhaps to lose sense of where the interface between them is. In Stanley Fish's terms, the "experience" of the passage is the meaning of the passage. This opening paragraph then, may mean that the reader is unable to get a consistent, definitive viewpoint on events. Fish's affective stylistics provide an interesting approach to the novel because the method enacts the subject: the developing responses of a person who tries to decipher a coded pattern that reveals itself progressively, temporally —a pattern whose meaning is finally inseparable from the subjective experience of it. The method also demonstrates that Pynchon can use prose style quite skillfully as a function of point of view, promoting sympathetic identification as well as ironic detachment. Here the narrator evokes in the reader Oedipa's experience of her day:

> Through the rest of the afternoon, through her trip to the market in downtown Kinneret-Among-The-Pines to buy ricotta and listen to the Muzak (today she came through the bead-curtained entrance around bar 4 of the Fort Wayne Settecento Ensemble's variorum recording of the Vivaldi Kazoo Concerto, Boyd Beaver soloist); then through the sunned gathering of her marjoram and sweet basil from the herb garden, reading of book reviews in the latest *Scientific American*, into the layering of a lasagna, garlicking of a bread, tearing up of romaine leaves, eventually, oven on, into the mixing of the twilight's whiskey sours against the arrival of her husband, Wendell ("Mucho") Maas from work, she wondered, wondered, shuffling back through a fat deckful of days which seemed (wouldn't she be first to admit it?) more or less identical, or all pointing the same way subtly like a conjurer's deck, any odd one readily clear to a trained eye. (49, p. 2)

The sentence makes the reader accompany Oedipa through a rhythm of routine action disrupted by a bit of suburban grotesquerie, action that is inconclusive, incomplete, or at least not expressed in complete clauses; he may be lulled, as perhaps Oedipa is, into forgetting that these fragments *should* add up to some coherent whole, but he feels a vague, almost subliminal suspense and dissatisfaction because of grammatical incompletion, just as she might from personal unfulfillment. The completing statement, when it comes, is "she wondered." She wonders without a precisely defined grammatical or mental object.

Aside from shifts in rhetorical attitude, the very presence of some statements may disturb the reader. At times, as in *V.*, a clearly separate omniscient narrator will intrude unexpectedly to make pronouncements: "If she'd thought to check a couple lines back in the Wharfinger play, Oedipa might have made the next connection by herself." Or "Your gynecologist has no test for what she was pregnant with" (49, pp. 68, 131). More typically, though, the all-knowing consciousness is not separable but suffused into the texture of the events or the prose, where it hovers malevolently. The punctured spray can seems to know where it is going, and Mucho does — as Oedipa suspects — "somehow" know about her affair with Metzger (49, p. 29). When she laughs out loud and helpless at her image of Inverarity's death, one reads: "You're sick, Oedipa, she told herself, or the room, which knew" (49, p. 2). But who says it knew? No quotation marks sort out her speech and thoughts from the editorial comments. The reader senses an ominous and omniscient presence but cannot tell if Oedipa is projecting it, enveloped by it, or a bit of both.

This uncertainty about who is knowing or speaking what pervades the book. Dr. Hilarius is full of "delightful lapses from orthodoxy," and then the narrative proceeds with a more attention-grabbing account of same, but the question remains — and unsettles when one realizes how easily one missed the hint of another consciousness — delightful *to whom?* Probably not to the distrustful Oedipa. Many other key lines break down into similar uncertainty on close inspection. At the end of the novel the men in the auction room, wearing black like Driblette's Tristero, "watched her come in, trying each to conceal his thoughts" (49, pp. 137–38). Is this Oedipa's version or someone else's? Are we viewing from the inside out or the outside in?

The subsequent description of crier Passerine notes "his eyes bright, his smile practiced and relentless" (49, p. 138). This recalls Oedipa's first view of Metzger, whose "enormous eyes, lambent . . . smiled out at her wickedly," and her image of the Tristero incarnate, whose "luminous stare locked to [hers], smile gone malign and pitiless" (49, pp. 16, 36). Other elements of the description tie the crier to the theme of imminent, awful, Pentecostal revelation. It would help immeasurably to crack the "mystery" of the book if one knew whether these impressions belonged to a paranoid Oedipa or an omniscient narrator, but the passage offers no help, only more confusions; it slides back and forth between these possibly subjective, unreliable descriptions of Passerine and objective accounts of Oedipa's movements. Speaking of Pynchon in general, Alfred Kazin makes a point relevant here: "the ambiguity of who-is-thinking-what gives the uncertainty an added touch of the sinister."[24]

The Narrator of Gravity's Rainbow

Gravity's Rainbow includes all of the above techniques to make point of view problematic and to disorient the reader. The perspectives become highly mobile and endlessly multiple as the narrator bounces back and forth between different coordinate systems so suddenly and irregularly that the reader cannot predict or even expect what might come next. He must adopt such diverse frames of reference as those belonging to the "other side" of death, to the insects in Christ's manger, or even to a rock, whose consciousness is described by analogy with film: the "shutter" trips so rarely that "we're talking frames per century [. . .] per millennium" (GR, p. 612). Pynchon builds his novel on an unbounded range of perspectives, each promising but imperfect. Somewhat like the contemporary atomic physicist, he resorts to "complementarity" in trying to give a fuller accounting of phenomena than any one interpretation can. Physicist Percy Bridgman explains the method:

> We know that there are situations which cannot be reproduced in language, but we nevertheless are constrained to say in language what it is that language cannot do. Always we run into these self-contradictions, and always we deal with them by shifting our point of view. This shift in the point

[24]Kazin, Book of Life, p. 277.

of view is nothing more nor less than a shift to the 'complementary' aspect of the situation.[25]

From his early short stories onward, Pynchon has been pleased to juxtapose sharply jarring complements — for example, the burlesque with the exalted or the terrible. In one of the many such instances that fill *Gravity's Rainbow*, the narrator jumps from the pathos of Stephen Dodson-Truck's confession to the ribaldry of "The Penis He Thought Was His Own" (apparently sung barbershop quartet style). Numerous scenes resembling Mack Sennett comedy are played against a backdrop of ugliness, perversion, filth, or the real possibility of death and destruction. Through such complementarity, the narrator forces the reader to shift suddenly, even violently, between opposing attitudes and tones: complacency, paranoia, derision, chumminess, pontification, perplexity, morbidity, obscenity, and many more. These leave the reader no sure ground from which to respond to the fictional events.

Such tactics cause unrest even when the narrator speaks as the same person — which he does not. In *Gravity's Rainbow*, he performs more impersonations and projects more voices than Herbert Stencil ever dreamed of, although Pynchon's point here is the same: to emphasize both the infinity of possible outlooks on a situation and the incompleteness of each one. The persona quick-changes narrative points of view to disorient the reader, compelling him at once to entertain many views and yet to resist any one — compelling him to be open and yet skeptical.

The narrator accomplishes these changes because he, like Pirate Prentice, can pass into the minds of others. As in the Zone, borders are illusory. As in twentieth-century science's models of the universe, separate entities dissolve into a continuum. Perfecting a technique from "Mortality and Mercy in Vienna," Pynchon's narrator glides through the permeable characters so smoothly that sometimes the reader may not recognize the shift from third person omniscient or objective to second person, first person, or interior monologue. For example, a third person narrator describes Teddy Bloat externally and conveys the ambience of a rainy wartime

---

[25]Percy W. Bridgman, *The Way Things Are* (Cambridge, Mass.: Harvard University Press, 1959), p. 179.

London day, mentioning that the Englishman "can't feel a bit of it." But then the voice, rather inconspicuously at first, adopts British phrasing, and soon the reader is inside the character looking out. Bloat feels nothing because "he's too busy running through plausible excuses should he happen to get caught, not that he will, you know [. . . .] Out wiv the old camera then, on with the gooseneck lamp, now aim the reflector just so . . . " (GR, pp. 17, 18).

Sometimes the narrator will perform such switches within switches within switches. The chapter beginning on page ninety-two opens with Katje's being filmed (and hence with film's usual implications for epistemology and illusion). As in Mondaugen's story, there are viewpoints within viewpoints. The narrator slides, as he did with Bloat, into Katje's head and eventually to thoughts of Blicero. He describes Blicero in the third person and then slides into his head, an interior space unavailable to Katje, who is left behind. There he encounters thoughts of Gottfried, whom he describes in the third person and then enters in his customary way.

At other times, the changing narrator will not mark his trail at all. Around the bottom of page 129 or the top of page 130 (it is hard to tell), he launches on a reverie comprising meditations, personal memories, and highly subjective descriptions, all delivered in what seems like a number of different but unidentified voices. Occasionally a voice will address "your" specific and detailed dreams, recollections, or desires, but the speaker and the listener remain unknown. In some of the most surreal episodes (for example, pages 640 and following), the narrator will describe a bizarre character, enter his fantasy peopled with other bizarre characters, transfer to a fantasy of one such, and continue, as freely as if he were transferring on bus lines. The lines need never lead back to the point of departure, nor, certainly, need they intersect with the plot lines of Katje, Slothrop, Enzian, and so on; but nonetheless, they echo those plot lines with common details like Kenosha, Wisconsin and toilet passages, giving the uncanny sense of some imperceptible tie-in, some "unedifying" connectedness, in William T. Lhamon's phrase.

The protean narrator, in short, is totally unpredictable in his transformations. Moreover, he appears taken with the powers of his position and with their arbitrary exercise. Often his voice will interrupt the story to give directions for staging a scene as if it were part of a film or music hall production instead of a novel; and the outlandishness of these directions, even for their appropriate media, underscores the free contrivance of the whole narrative. The narrator seems to have no controls or limitations placed on him or on what he can do.

And yet the narrator proves limited and fallible despite his ability to adopt different points of view. At times he claims foreknowledge, makes didactic pronouncements, or presumes to arbitrate in matters of musical taste (GR, p. 441). At other times he must confess ignorance, as when Pointsman and Mexico pass out of his range, or when the question arises as to why Katje left Blicero: "We are never told why" (GR, p. 107). Who "told" him what he knows, and how can a narrator enter the head of a character in one scene and suffer him to walk out of earshot in another?

Perhaps most disturbingly, there may be a voice or voices in back of the narrator's. And if so how can we tell how many there are, who they are, or when they speak? For example, the narrator begins quite rationally to explain the various meanings behind the double S shape of the Mittelwerke tunnels. As he becomes more fanciful, someone else comments, "(the voice speaking here grows more ironic, closer to tears which are not all theatre)" (GR, p. 302). This intrusion has two effects. First, it reveals that the narrator's account is not the authoritative, objective truth but just another limited and subjectively distorted version. We wonder if any of his other statements can be more reliable. Second, the narrator's account is not the only one we hear; it does not appear in quotation marks, nor does the sudden intrusion. The border between one and the other, like so many interfaces in the novel, is totally permeable and indistinct. As a result, we can never be quite sure which voice or perspective we are getting. With such disturbing inconsistencies, the reader can never fully have faith in anything in the narrative; he can never come to rest or settle on the meaning, the definitive version. The confusing inconsistencies in the narrative voice (or voices) could on the one hand be functional, brilliant devices to trap the reader in uncertainties and in versions he must question. On the other hand, the narrator or the author himself may simply lose control of his materials in places and succumb to confusions and irresolutions of his own. The narrator develops a contradictory attitude toward Slothrop in particular, belittling this central character (more or less fondly) from the outset but then in the "Counterforce" section presenting sharply opposed views of him. Slothrop is "closer to being a spiritual medium than he's been yet," but he is also a "dunce and drifter" (GR, pp. 622, 626). He ceases being "any sort of integral creature any more" as one by one people (and the narrator) cease "trying to hold him together" (GR, p. 740). As he falls apart and scatters, so does the important subplot that centers on him, and for this the narrator seems to feel somewhat accountable:

> —There ought to be a punch line to it, but there isn't. The plan went wrong. He [Slothrop] is being broken down instead, and scattered. His tarot cards have been laid down [. . .] but they are the cards of a tanker and feeb: they point only to a long and scuffling [Ian?] future, to mediocrity (not only in his life but also, heh, heh, in his chroniclers too, yes yes nothing like getting the 3 of Pentacles upside down covering the significator on the second try to send you to the tube to watch a seventh rerun of the Takeshi and Ichizo Show, light a cigarette and try to forget the whole thing). (GR, p. 738)

The narrator has identified himself with Slothrop on several occasions. Apart from the similarity of their tarot, Slothrop's "glozing neutrality" and missed revelation remind the narrator of his own shortcomings: "is it, then, really never to find you again? Not even in your worst times of night, with pencil words on your page only Δt from the things they stand for?" (GR, p. 510). He includes himself among "the rest of us, not chosen for enlightenment," who must "go on blundering inside our front-brain faith in Kute Korrespondences" (GR, p. 590), as Slothrop in particular does. Thinking that all of the Zone's plots form "an enormous transit system," Slothrop concludes "that by riding each branch the proper distance, knowing when to transfer, keeping some state of minimum grace though it might often look like he's headed the wrong way, this network of all plots may yet carry him to freedom" (GR, p. 603). Whatever success he achieves is severely qualified. In transferring from plot to plot, character to character, fantasy to fantasy, the narrator may act on a similar hope and yet feel that he has succeeded no better than Slothrop.

Mark Siegel has compared the narrator to a court jester, not a "charismatic leader" but, "by his own account, the Fool who fulfills his courtly role as an entertainer and advisor by disguising his meanings as 'mindless pleasures.' "[26] The self-deprecation, however, is not all feigned. If, as Mark Siegel claims, "the characters are facets of the narrator,"[27] then Slothrop is a major, or perhaps the major, facet: a clever but not quite clever enough observer/quester who gives over the quest to discover the secret of his own and his time's assembly because of fear, inability to take the strain, unwillingness to make the effort. The narrator *tries* "to forget the whole thing" and absorb himself in mindless pleasures, like the seventh rerun of the Takeshi and Ichizo show, but he cannot.

One can only speculate on whether Pynchon sees himself reflected in the narrator as the narrator sees himself reflected in Slothrop. Although rumors abound that he is working on a new book, he has not published one since 1973. He may now be on the seventy-seventh rerun. Yet I would argue that the confusions, inconsistencies, and scatterings in narrative viewpoint are mainly functional — not admissions that the authorial "plan went wrong" so much as demonstrations that full, objective, and certain knowledge is impossible, that *any* plan will go wrong. The narrator often mocks and frustrates the reader's desire for clear explanation: "You will want cause and effect," he says. "All right" (GR, p. 663). He then offers an outlandishly fanciful account of a Polish undertaker who rowed out in a storm to see if he could get struck by lightning. Any reader who has held some atavistic desire for logical development of character and plot must finally give up here.

Complement, Ambivalence, and Parody

Pynchon's narrative convolutions, transformations, and deceptions are aesthetic corollaries of a new scientific conception of the world and cosmos that he tries to represent "isomorphically" in the form of his book, in the patterns of his language. The radical, experimental styles and themes of his art closely parallel the advances in scientific concepts discussed in chapter 4. Consequently, Pynchon grounds his work in uncertainty and tension between unreconciled

[26]Siegel, *Pynchon*, p. 120.
[27]Ibid., p. 42.

complements, basic ambivalences. Somewhat like the Keatsian poet, his narrators have "no identity" and practice "negative capability"; that is, they entertain many contradictory points of view, assuming each one completely and seeing the world in its terms, usually without apologies, qualifications, or attempts to reconcile it with the other viewpoints subsequently assumed. Mark Siegel notes in writing of *Gravity's Rainbow*: "The narrator's ambivalent attitude toward such things as death, structure, and mindless pleasures manifests itself in conflicting sets of characters and philosophies, each representing one part of the narrator's attitude." Each point of view "is really a part of an entire spectrum which is the 'rainbow' of possibilities encompassed by Pynchon's vision."[28]

The narrators, and perhaps the author, arrive at their own tentative views, feelings, stances, and attitudes by exploring complementary perspectives. Almost any assertion will have an opposite and equal, or nearly equal, counterpart. As $\triangle t \to 0$ for Oedipa, she has a disturbing vision "in which change had to be confronted at last for what it was, where it could no longer disguise itself as something innocuous like an average rate . . . where death dwelled in the cell though the cell be looked in on at its most quick" (49, pp. 95 – 96). As $\triangle t \to 0$ for Leni, she finds "the moment, and its possibilities," loses fear of personal consequences, and can act purposefully. As $\triangle t \to 0$ for Slothrop, his "temporal bandwidth" shrinks and he scatters, becoming unable to perceive or do much of anything. Mark Siegel adds that "the $\triangle t$, itself a symbol for a means of transcendence, becomes in its technological application a device for perpetrating the 'pornography of flight' and the fragmentation of sensibility."[29]

A profound ambivalence about order and disorder is at the core of Pynchon's fiction. Which describes the nature of reality? Pynchon exploits the paradoxical schism between macro and micro perspectives to show that we cannot make a firm 1 or 0 answer (see chapter 5). Either description is potentially valid because the nature of reality depends on perspective, but Pynchon seems deeply divided about the implications of both. Disorder, on the one hand, characterizes randomness, entropy, heat death, *anomie*, the decadent

[28]Ibid., pp. 41, 16.   [29]Ibid., p. 93.

intermingling of animate and inanimate. But on the other hand, "salvation" and freedom may lie in accident, for accident allows surprise, wonder, spontaneity, singularities; it permits creativity, the chance to find or make something new, and as Enzian thinks, the magic is in the *act* of creating, not the finished product. Squalidozzi realizes that "in the openness of the German Zone," hope and danger are "limitless" (GR, p. 265). Chaotic assemblages appear in Pynchon's work as Slothrop's desk top and Pirate's topsoil, urban waste landscapes and dumps that preserve "somewhere, among the wastes of the World, [. . .] the key that will bring us back" (GR, p. 525). Discontinuity, "the change from point to no-point," always "carries a luminosity and enigma at which something in us must leap and sing, or withdraw in fright" (GR, p. 396).

Order and continuity also mix blessing and curse. On the one hand, they characterize the "relentless rationality" of Dennis Flange's pre-dump life (L, p. 33), the prison-hothouse shared by Callisto and Aubade, Stencil's hothouse of the mind, routinization, and Their network of oppressions. But on the other hand, order and continuity describe the improbable message; the printed circuit and hieroglyphic pattern; the necessary metaphorical model of the world; the integrating, "Messianic" gravitational field; the eternally returning Ouroboros; and the soil meshes and "living genetic chains" that flout Death by "assertion-through-structure" (GR, p. 10).

As a result of this fundamental ambivalence, nearly everything in the fiction becomes Janus-faced — especially attempts to discover, create, or describe some order in events. Paranoia, although better than anti-paranoia, is often denigrated. It resembles the Puritan mentality and the sequential, cause and effect mode of explanation, both of which Pynchon rejects. He characteristically attacks the Western habit of making systems that reduce variety and randomness to mechanical regularity and certainty. Also, paranoia is self-centered. Pynchon seems to believe that "*everything is connected*," but simultaneously and without center. Paranoia thus misrepresents the temporal and spatial structure of the world and cosmos. It lends an incomplete vision, marking only the "onset" of the mystic vision. Unlike the paranoid, the mystic can see a universe that embodies an infinity of discrete particles and moments, that belies systems of organization, and yet is "blindingly One." The mystic seems able somehow to comprehend the pattern all together and at once, not step by step as the paranoid must. Only the mystic attains thereby a vision of wholeness and binding love; only the mystic can sense gravity's rainbow beyond the parabolic V-2 flight, the serpent beyond the aromatic benzene ring, the cosmos beyond the apparent chaos or interlocking conspiracies. Yet even the mystic vision is undercut a little. Just as the revelatory stamps in *Lot 49* are handled by one Genghis Cohen, so our only mystic in *Rainbow* is somebody named Bland, formerly one of Them.

The very act of expressing visions, paranoid or mystic, is both championed and derided. Enzian and Fausto recognize a certain "magic" in the process: a "delusion" can inspire one to survive; a fiction can engender a new reality; a lie can produce a new truth. But by giving subjective reality too solid and seductive a form, one can solipsize oneself or, on a mass scale, justify atrocities. Moreover, language itself—like paranoia— may falsify the existence it seeks to describe, for it is sequential. Words, like molecules, "can be modulated, broken, recoupled, redefined, co-polymerized"—perhaps, Rathenau would say, as an "impersonation of life" (GR, pp. 355, 166). Like analysis, language can divide "the Creation finer and finer, [. . .] setting namer more hopelessly apart from named" (GR, p. 391). It can violate the all-important moment and bury rather than deliver its reality, its possibilities, as when the central Asian boy and girl have their singing-duel: "soon someone will come out and begin to write some of these [exchanges] down in the New Turkish Alphabet [. . .] and this is how they will be lost" (GR, p. 357).

Where do the narrators or their author finally stand on any of these questions? The speaking voice apparently believes in each position while giving it. Pynchon's work lives in its ambivalence about nearly everything, especially about detecting and communicating patterns, linking correspondences and making them linguistic, using metaphors to account for a reality that is not directly accessible. This puts Pynchon in a strange position, one he shares with other contemporary writers who self-consciously recognize the severe limits of human knowledge and expression: he writes, just as Mehemet's sailor paints the side of a sinking ship, knowing that he cannot complete his task, knowing that his

vessel will not long bear contact with external "reality,"
knowing that it sinks even as he ornaments its surface. But
despairing of final accomplishment, he may find some value
in the sheer activity. "Like Stencil," Robert Golden observes,
"Pynchon seems to feel that only the search for meaning, and
not its final achievement, is a real possibility."[30]

In being more conscious and controlled than Stencil, the
author is only more aware that he cannot rest satisfied in any
hothouse fiction that he constructs for himself. He must keep
knocking holes in the walls as he makes them, and he must
keep moving through them because stasis offers no possibility
or surprise. Pynchon, of course, leaves himself openings
through self-parody. *V.* does undercut the human compulsion
to find patterns in events, but what is the novel if not the
author's response to the patterns he finds in the events of our
recent history? Aware of his paradoxical position, Pynchon
avoids censure by not allowing his response to assume a
final, closed form. He will employ any vantage point on the
Situation, but he will settle for none and leave none unscathed.

Max Schulz remarks that "Whereas a Blake, a Coleridge, or a
John Stuart Mill could still believe in the intellectual systems
of his own making," contemporary man, as Pynchon shows
him, cannot do so without fatuousness, irony, or parody.[31]
Such systems will continue to be made, however; the plots of
fiction makers and pattern detectors will not be formless and
meaningless, for they exist to help discover form and meaning,
to supply them, or at least to give illusions of them. Parody
allows the writer to draw on the coherence and orderly
framework of a system, to have for a time a fixed vantage point
on the world, and yet to liberate himself from all systems by
playfully demonstrating his knowledge of their insufficiency.

As early as "Low-lands," Pynchon began his practice of
building a scene that can arouse any number of serious feelings
and then debunking it. For example, the narrator first describes
Nerissa in cosmic imagery:

> her face, floating wide-eyed and anxious . . . and the stars caught
> in her hair. . . . In the starlight she was exquisite: she wore a dark

[30]Robert E. Golden, "Mass Man and Modernism: Violence in Pynchon's *V.*,"
Critique 14, no. 2 (1972), 13.
[31]Max F. Schulz, *Black Humor Fiction of the Sixties: A Pluralistic Definition
of Man and His World* (Athens, Ohio: Ohio University Press, 1973), p. 62.

dress, her legs and arms were bare, slim, the neck arching and delicate, her figure so slender it was almost a shadow. Dark hair floated around her face and down her back like a black nebula; eyes enormous . . . (L, p. 104)

Then he concludes bathetically, "nose retroussé, short upper lip, good teeth, nice chin," adding also that she was "roughly three and a half feet tall" (L, p. 104). As if this is not bad enough, Flange scratches his head, introduces himself, and wonders if she might not want to "discuss the Midget Problem" (L, p. 105).

Characteristically, Pynchon prizes and often succeeds at the incongruous juxtaposition of the ridiculous and the sublime, but in this early attempt the undercutting seems forced and clumsy. Still, his need of it may reveal something about his intentions. He can use an image like Nerissa-of-the-Dump to suggest that only in the cast off and passed over can we still hope to find possibility, wonder, and surprise, but in mocking this same image he can protect himself from charges of writing sentimental fairy tales. He can laugh at himself and so be liberated from himself while still putting his themes before us for consideration. If we take anything too seriously, he is not accountable — we are. Perhaps such frivolity allows him to range about incognito, to explore a variety of weighty problems and posit tentatively a number of grave answers without being committed to or trapped in any restricting one.[32]

This tactic also liberates Pynchon so that he can recycle literary materials and methods that might be considered obsolete or unoriginal by an *avant-garde* audience. For example, the story could hardly exist without the fetal motif, but Pynchon guards himself from appearing to take Freudianism too seriously by suggesting that Dennis Flange's generation finds it *passé*, even comically so. He handles literary allusion and myth in a like manner. His evocations of Eliot and Dante here enforce certain parallels and add certain resonances to the action and characters; but, as Joseph Slade notes, "Low-lands" is almost a parody of "The Waste Land," taking the mythic underpinnings of that poem and thrusting them into grotesque or burlesque contexts. In this way, Pynchon

[32]William Vesterman makes a similar point about the author's "songs" in "Pynchon's Poetry," in *Mindful Pleasures: Essays on Thomas Pynchon,* ed. George Levine and David Leverenz (Boston: Little, Brown and Co., 1976), pp. 101–12.

reveals a post-modern sensibility: while he may draw on myth, he debunks it and questions whether it is viable, as T. S. Eliot postulates, as "a way of controlling, of ordering, of giving a shape and a significance to the immense panorama of futility and anarchy which is contemporary history."[33] For Eliot, an intellectual feat such as *The Golden Bough* opens a realm of possibility. Pynchon wonders, especially in the early fiction, if it might only lock the seeker into a hothouse from which he imposes a falsifying and perhaps destructive teleology on chaos.

Pynchon, then, borrows heavily from our cultural heritage, but often to parody it or chart its disintegration. Through Herbert Stencil, he invokes the ancient tradition of making a woman the emblem of Western culture. Robert Graves, with whom Stencil feels some affinity, argues in *The White Goddess* that Western civilization has determined its course largely by the ways in which it has responded to this mythic figure in her various embodiments. As her status, power, and centrality decline, so does our culture. The mythographer plots that decline by tracking her through cryptograms, anagrams, numerology, and so on. Pynchon, like Graves, uses a female emblem to trace Western decay, but unlike his predecessor, he also employs her to burlesque such an enterprise. For just as V. is a travesty of the White Goddess, so V. (through Stencil) is in part a parody of *The White Goddess* and of any attempt by the human imagination to formulate a myth that organizes history or society. Likewise, Pynchon practices and parodies the historiography of Henry Adams, who sought the track of the energy and described it with a metaphor. Pynchon himself describes the track of the energy through metaphor, but he creates characters such as Callisto and Stencil who look ridiculous in their similar efforts and who even refer to themselves in the third person, as did Adams in *The Education*.

Pynchon also uses parody to recycle literary modes. Robert Sklar calls the book a "collage, an abstract composition put together with parodies of spy novels, political novels, adventure novels, decadent novels, romances, utopias and whatever other category the ingenious mind can find."[34] Good

[33]T. S. Eliot, "*Ulysses*, Order, and Myth," *Dial*, November 1923.
[34]Robert Sklar, "The New Novel, USA: Thomas Pynchon," *Nation* 205 (25 September 1967), 277.

cases have been made for *V.* as a parody of everything from
Modernism to McCarthyism to itself. Actually, parody is an
ongoing force in the novel; to paraphrase Stencil's notion of V.,
its particular shape is governed only by the surface materials of
each episode. The laughter extends toward the reader, who
often gets seduced into imitating Stencil's obsessive search for
design and meaning in the act of reading about it.

In *The Crying of Lot 49*, the reader and the author are
pictured and parodied in the main character. Through Oedipa's
meditation on "the act of metaphor," the novel admits itself to
be "a thrust at truth and a lie," depending on "where you
were" (49, p. 95). Metaphor cannot deliver a final truth, but it
can guide or misguide. For example, Pynchon notes that many
of the works at the Watts festival "were fine, honest rebirths."
But then again, "if there is any drift away from reality, it is by
way of mythmaking. As this summer [1966] warms up, last
August's riot is being remembered less as chaos and more as
art" (W, p. 157). Art can lead or mislead: consequently,
Pynchon demonstrates both a playfulness and a seriousness
about making fiction.

Gravity's Rainbow regards myth somewhat as *The Crying
of Lot 49* regards metaphor. Because it exists in the imperfect,
sequential medium of language, myth, like paranoia, cannot
perfectly depict the truth that perhaps only mystics can
approach. Pynchon might also feel that myth, like paranoia,
may rigidify and so obscure perception, imposing a partially
congruent structure on events and hiding the "magic" of
naming behind the opacity of time-encrusted names. Richard
Poirier interprets him as saying that "the inherited ways of
classifying experience are no longer a help but a hindrance. All
of the formulas by which experience gets shaped or organized
around us are themselves a part of the chaos of experience with
which one has to deal."[35] Similarly, Richard Wasson argues
that Pynchon's distrust of myth helps to distinguish him from
his modernist predecessors.[36]

By parodying myth, Pynchon can exploit it and attack it at
the same time, as he has done ever since "Low-lands." Tyrone
Slothrop, the unheroic hero of *Gravity's Rainbow*, makes the

---

[35]Poirier, "The Importance of Thomas Pynchon," p. 20.
[36]Richard Wasson, "Notes on a New Sensibility," *Partisan Review* 36, no. 3
(1969), 460–77.

conventional descent to the underground, but he descends via a toilet in the Roseland ballroom (the episode is part of his hallucination). In the subterranean Mittelwerke, he is chased by demented American technical intelligence men singing their grotesque "Rocket limericks." Through parody, Pynchon can tap the psychological and cultural reservoir of myth while building on its structure, as he does with allusions to various religious works, to Orphic myth, to Wagnerian opera, and so on. Yet while giving "shape and significance" to contemporary history as it appears in his novel, he puts himself and his reader at a safe remove; his incessant comic attack ventilates the structure, not allowing the shape to solidify and seal reader or author into a hothouse, or to thrust a hardened form unchallenged on a fluid reality.

Plot, Structure, and Relation

Still, something survives all of the ambivalence, relativism, and parody. As paranoia seems preferable to anti-paranoia, so myth seems to anti-myth, or, more generally, structure to anti-structure, system to anti-system. Myth—as the "*act* of naming" rather than the names—"obeys" and suggests the pattern by "isomorphic representation." In the pattern may lie the essence or at least the basis of life; in obeying it may lie the main hope of opposing death. Death *can* be opposed, says Pynchon, by "assertion-through-structure"—by the persistence of some complex system that extends through space (as the aromatic molecular weave of Pirate's banana breakfast wafts through blasted London) or that endures through time (as "the living genetic chains prove even labyrinthine enough to preserve some human face down ten or twenty generations" [*GR*, p. 10]). Pynchon, of course, asserts structure through words in the very form of his novel.

In revealing the path our world has taken, the spirit of Rathenau pointed to "the persistence [. . .] of structures favoring death" (*GR*, p. 167). Certainly Pynchon has urged his readers to consider the deadening effects of structure: abstraction, analysis, rationalized systems, labyrinths, and interlocking conspiracies. At times he clearly seems to share Squalidozzi's desire to efface the "ever more complex patterns on the blank sheet," to "return to that first unscribbled serenity

. . . that anarchic oneness of pampas and sky" (GR, p. 264). And yet how many modern novelists have employed patterns more complex or lengthy than Pynchon's? It is wrong simply to say that he composes books which indict their own complexity and thus turn upon themselves, questioning or attacking their own processes and dissolving in self-parody.[37] It is exactly the labyrinthine form that allows the genetic chains to preserve human life; "the high intricacy" of structure is "the conjuror's secret by which [. . .] Death is told so clearly to fuck off" (GR, p. 10).

In the form of his fiction, especially *Gravity's Rainbow*, and even in his sentence construction, Pynchon vindicates and practices a certain kind of system: he asserts the structure of the cosmos as he understands it—especially as contemporary science has led him to understand it. His work does not unfold according to Newtonian mechanics in straight lines of causal sequence, chronology, or character and plot development proceeding from an absolute reference point. Rather it approximates the universe of geodesy and relativity, in which aligned stresses and matched internal oppositions balance themselves to form a sphere around some hypothetical "center" that exists only as their relations imply it. These balanced oppositions testify to the multiplicity of the cosmos and the need for complementary perspectives. Hence one finds in Pynchon not only self-parody but also multiple plot lines. He has a predilection for building mutually informing subplots around very different types of characters: the schematizers or systems makers (such as Callisto, Stencil, and Weissmann) and the moment-to-moment men (such as Meatball, Profane, and Slothrop). Sometimes, as in "Entropy," one type is a corrective for the other, but often they just have opposing flaws.

Characteristically, Pynchon will alternate contrapuntally between the subplots, using various technical devices to augment the duality but provide a connecting link at the same time. For example, in "Entropy" he uses the music motif and differing prose styles to characterize each scene. The jazz at Meatball's party is open, spontaneous, unpredictable, and unpatterned—sometimes to the point of cancelling itself out;

---

[37]George Levine gives a very good discussion of Pynchon's anarchism in "Risking the Moment." But he does not consider the author's complementary attraction to structures and systems.

the classical references to Callisto, on the other hand, suggest closure, pattern, planning, and contrived order. Similarly, Pynchon's writing embodies a schizophrenia of styles to reflect the different personae: simple parataxis for Meatball and intricate, cerebral, overwrought hypotaxis for Callisto and Aubade. The hierarchical structure of their expression reveals their attempt to forestall entropic levelling.

The two basic subplots and character types recur in V. In fact, Pynchon separates the hothouse quest of Herbert Stencil and the street meanderings of Benny Profane into subplots that, although they inform one another, touch only on one plane, as do the living quarters of Meatball and Callisto. Here Benny's story constitutes "ground level" for Stencil's airy abstraction. The decadent fascination with the inanimate is Benny's ceiling, the closest he ever comes to thinking and inference, and it is Stencil's floor, the closest he ever gets to verifiable reality. The dual prose styles also reappear. George Levine nicely observes that the writing in V. "seems to live the tension between the resolute, Profane-like, commitment to the separateness of things and the overpowering, Stencilish, sense of their connectedness."[38] The sentences relating the Whole Sick Crew episodes are generally simple (sometimes compound) and rather straight-forward. But let a Stencil or a Fausto or a Mondaugen (especially Stencilized) enter the scene, and the prose becomes quite different. For example, Pynchon often employs periodic or suspended sentences in depicting a character's attempt to give structure and meaning to his impressions:

> It was her inability to come to rest anywhere inside plausible extremes, her nervous, endless motion, like the counter-crepitating of the ball along its roulette spokes, seeking a random compartment but finally making, having made, sense only as precisely the dynamic uncertainty she was, this that upset Mondaugen enough to scowl quietly and say with a certain dignity no, turn, leave her there and return to his sferics. (V., p. 238)

This rather Jamesian type of sentence recurs throughout V., for it gives form to one of the novel's main themes: the human propensity for making patterns, interpreting symbols, working

---

from inert facts toward a summary statement that circumscribes, defines, resolves them. Fausto Maijstral writes:

> But the desert, or a row of false shop fronts; a slag pile, a forge where the fires are banked, these and the street and the dreamer, only an inconsequential shadow himself in the landscape, partaking of the soullessness of these other masses and shadows; this is the 20th Century nightmare. (V., p. 303)

As discussed above, *The Crying of Lot 49* has a single plot line viewed from a variety of perspectives and filtered through a polarity of styles. *Gravity's Rainbow*, which returns to multiple plot lines, retains the clashing syntactical modes and levels of diction:

> [. . .] Slothrop's dumb idling heart sez: The Schwarzgerät is no Grail, Ace, that's not what the G in Imipolex G stands for. And you are no knightly hero [. . . .] You play because you have nothing better to do, but that doesn't make it right. And where's the Pope whose staff's gonna bloom for you? (GR, p. 364)

Blicero says:

> Out here, they wanted to dive between the worlds, to fall, turn, reach and swing on journeys curved through the shining, through the winter nights of space—their dreams were of rendezvous, of cosmic trapeze acts carried on in loneliness, in sterile grace, in certain knowledge that no one would ever be watching, that loved ones had been lost forever. . . . (GR, p. 723)

Gravity's Rainbow is Pynchon's most faithful "isomorphic representation" of the new cosmos. As noted, the novel defies a 1 or 0 method of reading. It comprises so many internal oppositions and complements that, as a structure, it exists in a seeming infinity of moments, things, details, and events. It allows uncertainty and possibility, yet its apparently disparate elements coalesce in a field that they create about themselves; insofar as they hold together, they do so by the gravity—the geometry of relations—of that field. Like all patterns, that geometry appears to vary with perspective. Taking a micro perspective and regarding individual moments or details, one sees apparent discontinuity. One may feel in reading the novel like a paranoid reading the world, groping through "front-brain" perceptions, "hoping to zero in on the tremendous and secret Function," feeling "the onset" of the discovery that "*everything is connected, everything in the Creation*" (GR, pp.

590, 703). As one steps back a little from the micro perspective and studies Pynchon's creation, connections appear between the countless impressions, episodes, fantasies, and reveries that may have looked quite isolated and fragmentary at first. But these connections are very loose and unrestricting; although the elements of the novel reflect or echo one another, they do not form what Pointsman would call "a clear train of linkages" (GR, p. 89). They belie causal sequence, chronology, and linear organization, the Newtonian mechanics of the traditional novel, thus suggesting "probable associations" and "tendencies to be related," less confining notions which contemporary science has preferred in making its own models of reality. Pynchon's model of reality, his novel, works like Leni's astrology: by "parallel, not series. Metaphor. Signs and symptoms. Mapping on to different coordinate systems." Franz scoffs at Leni: "Try to design anything that way and have it work" (GR, p. 159). He may as well have challenged his author.[39] Relativity theory supports Leni and Pynchon, declaring that all reference systems are equivalent for description of natural laws and phenomena.

Pynchon revels in the freedom of invention that such a design principle affords him, zooming between coordinate systems, flashing reflections, sounding echoes, coining metaphors, drawing parallels, making analogies, playing with microcosms and macrocosms at will. To cite just one example (GR, p. 147 – 49), the narrator launches off on a fantastic account of the central nervous system, describing its processes in terms of colonization, the Kingdom of God, and a "CNS" bureaucracy (the connotation of which undercuts faith in the efficiency of human perception). Many episodes, especially late in the novel, are related but not logically necessary for development of plot, character, or theme. There is no suggestion of causal connection but rather of parallel movement in accordance with some all-subsuming process that makes it possible to talk of one thing in terms of another. Pynchon's method of parallel construction extends from his scenes to his sentences. Examples appear on every page of his works, from first to last.

[39]Marjorie Kaufman has expressed a similar view in "Brunnhilde and the Chemists: Women in Gravity's Rainbow," in *Mindful Pleasures: Essays on Thomas Pynchon*, ed. George Levine and David Leverenz (Boston: Little, Brown and Co., 1976), pp. 197– 227.

Here is the second sentence from "Mortality and Mercy in Vienna":

> All day rain clouds had hung low and ragged-edged over Washington, ruining the view from the top of the Monument for the high-school kids on their senior trips, sending brief squalls which drove tourists squealing and cursing in to find shelter, dulling the pink of the cherry blossoms which had just come out. (MMV, p. 195)

He closes Gravity's Rainbow with the syntactic parallels of a William Slothrop hymn.

But from a macro perspective, parallels are an illusion because straight lines are an illusion. Considering the shape of the entire field, cosmos or novel, one needs a non-Euclidean geometry to describe the relational pattern wrought by its gravity. According to Einstein, there are only curved lines in space because matter warps space-time into a curvilinear gravitational field that bends even light. The space-time continuum arches back upon itself, and so a beam of light will eventually return to its source after tracing a gigantic circle. This compares to "the Great Serpent holding its own tail in its mouth [. . . .] The Serpent that announces, 'The World is a closed thing, cyclical, resonant, eternally-returning' " (GR, p. 412). As noted in chapter 3, Pynchon has associated the Serpent with gravity through images, for example the "rainbow lashings" of both their coils.

And Pynchon tries to make his novel function the same way. As a gravitational field, it is a geometry of relations curved back upon itself by its own matter. The end is in the beginning, the beginning in the end, for the novel opens with an aftermath and closes with an advent. What immediately follows and precedes is "all theatre." The novel, in this sense, is "eternally-returning" — also in the sense that its gravity recycles the fragments, detritus, and exhausted materials of our culture: "the wastes of dead species, gathered, packed, transmuted, realigned, and rewoven" into new combinations and associations (GR, p. 590). In the relativistic cosmos, everything bears on everything else, in all directions at once, somewhat as is the case in this novel. Hence Gravity's Rainbow often dispenses with "the one-way flow of European time" (GR, p. 724). Einstein argued that time is not absolute; it is subjective, a sense impression like color or shape, a variable quantity that depends on the observer's motion. The chapter which introduces Leni flashes back and forth between her past and present experiences. The time sequence is deliberately obscure and unexplained because it is not the point. The interface between the past and the present is permeable, fading, as are the interfaces between the living and the dead, the inside and the outside, the subject and the object, one character or narrator and another. The chronology of the memories, experiences, and reveries is unimportant because "they are part of the same movement. Not A before B, but all together" (*GR*, p. 159).

"*Everything is connected.*" As a corollary, *everything signifies,* as the imagery of the book attests: "The trees grow heavy with black birds, branches like dendrites of the Nervous System fattening, deep in twittering nerve-dusk, in preparation for some important message. . . ." (*GR*, p. 364). One cannot help but read or try to decode such a world. And yet how can one read it? How can one write about it? One must start and end. But with no absolute reference points, just endless equivalent ones, any starting and ending points, and any arrangement of points between, will be an arbitrary distortion of the way things are. W. T. Lhamon, Jr. remarks that the pressures of endless and simultaneous relation "make linear communication inadequate, chronology a joke, and organization destructive."[40] The very volume of detail suggests hidden patterns and latent connections that stretch beyond one's ability to process them — meanings concealed and yet, in Oedipa's terms, intended to communicate.

In the novel as in the cosmos, everything seems potentially revealing because everything affects the field and is affected in return: everything exerts an influence that it receives back. Lines, beams of light, epistemological inquiries, or whatever ultimately refer back to their point of origin. Because of this radical equality, this total reciprocity, Einstein suggested that the four-dimensional space–time continuum is like a sphere on which a line returning to its starting point suggests the surface. On the surface of the sphere all points are equivalent,

[40]W. T. Lhamon, Jr., "Pentecost, Promiscuity, and Pynchon's V.: From the Scaffold to the Impulsive," In *Mindful Pleasures: Essays on Thomas Pynchon,* ed. George Levine and David Leverenz (Boston: Little, Brown and Co., 1976), p. 69.

defining an imaginary center with uniform radii. Similarly, the surface points of *Gravity's Rainbow* can be seen as equivalent — not linked in sequence but all related, all bearing alike on one another and implying some felt but unarticulated tie-in. Einstein proposed that the universe is finite and yet unbounded. *Gravity's Rainbow*, by analogy, has only so many words, but an indefinite number of relations obtain among all of its equivalent parts and coordinate systems. Also, because the novel is structured by relations, not causal sequences, there is no limit to the number of equivalent episodes, metaphoric analogies, and parallel fantasies that could have served. Leni sees Lang's "dream of flight" as "one of many possible" (GR, p. 159), and so are any of Pynchon's dreamt moments. In reading or writing about the world, the author faces a problem (similar to one the critic faces in reading or writing about this book): if everything signifies, what do you keep and what do you toss out? If everything is connected, at once and without fixed center, how do you choose and order the parts?

Pynchon acknowledges these problems with the structure of both novels and sentences. In *Gravity's Rainbow* particularly, all moments and viewpoints seem equally present, available, capable of revealing or deluding. A reviewer for the *Times Literary Supplement* laments that the book is "very hard to read — impossible, it has to be said, to read continuously — not because of density or obscurity, but because it's so nearly devoid of hierarchy or perspective. . . . You couldn't find a more democratic novel."[41] Actually the novel has so *many* perspectives that it appears to have none. Apart from the transformations and inconsistencies of the protean narrator, the work itself seems a junkpile "of such different things as pantomime, burlesque, cinema, cabaret, card games, songs, comic strips, spy stories, serious history, encyclopaedic information, mystical and visionary meditations, the scrambled imagery of dreams, the cold cause-and-effect talk of the Behaviourists, and all the various ways men try to control and coerce realities both seen and unseen — from magic to measurement, from sciences to seances."[42] This range itself demonstrates how Pynchon's world comprises unlimited complementary perspectives.

[41]"Waiting for the Bang," review of *Gravity's Rainbow*, *Times Literary Supplement*, 16 November 1973, p. 1389.
[42]Tony Tanner, "V. and V-2," *London Magazine* 13 (Feb.– March 1974), 83.

Because Pynchon asserts a radically new type of structure, he seems to throw these diverse components together at random, without system or coherent design, like items in a junkpile. But Pynchon's junkpiles have held possible redemption ever since the first one appeared in "Low-lands." Why shouldn't he make his novel into one, an assemblage of all the genres, games, stances, and perspectives of his cultural heritage, scrapped and yet not lost, ready to be salvaged? His junkpiles have always opposed the rigid world of programming, rationalization, and routinization with the chaotic virtues of spontaneity, surprise, and discovery; they have always countered the linear motion of entropy and exhaustion with the circular motion of recycling.

Such beliefs could explain not only the novel's junkpile slew of jumbled perspectives but also its sheer bulk of apparently unorganized detail. Often the narrator will simply begin listing *things* so as to reveal an attitude toward them but not a conceptual framework that can order them into any kind of logical or meaningful progression. Such catalogues are, in the words of George Levine, "imagined with the particularity that always offers more than can be systematized."[43] The narrator seems overwhelmed in a universe made complex by things, unable or perhaps unwilling to pattern the myriad items and events.

Because he senses the value lurking in junkpiles, the narrator may be unwilling to discard anything. Objects and events become important in and for themselves, take on lives of their own, even (or especially) if there is no system to arrange them, to give them a shape or meaning. In each of his works, Pynchon will build sentences simply by piling up a long list of items or examples when just a few would do. Typically a loose parallel runs through the clauses, but the clauses, like the items and examples, are separate and unconnected, randomly ordered, accreting indefinitely without pattern, progression, or apparent purpose; no logical form prescribes a direction or end point. Thus the sentence may structurally mimic what it describes: for example, the detritus in Mucho's cars (*49*, pp. 4–5), the contents of Mr. McAffee's wallet or the events of his life (SI, p. 49), Slothrop's desk top (GR, p. 18), or the "great frontierless streaming" of refugees across the Zone (GR, pp. 549–51). Pynchon will often build such sentences out of absolute

[43]Levine, "Risking the Moment," p. 127.

constructions, for then the events are not limited and past but immediate, simultaneous, and frozen in an eternally present moment: here Pökler stares at the naked corpses stacked in front of the crematoriums, "the men's penises hanging, their toes clustering white and round as pearls . . . each face so perfect, so individual, the lips stretched back into death-grins, a whole silent audience caught at the punch line of the joke . . ." (GR, p. 432). The absolute construction is Pynchon's "double integral" in prose, operating so that "time falls away: change is stilled [. . . .] to become architecture, and timeless" (GR, p. 301).

Pynchon also manipulates sentence construction to rehearse the movement of "time's arrow":

> A screaming comes across the sky. It has happened before, but there is nothing to compare it to now.
> It is too late. The Evacuation still proceeds, but it's all theatre. There are no lights inside the cars. No light anywhere. Above him lift girders old as an iron queen, and glass somewhere far above that would let the light of day through. But it's night. He's afraid of the way the glass will fall — soon — it will be a spectacle: the fall of a crystal palace. But coming down in total blackout, without one glint of light, only great invisible crashing.
> Inside the carriage, which is built on several levels, he sits in velveteen darkness, with nothing to smoke, feeling metal nearer and farther rub and connect, steam escaping in puffs, a vibration in the carriage's frame, a poising, an uneasiness, all the others pressed in around, feeble ones, second sheep, all out of luck and time: drunks, old veterans still in shock from ordnance 20 years obsolete, hustlers in city clothes, derelicts, exhausted women with more children than it seems could belong to anyone, stacked about among the rest of the things to be carried out to salvation. Only the nearer faces are visible at all, and at that only as half-silvered images in a view finder, green-stained VIP faces remembered behind bulletproof windows speeding through the city . . . . (GR, p. 3)

One might say that the sentence beginning the third paragraph enacts a progressive, entropic levelling. At first the sentence, like the carriage, "is built on several levels." But it moves from subordination to coordination, hierarchy to equivalence, logical connection to disorganized accretion. With a "great invisible crashing," it falls into a rubble of fragments, stacked randomly, haphazardly, as the people described are stacked by the military. The sentence construction mimics a patterned as well as a chaotic reality, and again, the nature of that reality depends on perspective. The more distant or macro view reveals pattern, as represented in the tightly organized subordinate structure of the sentence opening. But when one zooms close up, inside the carriage and the character to share "feeling" and perception, the micro view reveals another jumbled catalogue of disconnected parts, much as Oedipa's printed circuit becomes a scatter of buildings when she descends from the mountain into San Narciso.

Pynchon also enforces his epistemology here by deliberately confusing perspectives or attempted approaches to the situation. The passage quickly juxtaposes the appeals of space and time, sound and sight; it asks the reader to visualize while telling him that he cannot visualize, that there is "no light anywhere." Pynchon forces the reader to adopt inappropriate strategies, and these felt mistakes or disorientations become part of the experience—the meaning. As with the Rocket, the jarring impact comes first, then the recognition of what happened. Maybe. In the final sentence of the passage, the point of view seems to switch from the mind of the unspecified "him" in the carriage (it turns out to be Pirate Prentice), to the mind and memory of . . . who knows? The *reader* knows only that he is out of the carriage and into a car which is "speeding" along like the mobile point of view that changes everything as it moves, both the apparent structure of reality and of the sentences that would render reality.

Significant Collections, Ellipses, and Revelation

Pynchon's manipulations of structure suggest that there is no stable perspective from which we can know and describe the world. Both the fictional and rhetorical forms reinforce Pynchon's epistemology and mirror it in their complementary expressions. In places the episodes, like some clauses, are ordered logically, even knit together into a paranoid history; in other places the episodes, like some clauses, are piled together loosely, as in much of "The Counterforce" section of *Gravity's Rainbow*. Many open-ended catalogue sentences illustrate an entropic levelling and dispersal, but other catalogue sentences demonstrate "a progressive *knotting into*" (GR, p. 3), moving from relative chaos toward hierarchy and concentration, gathering fragments into a deliberate grammatical and logical closure. The structure of the sentence below becomes increasingly intricate; the prose enacts the ordering impulse while stating its rationale:

> Now there grows among all the rooms, replacing the night's old smoke, alcohol and sweat, the fragile, musaceous odor of Breakfast: flowery, permeating, surprising, more than the color of winter sunlight, taking over not so much through any brute pungency or volume as by the high intricacy to the weaving of its molecules, sharing the conjuror's secret by which—though it is not often Death is told so clearly to fuck off—the living genetic chains prove even labyrinthine enough to preserve some human face down ten or twenty generations . . . so the same assertion-through-structure allows this war morning's banana fragrance to meander, repossess, prevail. (GR, p. 10)

The nature of both the sentence and the reality it portrays varies with perspective. Moving from the micro to the macro, from the cramped rooms to the larger outdoors, from the human face to the scope of generations, the isolated parts form an integrating pattern.

Any isolated part, regardless of how minor, could prove to be a resonating clue, to bear illuminating relations to the other elements in the world of the novel. *"Everything is connected,"* though neither the character, the reader, the narrator, nor perhaps the author can ever fix his view of this world and establish a standard by which some details are clearly important and others are not. The relative universe forces one to admit that *anything* could be highly significant. Alfred North Whitehead writes: "Universality of truth arises from the universality of relativity, whereby every particular actual thing lays upon the universe the obligation of conforming to it. Thus in the analysis of particular fact universal truths are discoverable, those truths expressing this obligation."[44] The smallest item in the greatest catalogue, like the briefest moment, thus has its "possibilities," possibilities one may ignore at a great loss. Perhaps the sense of so much wasted potential and lost information gives Pynchon's fiction its characteristic poignancy. Edward Mendelson speaks of "the *tristesse* that must accompany any sense of coherence and

[44] Alfred North Whitehead, *Symbolism: Its Meaning and Effect* (New York: Macmillan, 1927), p. 39.

fullness. For if even the smallest event carries large significance, then even the smallest loss, the most remote sadness, contains more grief than a secular vision can imagine."[45] Recall the detritus in the back seats of Mucho's cars or the stuffing of the old sailor's mattress in *The Crying of Lot 49*, the brassiere Jessica finds in the rubble or the "old used toothpaste tubes" in *Gravity's Rainbow* (pp. 43, 130); anything and everything can speak to "the sensitive," but few can endure such sensitivity.

The catalogues and their seemingly endless cumulative sentences cannot include everything. *Gravity's Rainbow*, for all its depth, hints that undisclosed realms lie just beneath even the tiniest patches on its huge surface. Infinite regresses and worlds of bizarre experience lurk below the prosaic account of the reunion between Franz Pökler and Kurt Mondaugen. On graduating, the latter had "gone off to South-West Africa, on some kind of radio research project. They had written for a while, then stopped" (GR, p. 161). The reader of *V.* knows the complexity of Mondaugen's Africa experience lying buried under the innocuous phrase. What lies under any of the thousands more suggestive ones? What do all the ellipses cover? The pervasive ellipses acknowledge Goedel's theorem: "there is bound to be some item around that one has omitted from the list" (GR, p. 320). They suggest the inconceivable number of things left unnamed, paths left unexplored, realities left untouched; they demonstrate the pitiful inadequacy of language in the face of the endless relation and ramification that is our cosmos; they testify to the insufficiency of the words from which the book is made. This passage describes the approach of Tchitcherine and Džaqyp Qulan to the Kirghiz light: "Waiting, out in sunlight which is not theirs yet, is the ... The ..." (GR, p. 343).

Pynchon's narrator has compared the Kirghiz light to the Rocket and the Rocket to the Word in several places (GR, pp. 25, 357–59, 510, 760). With words, as with rockets or revelations, "chances are astronomically against a perfect hit"; the attempted strikes "disperse about the aiming point in a giant ellipse—the Ellipse of Uncertainty" (GR, p. 425). But there are

[45]Edward Mendelson, "The Sacred, the Profane, and *The Crying of Lot 49*," in *Individual and Community: Variations on a Theme in American Fiction*, ed. Kenneth H. Baldwin and David K. Kirby (Durham: Duke University Press, 1975), p. 216.

other possibilities in language—even a "high magic to low
puns," a "sympathetic magic, a repetition high and low of
some prevailing form" (49, p. 96; GR, p. 232). On the strength
of that sanction, one might say that Pynchon substitutes the
Ellipses of Uncertainty for a perfect hit. For these ellipses are
as close as one gets to revelation. Pynchon never presents the
crying of lot 49 or the Kirghiz light. He never presents the
Rocket explosion: the book ends with an apocalyptic vision
of the Rocket poised to strike; it opens with a dream of the
Rocket's immediate aftermath, the sound of the approach, like
words, racing to catch up to the "reality." But that moment of
unmediated revelation, perhaps beyond subjectivity and
versions, never appears in *Gravity's Rainbow.*

Unmediated revelation may never appear in any body of
language. Yet Pynchon seems to feel that language can suggest
what it cannot present. Hence he attempts an "isomorphic
representation" of the world and cosmos as seen through
modern art, recent history, and contemporary science. His
creations appear to his readers and characters alike as a
plethora of intricately woven hieroglyphic patterns, patterns
that phase at some uncertain latitude into random congeries of
things and events, patterns that promise but never quite yield
the final answer. In place of revelation, Pynchon gives the
Ellipses of Uncertainty. Dispersed about them is some of the
most challenging and remarkable fiction in our literature.

Selected Bibliography

To record again all of the works cited in the chapter notes strikes me as a great waste of time and trees. Bibliographic information on the primary texts is summarized under "Abbreviations" at the front of this book. What follows is a selected list of criticism or related readings not mentioned in the notes but still helpful to me in my study of Pynchon and contemporary American fiction.

Contemporary American Fiction

Buckeye, Robert. "The Anatomy of the Psychic Novel." *Critique* 9, no. 2 (1967), 33 – 45.

Detweiler, Robert. "Games and Play in Modern American Fiction." *Contemporary Literature* 17, no. 1 (1976), [44]– 62.

Friedman, Bruce Jay. "Black Humor." In *The Sense of the Sixties,* edited by Edward Quinn and Paul J. Dolan, pp. 435 – 59. New York: Free Press, 1968.

Galloway, David. "Clown and Saint: The Hero in Current American Fiction." *Critique* 7, no. 3 (1965), 46 – 65.

Greenberg, Alvin. "The Death of the Psyche: A Way to the Self in the Contemporary Novel." *Criticism* 8 (1966), 1 – 18.

Hassan, Ihab. "Laughter in the Dark: The New Voice in American Fiction." *The American Scholar* 33 (1964), 636 – 38, 640.

Kostelanetz, Richard. "American Fiction of the Sixties." In *On Contemporary Literature,* edited by Richard Kostelanetz, pp. 634 – 52. New York: Avon Books, 1969.

LeClair, Thomas. "Death and Black Humor." *Critique* 17, no. 1 (1975), 5 – 46.

McConnell, Frank D. *Four Postwar American Novelists: Bellow, Mailer, Barth, and Pynchon.* Chicago: University of Chicago Press, 1977.

McNamara, Eugene. "The Absurd Style in Contemporary American Literature." *Humanities Association Bulletin* 19, no. 1 (1968), 44 – 49.

Vinson, James, ed. *Contemporary Novelists.* London: St. James Press, 1972.

Thomas Pynchon

BACKGROUND

Adams, Henry. *The Degradation of Democratic Dogma.* New York: Macmillan, 1919.

Bohm, David. *Causality and Chance in Modern Physics.* London: Routledge and Kegan Paul, 1957.

Bohr, Niels. "Discussion with Einstein on Epistemological Problems in Atomic Physics." In *Albert Einstein, Philosopher-Scientist,* edited by Paul Arthur Schlipp. New York: Library of Living Philosophers, 1949.

Bork, Alfred M. "Randomness and the Twentieth Century." *Antioch Review* 27 (1967), 40–61.

Brown, Norman O. *Life Against Death: The Psychoanalytic Meaning of History.* Middletown, Conn.: Wesleyan University Press, 1970.

Cassirer, Ernst. *Determinism and Indeterminism in Modern Physics: Historical and Systematic Studies in the Problem of Causality.* New Haven, Conn.: Yale University Press, 1956.

Einstein, Albert. *Relativity.* Translated by Robert W. Lawson. New York: Henry Holt, 1920.

Goldman, Stanford. *Information Theory.* New York: Prentice-Hall, 1953.

Heisenberg, Werner. *Physics and Philosophy.* New York: Harper and Brothers, 1958.

Rubinoff, Lionel. *The Pornography of Power.* New York: Ballantine Books, 1968.

Weber, Max. *The Protestant Ethic and the Spirit of Capitalism.* Translated by Talcott Parsons. New York: Charles Scribner's Sons, 1958.

BIBLIOGRAPHIES

Herzberg, Bruce. "Selected Articles on Thomas Pynchon: An Annotated Bibliography." *Twentieth Century Literature* 21, no. 2 (May 1975), 221–25.

———. "Bibliography." In *Mindful Pleasures: Essays on Thomas Pynchon,* edited by George Levine and David Leverenz, pp. 265–69. Boston: Little, Brown and Co., 1976.

Mendelson, Edward, ed. *Pynchon: A Collection of Critical Essays.* Twentieth Century Views. Englewood Cliffs, N.J.: Prentice-Hall, 1978. Pp. 223–25.

Weixlmann, Joseph. "Thomas Pynchon: A Bibliography." *Critique* 14, no. 2 (1972), 34–43.

COLLECTIONS OF ESSAYS

Critique 16, no. 2 (1974). See also 18, no. 3 (1977).

Levine, George, and Leverenz, David, eds. *Mindful Pleasures: Essays on Thomas Pynchon.* Boston: Little, Brown and Co., 1976.

Mendelson, Edward, ed. *Pynchon: A Collection of Critical Essays.* Twentieth Century Views. Englewood Cliffs, N.J.: Prentice-Hall, 1978.

Pearce, Richard, ed. *Critical Essays on Thomas Pynchon.* Boston: G.K. Hall, 1980.

Twentieth Century Literature 21, no. 2 (1975).

PERIODICALS

Krafft, John, and Khachig, Tölölyan, eds. *Pynchon Notes.* Suffolk County Community College and Wesleyan University. October 1979—Serial Bibliography.

GENERAL

MacAdam, Alfred. "Pynchon as Satirist: To Write, to Mean." *The Yale Review* 67 (1978), 555—66.

Schaub, Thomas H. *Pynchon: The Voice of Ambiguity.* Urbana: University of Illinois Press, 1981.

Stark, John O. *Pynchon's Fictions: Thomas Pynchon and the Literature of Information.* Athens, Ohio: Ohio University Press, 1980.

Weissenburger, Steven. "The End of History? Thomas Pynchon and the Uses of the Past." *Twentieth Century Literature* 25 (1979), 54—72.

V.

Balliett, Whitney. "Wha." *The New Yorker* 39 (15 June 1963), 113—14, 117.

Fahy, Joseph. "Thomas Pynchon's V. and Mythology." *Critique* 18, no. 3 (1977), 5—18.

Greiner, Donald J. "Fiction as History, History as Fiction: The Reader and Thomas Pynchon's V." *South Carolina Review* 10 (November 1977), 4—18.

Hassan, Ihab. "The Futility Corner." *Saturday Review* 46 (23 March 1963), 44.

Hoffman, Frederick J. "The Questing Comedian: Thomas Pynchon's V." *Critique* 6, no. 3 (Winter 1963/64), 174—77.

Meixner, John A. "The All-Purpose Quest." *The Kenyon Review* 25 (Autumn 1963), 729—35.

"Pieces of What?" *Times Literary Supplement,* 11 October 1963, p. 813.

Richardson, Robert O. "The Absurd Animate in Thomas Pynchon's *V.*: *A Novel.*" *Studies in the Twentieth Century* 9 (1972), 35–58.

Richter, David. "The Failure of Completeness: Pynchon's *V.*" In his *Fable's End*, pp. 101–35. Chicago: University of Chicago Press, 1974.

Young, James Dean. "The Enigma Variations of Thomas Pynchon." *Critique* 10, no. 1 (1968), 69–77.

THE CRYING OF LOT 49

Alter, Robert. "The Apocalyptic Temper." *Commentary* 41 (June 1966), 61–66.

Davis, Robert M. "Parody, Paranoia, and the Dead End of Language in *The Crying of Lot 49.*" *Genre* 5 (1972), 367–77.

Hiebert, E. N. "The Uses and Abuses of Thermodynamics in Religion." *Daedalus* 95 (1966), 1046–80.

Leland, John P. "Pynchon's Linguistic Demon: *The Crying of Lot 49.*" *Critique* 16, no. 2 (1974), 45–53.

Mangel, Anne. "Maxwell's Demon, Entropy, Information: *The Crying of Lot 49.*" *Tri-Quarterly* 20 (1971), 194–208.

Nohrnberg, James. "Pynchon's Paraclete." In *Pynchon: A Collection of Critical Essays*, edited by Edward Mendelson, pp. 147–61. Englewood Cliffs, N.J.: Prentice Hall, 1978.

Puetz, Manfred. "Thomas Pynchon's *The Crying of Lot 49*: The World is a Tristero System." *Mosaic* 7, no. 4 (1974), 125-37.

Schmitz, Neil. "Describing the Demon: The Appeal of Thomas Pynchon." *Partisan Review* 42 (1975), 112–25.

Young, James Dean. "The Enigma Variations of Thomas Pynchon." *Critique* 10, no. 1 (1968), 69–77.

GRAVITY'S RAINBOW

Fowler, Douglas. *A Reader's Guide to Gravity's Rainbow.* Ann Arbor, Mich.: Ardis, 1980.

Fussell, Paul. "The Brigadier Remembers." In *Pynchon: A Collection of Critical Essays*, edited by Edward Mendelson, pp. 213–19. Englewood Cliffs, N.J.: Prentice Hall, 1978.

Kappel, L. "Psychic Geography in *Gravity's Rainbow.*" *Contemporary Literature* 21 (1980), 225–51.

Krafft, John M. "'And How Far-Fallen': Puritan Themes in *Gravity's Rainbow.*" *Critique* 18, no. 3 (1977), 55–73.

Leverenz, David. "On Trying to Read *Gravity's Rainbow.*" In *Mindful Pleasures: Essays on Thomas Pynchon*, edited by George Levine and David Leverenz, pp. 229–49. Boston: Little, Brown and Co., 1976.

LeVot, André. "The Rocket and the Pig: Thomas Pynchon and Science Fiction." *Caliban* 12 (1975), 111–18.

Lhamon, W. T., Jr. "The Most Irresponsible Bastard." *New Republic,*
11 March 1973, pp. 12, 14.

Mendelson, Edward. "Gravity's Encyclopedia." In *Mindful Pleasures:*
Essays on Thomas Pynchon, edited by George Levine and David
Leverenz, pp. 161– 95. Boston: Little, Brown and Co., 1976.

Morgan, Speer. "*Gravity's Rainbow:* What's the Big Idea?" *Modern*
Fiction Studies 23 (1977), 199– 216.

Morrison, Philip. Review of *Gravity's Rainbow. Scientific American*
229 (October 1973), 131.

Sanders, Scott. "Pynchon's Paranoid History." In *Mindful Pleasures:*
Essays on Thomas Pynchon, edited by George Levine and David
Leverenz, pp. 139– 59. Boston: Little, Brown and Co., 1976.

Schmitz, Neil. "Describing the Demon: The Appeal of Thomas
Pynchon." *Partisan Review* 42 (1975), 112– 25.

Schwarzbach, F. S. "A Matter of Gravity." In *Pynchon: A Collection of*
Critical Essays, edited by Edward Mendelson, pp. 56– 67.
Englewood Cliffs, N.J.: Prentice Hall, 1978. Note reply by Jonathan
Rosenbaum, pp. 67– 68.

Seidel, Michael. "The Satiric Plots of *Gravity's Rainbow.*" In
Pynchon: A Collection of Critical Essays, edited by Edward
Mendelson, pp. 193– 212. Englewood Cliffs, N.J.: Prentice Hall,
1978.

Siegel, Mark R. "Creative Paranoia: Understanding the System of
Gravity's Rainbow." *Critique* 18, no. 3 (1977), 39– 54.

Simmon, Scott. "*Gravity's Rainbow* Described." *Critique* 16, no. 2
(1974), 54– 67. Also note his "A Character Index: *Gravity's*
Rainbow," pp. 68– 72.

works of, 12; epistemology of, 20, 26; unreliable narrator in works of, 29; mentioned, 2

Entropy: counterrealistic and neorealistic treatment of, 6 – 7; Manichean view of, 12; metaphorical use of, 45 – 46, 48, 51, 54, 61, 65, 66, 112, 114, 115, 157; definitions of, 46; automatonism and, 47; manifest in landscape, 54 – 55, 56; reversibility of, 73 – 74, 77 – 78, 80, 88, 114 – 17; assumed irreversibility of, 112; development of the scientific concept of, 112 – 15

Enzian (GR): utilization of waste of, 91 – 92; responsiveness to metaphor of, 154, 173; on myth and language, 173

Epistemology, 131 – 53 passim; counterrealistic treatment of, 13 – 21, 26; as a function of perspective, 21; implications for narrative structure of, 29 – 38 passim; and knowledge of ultimate reality, 122 – 23, 171 – 73, 188 – 89; and quantum mechanics and relativity, 130, 171 – 72; influence of science and pseudoscience on, 154 – 56, 162 – 63, 165, 171 – 72; influence of on Pynchon's symbolism, 187 – 88; influence of on narrative technique, 189. *See also* Perspective

Esther (V), 48

Fariña, Richard, 29
Faulkner, William, 181
Film, 117 – 18, 131, 169, 178
Fish, Stanley, 194
Flange, Dennis (L): apocalyptic vision of, 65; need for love of, 77; tendency to withdraw of, 96 – 97; sense of possibilities of, 128; rationale of for passivity, 135, 139; multiple selves of, 139; questionability

of his meeting with Nerissa, 139 – 40; responsiveness to metaphor of, 154, 157, 173

Force, 119, 120
Forster, Edward Morgan, 2, 179, 180
Fourier, Jean Baptiste Joseph, 112
Freud, Sigmund, 48, 54, 206

Gaddis, William, 3, 36
Gaines, Ernest, 3
Galileo, 171
Gardner, John, 3
Gibbs, Willard, 113 – 16 passim, 140
Godolphin, Hugh (V), 26, 136
Goedel, Kurt, 29, 137, 221
Gold, Herbert, 3
Golden Bough, The, 207
Graves, Robert, 207
Gravity: significance of, 82 – 83; regenerative power of, 85, 91; Einstein's theory of, 126
Great Serpent: travestied, 50; as symbol of unity, 63, 83, 84; associated with gravity, 83
Grotesque the: and automatons, 7; and technology, 7 – 8, 60; and causality, 8, 9; and the absurd, 9; conventions of updated, 51; Montaigne's definition of applied to San Narciso, 55

Hammett, Dashiell, 142
Hawkes, John: entropy in works of, 6; invented realities in works of, 22, 23, 26, 27; unreliable narrators in works of, 30; fabulism in works of, 33; ambivalence about structure of, 35 – 36; mentioned, 3, 11
— *The Beetle Leg*, 6
— *The Lime Twig*, 36
Heisenberg, Werner: Pynchon's allusions to, 40; indeterminacy principle of, 121, 122 – 23, 134; on the subjectivity of knowledge, 135, 136; mentioned, 29, 140, 163, 168

Designer: Marilyn Perry
Compositor: Innovative Media, Inc.
Printer: Thomson-Shore, Inc.
Binder: John H. Dekker & Sons
Text: 10/12 Melior Roman
Display: Melior Roman